Pools

Photography by Pere Planells

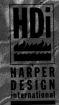

HDi

**HARPER
DESIGN
international**

An Imprint of HarperCollins*Publishers*

POOLS: Good Ideas

Publisher: Paco Asensio

Editor: Haike Falkenberg

© Photos: Pere Planells

Art Director: Mireia Casanovas Soley

Text: Cristina Montes, Fanny Tagavi

Translation: Wendy Griswold

Layout: Kike Vergés, Gisela Legares

2003 © Loft Publications S.L. and Harper Design International

First published in 2002 by LOFT and HBI,
an imprint of HarperCollins International
10 East 53rd St. New York, NY 10022-5299
Now published by Harper Design International

Distributed throughout the world by
HarperCollins International
10 East 53rd St. New York, NY 10022-5299
Fax: (212) 207-7654

HarperCollins books may be purchased for educational, business, or sales promo-
tional use. For information, please write: Special Markets Department, HarperCollins
Publishers Inc., 10 East 53rd Street, New York, NY 10022.

LOFT Publications
Via Laietana, 32 4t Of.92. 08003 Barcelona. Spain
Tel.: +34 93 268 80 88
Fax: +34 93 268 70 73
loft@loftpublications.com
www.loftpublications.com

ISBN: 0-06-058909-4

D.L. B- 51.023-03

If you would like to suggest projects for inclusion in our
next volumes, please e-mail details to us at:
loft@loftpublications.com

First paperback printing, 2003

Sophisticated Geometry *Cádiz, Spain* **10**

20 The Value of the Past *Marrakech, Morocco*

Water in Continuous Motion *Saint Tropez, France* **26**

34 In the Heart of a Quarry *Barcelona, Spain*

Play of Shapes *Nimes, France* **42**

50 Chromatic Personality *Jalisco, Mexico*

Perfect Blend *Ibiza, Spain.* **58**

66 Inspired by the Past *Mallorca, Spain*

Bordering on the Theatrical *Marseilles, France.* **70**

78 A Small Oasis *Mallorca, Spain.*

Passion for the Traditional *Seville, Spain* **86**

94 The Eternal Cycle of Water *Mallorca, Spain*

The Reinterpretation of Water *Marrakech, Morocco* **100**

108 In the Garden of the Imaginary *Provence, France*

Recovering the Past *Mallorca, Spain* **116**

124 A Stream Amid the Rocks *Ibiza, Spain*

Color Contrasts *Mallorca, Spain* **132**

140 Hidden in a Garden *Marrakech, Morocco*

A Mirror Between the Earth and Sky *Mallorca, Spain* **148**

158 Hymn to Sensuality *Cádiz, Spain*

Traditional Inspiration *Douar Abiat, Marocco* **166**

172 Exercise in Contrasts *Girona, Spain*

Zen Symmetry *Barcelona, Spain* **180**

186 Classical Personality *Les Beaux de Provence, France*

To Live in Paradise *Cádiz, Spain.* **194**

202 Classical Spirit *Saint-Rémy de Provence, France*

Vantage Point *Ibiza, Spain* **212**

218 The Patina of Time *Ibiza, Spain*

The Magic of a Setting *Ibiza, Spain* **228**

236 Minimalist Character *Miami, USA*

Rural Symmetry *Santorini, Greece* **244**

252 Carpet of Water *Girona, Spain*

Dressed in Blue *Barcelona, Spain.* **258**

262 Between two Worlds *Tuscany, Italy*

Urban Essence *Barcelona, Spain* **270**

274 Private Space *Ibiza, Spain*

An Urban Oasis *Barcelona, Spain* **280**

288 Memories of the Past *Córdoba, Spain*

Nomadic Sensations *Mallorca, Spain* **294**

300 Peaceful Pool *Marrakech, Morocco*

Soft Murmur of Water *Marrakech, Morocco* **306**

314 Renewed Tradition *Marrakech, Morocco*

Captivating Calm *Ouled Ben Rahmoune, Morocco.* **320**

I n ancient times, water was considered a gift from the gods. Control and command of water stood for power, as we have learned by studying the Egyptian and Assyrian civilizations and the kingdom of Sheba. No one dared to change the cycle of nature, not even the Romans. Even Rome, shortly before the decline of the Empire, was known as "the city of water," inasmuch as eleven major aqueducts supplied it. When the Empire collapsed, Constantinople perpetuated the pleasure of the thermal baths, the love of fountains, and the play of water –the splendor of which was perfected by the Muslim world.

This affinity for water extended into Europe when the Baroque style gained in popularity and was incorporated into the architecture, and grew during the eighteenth and nineteenth centuries, when taking the waters became fashionable and personal hygiene and body culture enjoyed a resurgence, as is happening again today.

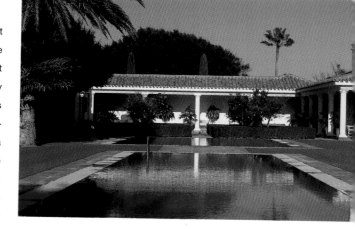

This brief history demonstrates that water has always been present, in one way or another, in human life, and that the history of civilization is necessarily linked to the history of water. While it is true that its principal and most common use is for human consumption, a look at the history of architecture also makes it clear that water has played many other roles. In an attempt to dominate part of nature, to mold it, as far as possible, to his will and bend it to his service, man has used water as a decorative element throughout history.

With the passage of time, water was brought under public control (we should never forget that, at certain times, water was the property of the privileged few and, since it did not belong to the majority, its presence in a civilization had a totally different significance) and was made available to all. What was once a status symbol—since until recently having a pool was a privilege that only a very few could aspire to—is now commonplace.

The pool, as we now think of it, with all its connotations, is a relatively recent phenomenon. Its earliest predecessors in nature are ponds, lakes, and even gently-flowing rivers, natural settings which, over the centuries, man chose for bathing, swimming, and enjoying the water—almost the same purposes we use pools for today.

In other eras, the word "pool" meant a receptacle of varying sizes which, in addition to being used for swimming was also employed as a cistern, hatchery, rainwater repository, and fishpond... The term originated with the Roman Empire, and thermal baths flourished with the ritual of the bath and the worship of water in Moorish cultures, and evolved as a structure over the ages, as architectural progress and styles changed it.

Today's pools can be described with an infinite number of adjectives. Perhaps one of the characteristics they share is having been individually designed and planned for the space they occupy.

This book takes us on a tour of very different structures, all appealing, in which the pool is seen as that private blue space that

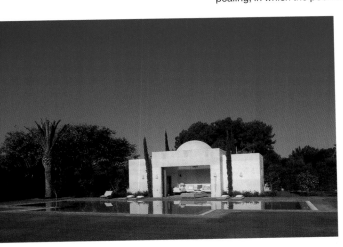

transports us to a paradise which is dreamed of and, often, lost. There are pools with geometric lines, irregular shapes, small, enormous, and understated. Pools inspired by nature, imitating ponds surrounded by plant life as overwhelming as it is lush, pools atop cliffs that look out at the sea and whose waters overflow in search of the infinite. Structures inspired by tradition, recreating lost epochs when water was the most valuable asset and an object of worship. Pools with turquoise water, genuine repositories of cool water in constant motion, pools with a natural beauty that seem to merge with sky and sea, pools whose water gushes from spouts, making evocative, hypnotic music that carries us far from this world...and, finally, pools that lie tranquil, seductive, and proud, amid their surroundings. Pools recall the magical, transparent, ever-changing spectacle of water. They are all intimate niches in which to discover new pleasures and submerge oneself in a dreamlike world.

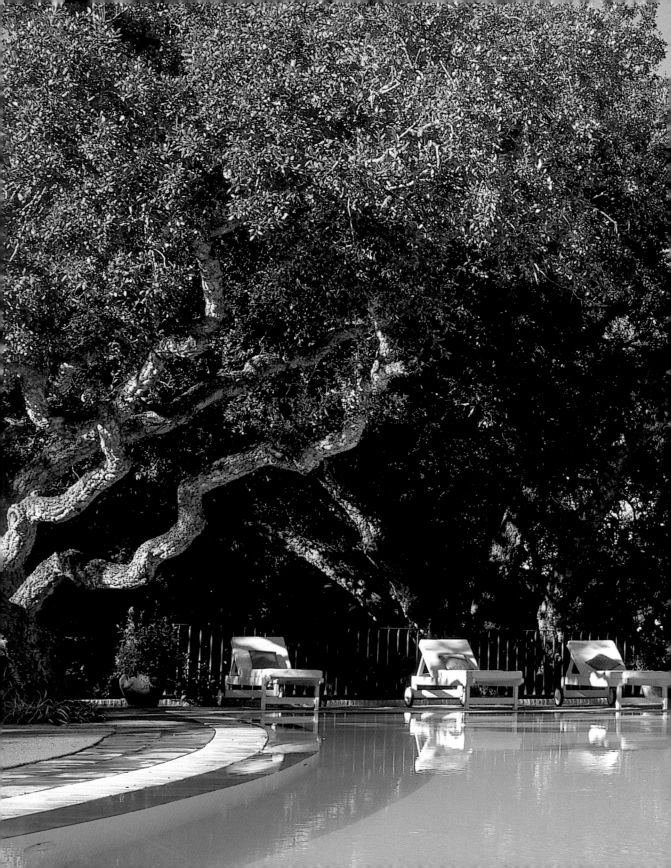

In front of a solid structure that recalls the architectural styles of other eras and other parts of the world lies this pool, whose lines mirror those of the building. The grouping is next to a golf course, so it is surrounded by green, which dominates the local landscape. Just a strip of vegetation separates the garden from the golf course, and the pool respects its setting.

The materials create an imaginary division between the pool and garden. Lush grass is interrupted by terra-cotta stones, which outline the pool. Another strip, this one of embossed marble—marble mixed with lime and pigments—creates a non-slip surface, rough but pleasant to the touch, just at the edge of the pool. The intense blue color of the water was achieved by coating the interior of the pool with light blue gresite.

Directly in front of the pavilion, the narrowest part of the pool is transversed by submerged steps that tempt the visitor to enter the water calmly and gradually. Opposite these are narrower steps made of stainless steel framed by two austere parallel poles topped by round wooden hand rests. These invite the visitor, when he has finished enjoying the water, to lose himself in the shade of the covered porch that occupies the widest part of the pavilion, crowned by a dome and attached to the main house. Each end of this lounging area, equipped with warm, comfortable furniture, has a changing room and a shower.

Orange trees, palms, cypresses, and typical Mediterranean trees complete an enchanting composition in which traditional and modern elements combine to create a relaxing, charming spot, filled with evocative touches inspired by Moorish and Andalusian styles.

Cádiz, Spain

Sophisticated
Geometry

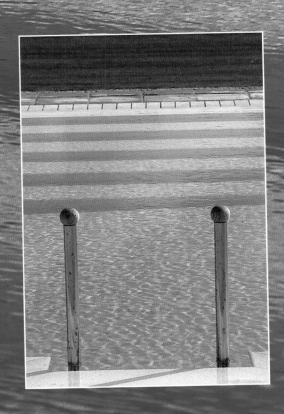

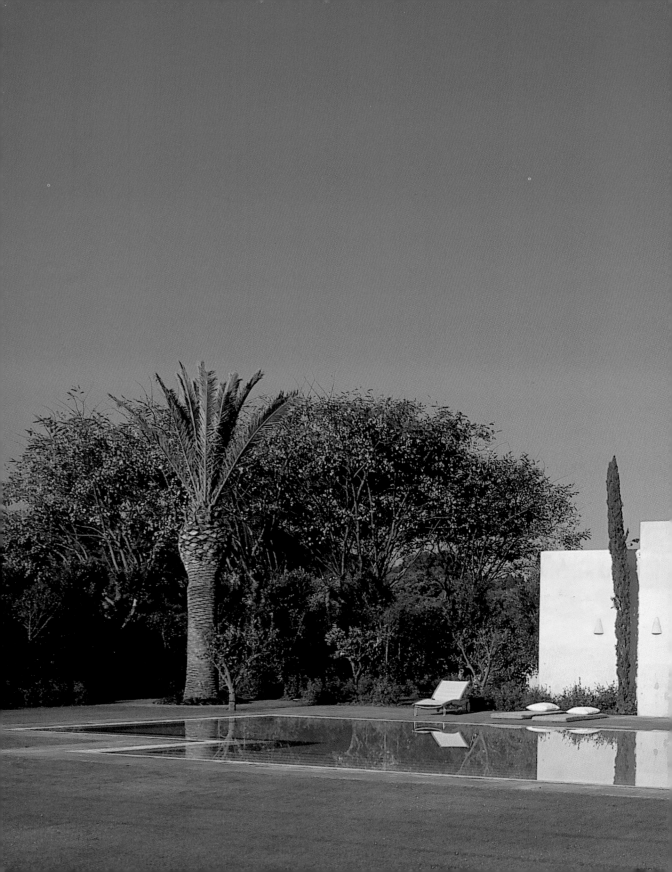

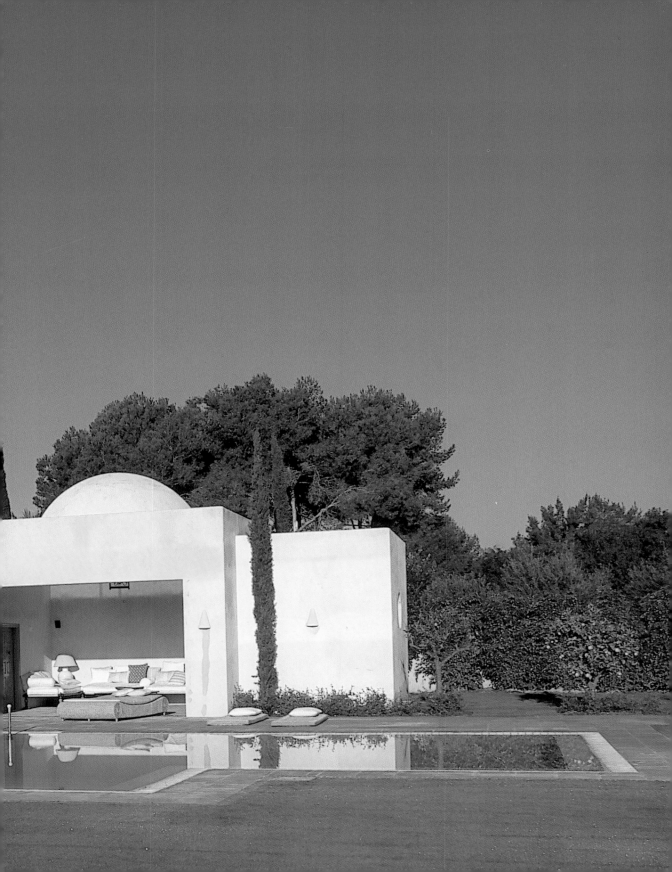

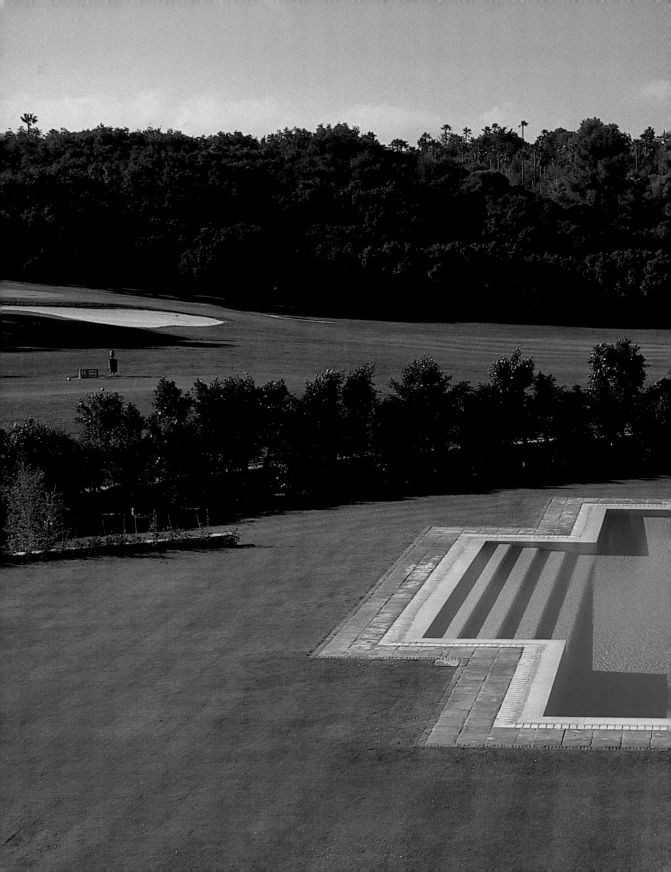

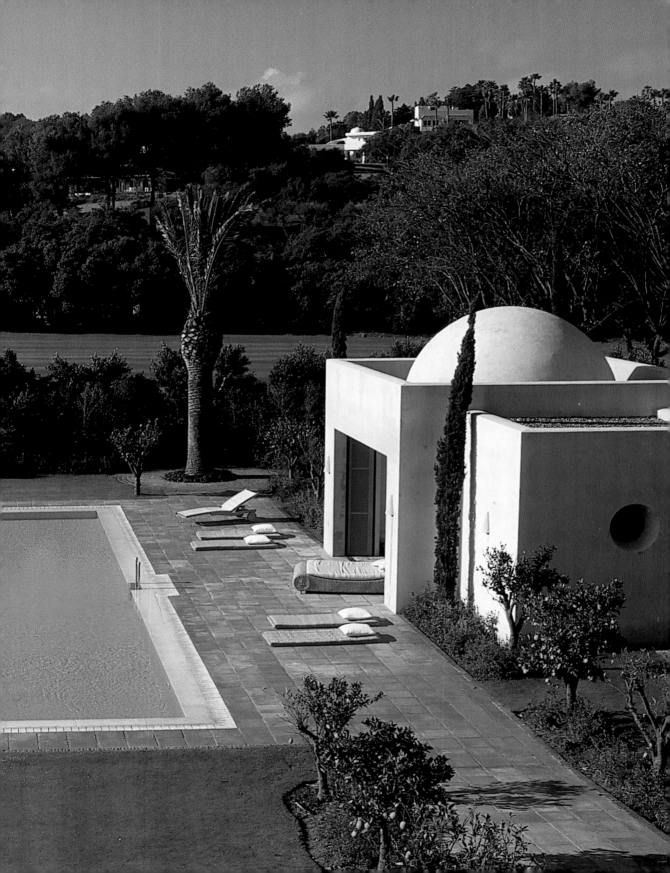

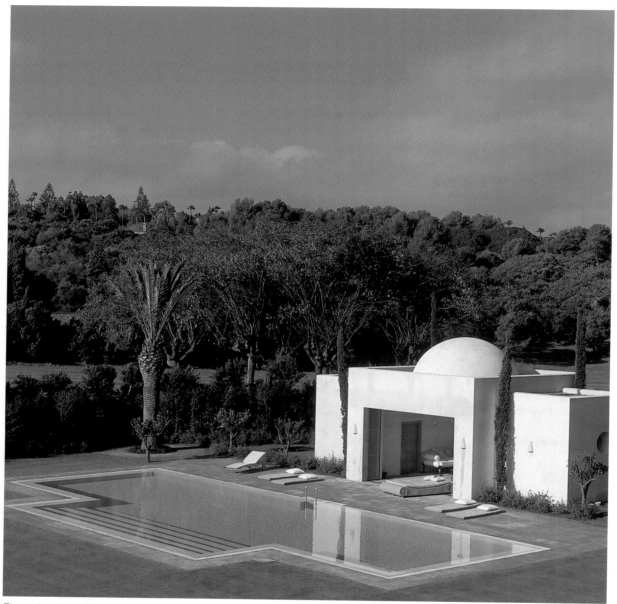

The pool sits in an elegant setting. The blue water stands out against the inviting landscape. The serene Mediterranean structure, cool and flooded with light, stands ready for relaxation and enjoyment.

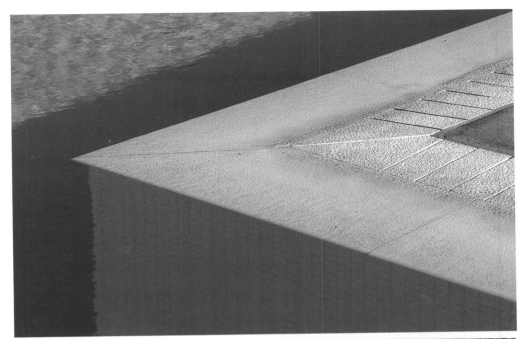

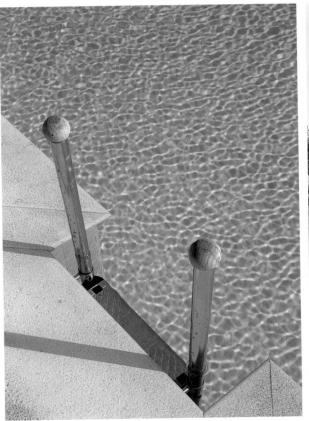

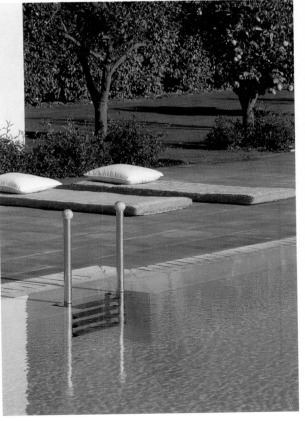

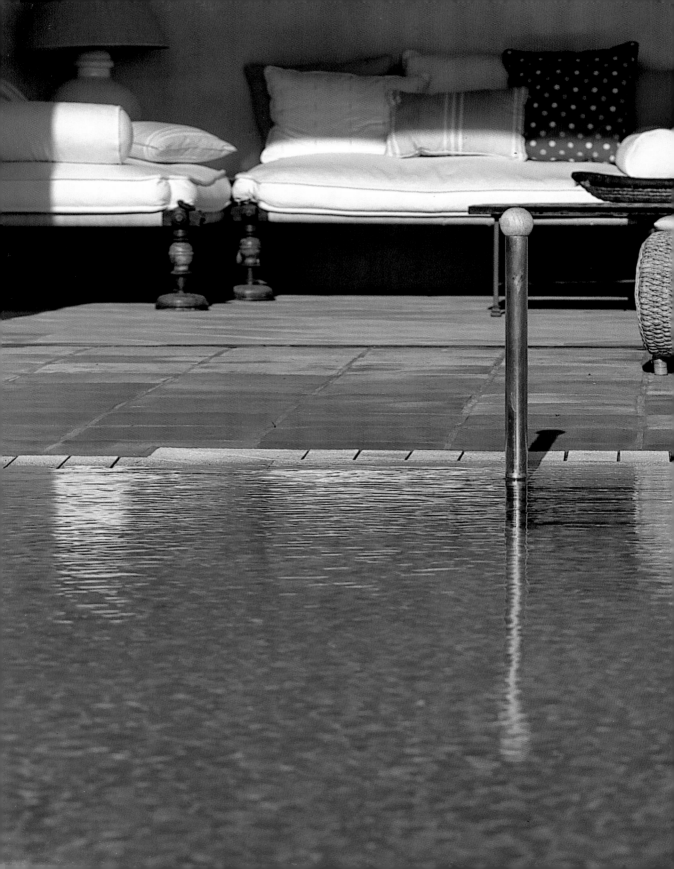

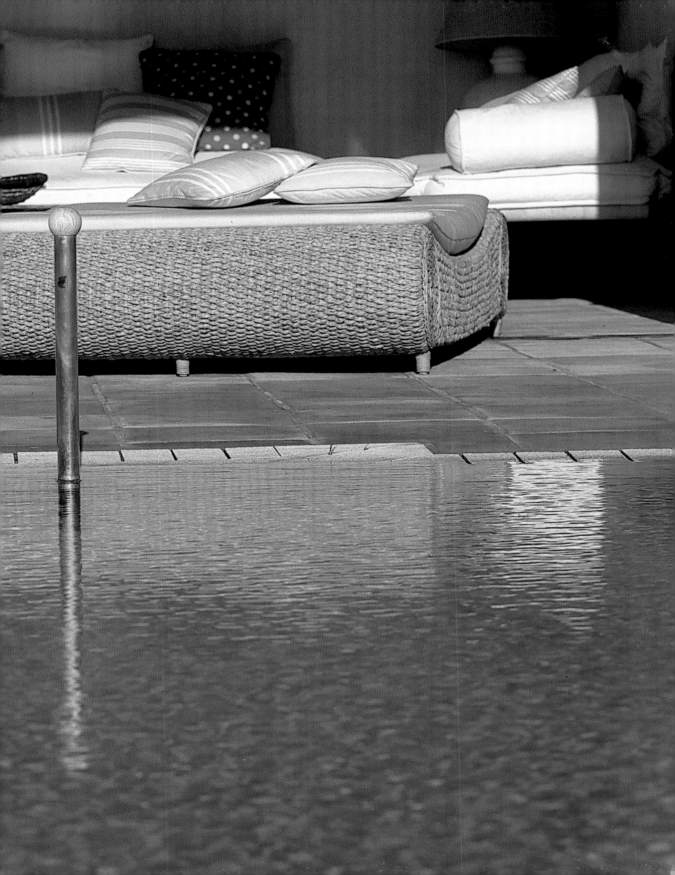

This spectacular project evolved from a few ruins, now formally integrated into the pool. The recovery and reinterpretation of ancient construction systems is an outgrowth of the traditional habitat, based on one material, earth, and one process, adobe, which involves building with bricks made of earth mixed with straw and dried in the sun.

Used by man for approximately 10,000 years to build houses and cities, adobe is enjoying a strong resurgence because it is environmentally friendly and insulating, keeping the structure cool in summer and warm in winter in a totally natural manner. Nevertheless, the resurgence of adobe architecture stems not just from interest in the tradition, but also from a very modern concern for the ecology.

For this project, located in a Moroccan paradise—the Marrakech palm grove—a group of ancient ruins was converted into an evocative sculpture, perfectly integrated with the setting and the pool.

The walls were restored with adobe brick, then covered by hand with unbaked adobe, and finally coated with plant oils for protection and preservation.

A pavilion in a restrained style presides over the pool, united chromatically with the grouping through an intense ochre, the color of earth, also used in the coating of the dividing walls.

Marrakech, Morocco

The Value of the Past

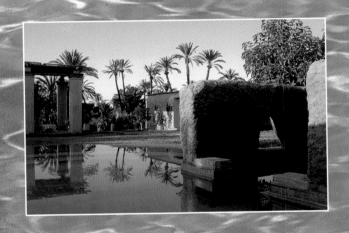

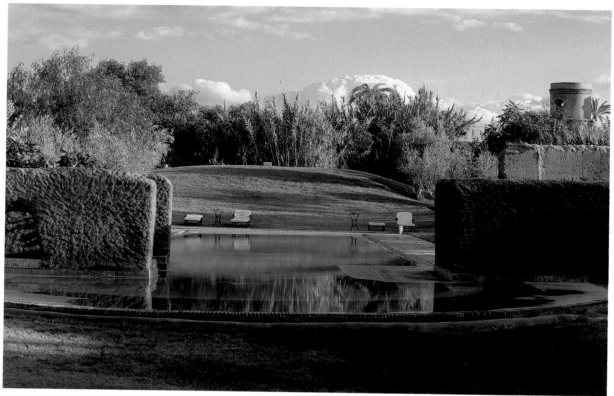

A wide view of the pool, showing the
unusual overflowing effect. This pool
design is a series of levels centered
around a group of ancient ruins, now
restored and integrated into the project
by architect Charles Boccara.

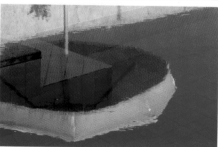

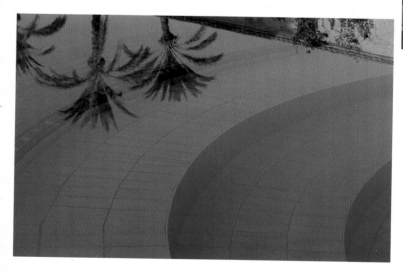

The pavilion that presides over the pool
has been done in an earth tone to unite
with its surroundings.

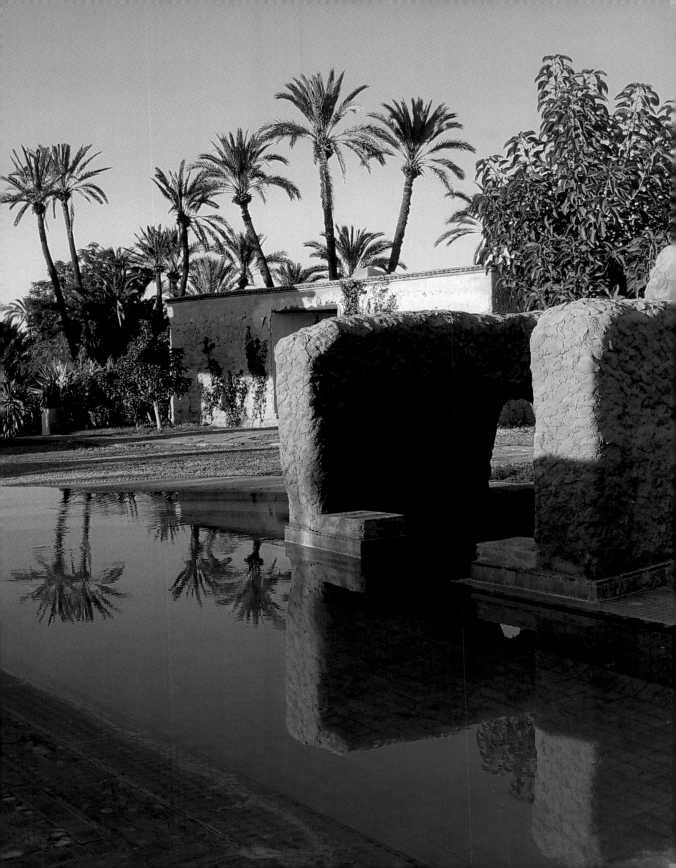

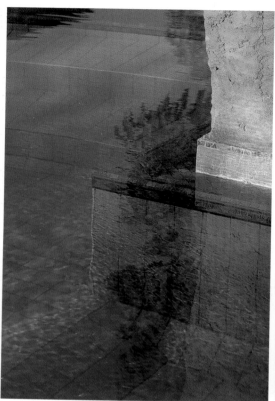

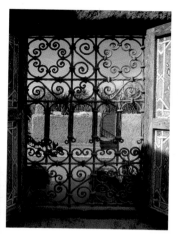

Sophisticated ornamentation decorates the base of the pool entrance. The walls are covered with adobe applied by hand and coated with plant oils for protection and preservation.

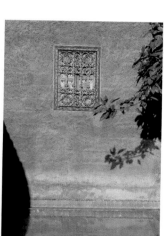

On the page to the right is a look at the special texture of the hand-applied adobe, which appears superimposed.

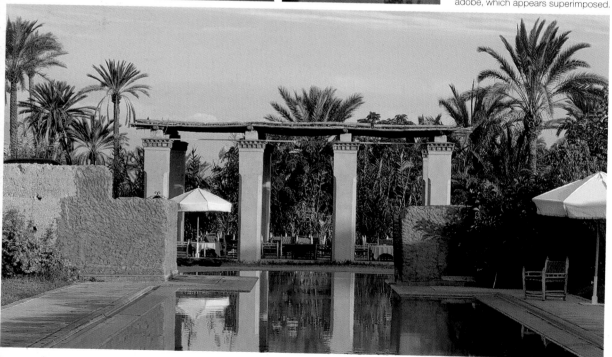

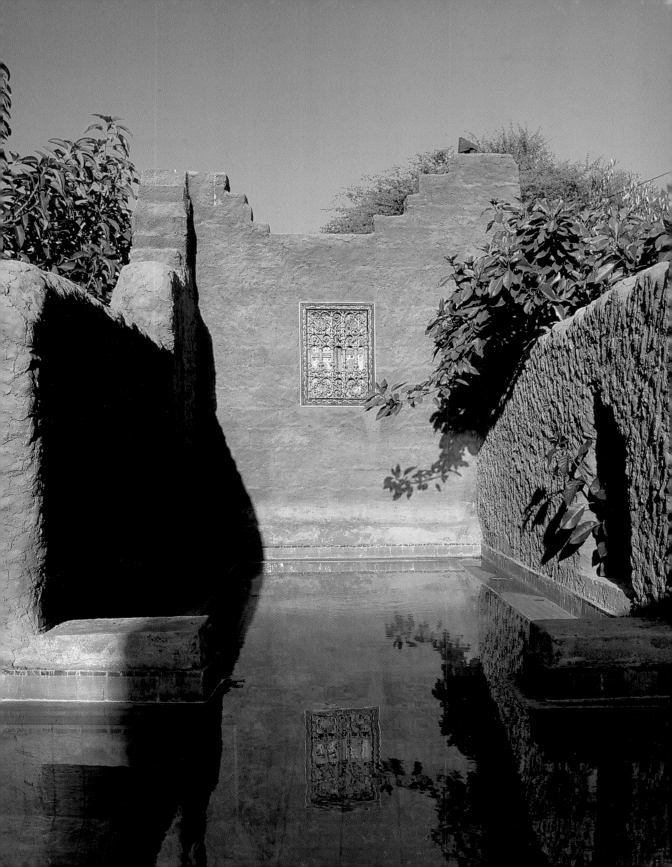

This pool is inspired by traditional ponds. It extends from the house and, when the light cooperates, reflects the house's image like a mirror.

It is an indoor–outdoor pool located in the space between the main building and the guest house.

The geometric shape of this stone structure, carefully integrated into its natural and architectural surroundings, breaks the green expanse of grass. Not impeded by any of the physical obstacles in its path, the water is guided by the stone as it flows. It even goes through doors, as if seeking the path to the sea, which it will never reach, but which is not far away. Protecting it and defining its shape are the flowerpots and the orderly, restrained landscaping that surround it. Since the pool's design stresses tradition and the past, it makes use of fragments that were already on the estate, such as an old water pump and a small pond once used for irrigation.

Complementing the grouping is a building attached to the main house. Its façade boasts straight lines and a series of symmetrical arches framing large doors. One of these doors opens onto the water, which passes smoothly by, creating a visual play of contrasts and shapes.

The constant presence of water and the choice of materials evoke ancient, lost eras, albeit in the context of a modern pool. The pronounced straightness and geometry of the entire complex is broken by the chromatic harmony and the natural setting that surrounds it and protects it from the eyes of strangers and anything else that might upset the peace and quiet.

Saint Tropez, France

Water in Continuous Motion

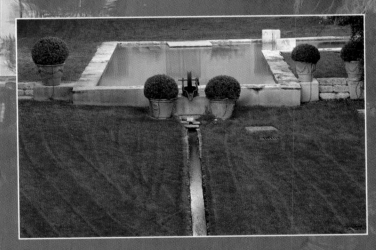

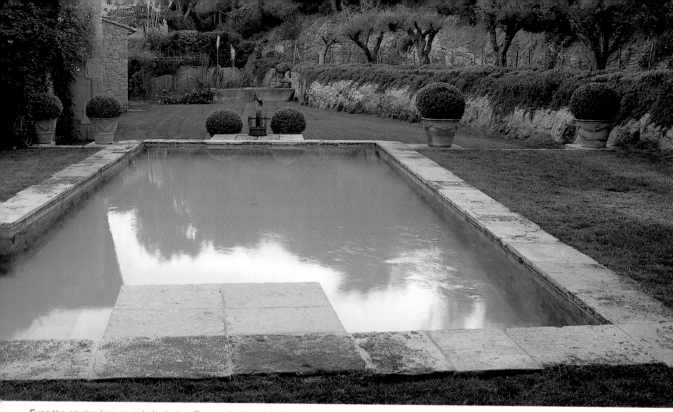

Even the garden has an orderly design. Surrounded by abundant vegetation, the water flows into the pool from its ancient source.

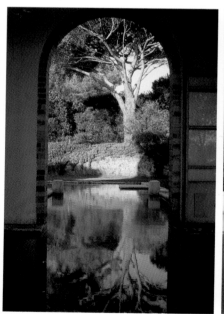

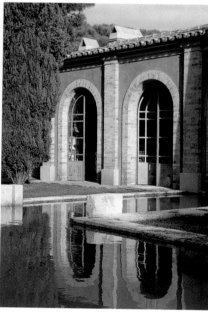

A generous arch is the entryway for the water, which stops for nothing in its path. The result is a spectacular composition.

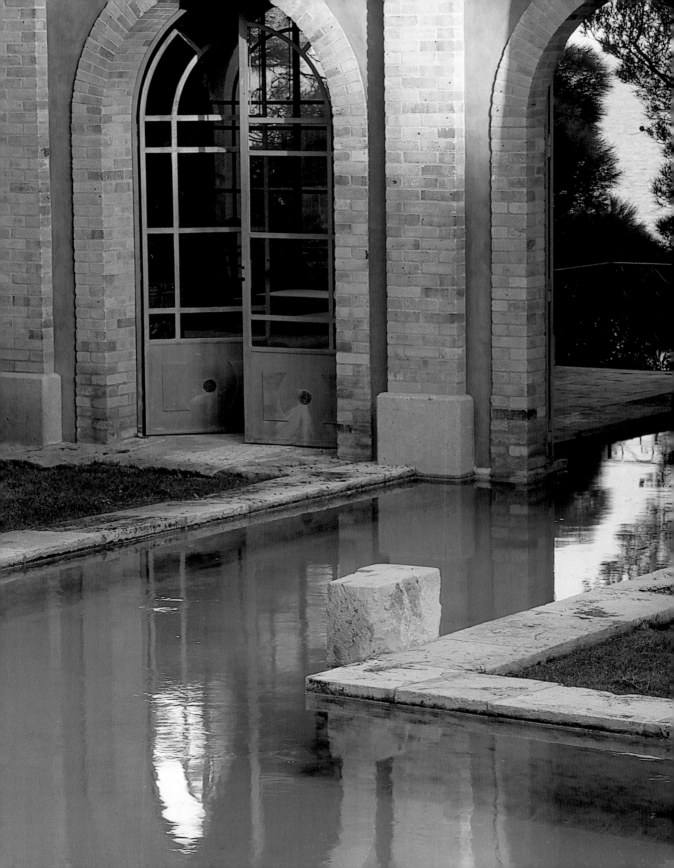

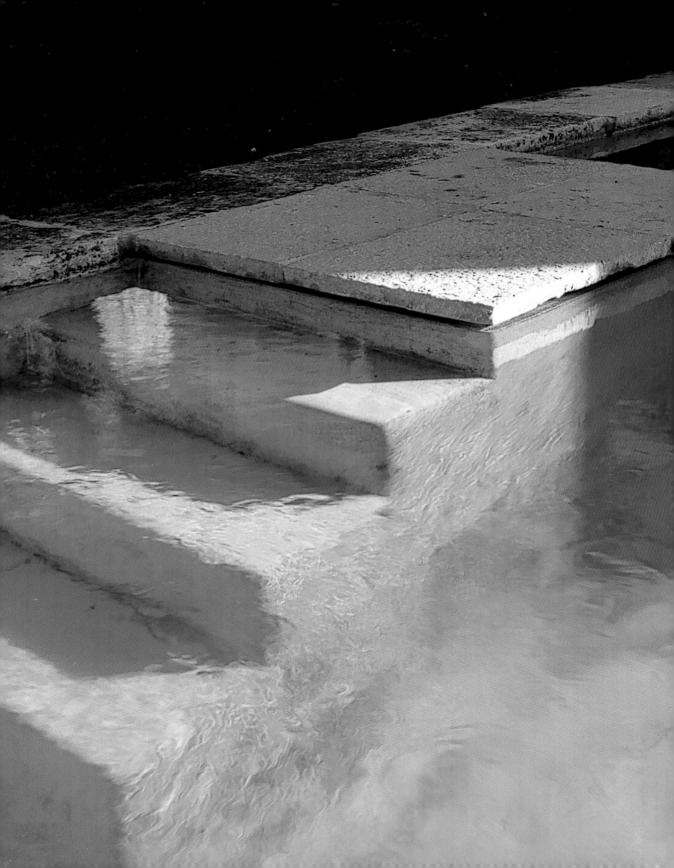

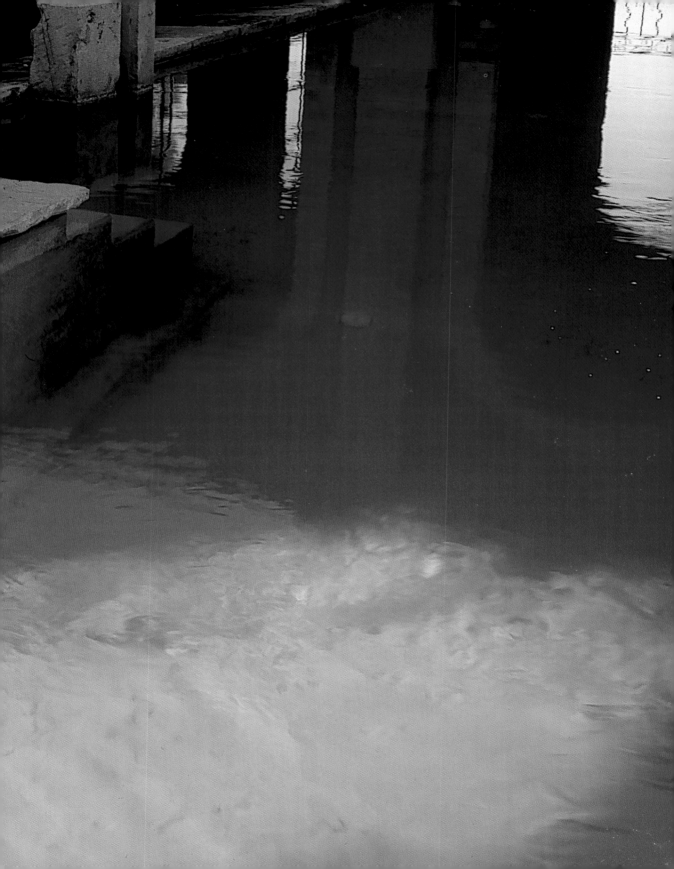

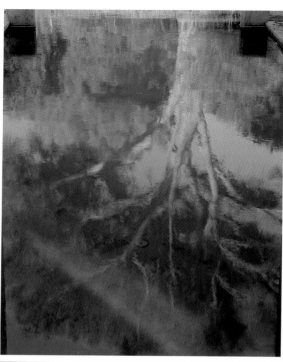

The water reflects some of the house's architecture and its surroundings, creating a very evocative play of shadows.

Like a protective cloak, the unpolished stone shapes the water's path. The cement at the bottom was tinted with light colors to give the water its special hue.

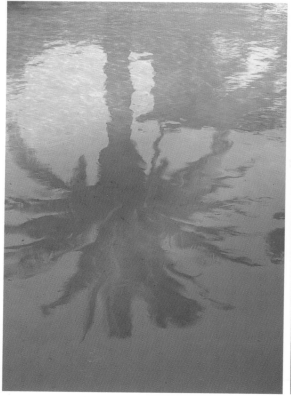

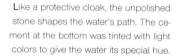

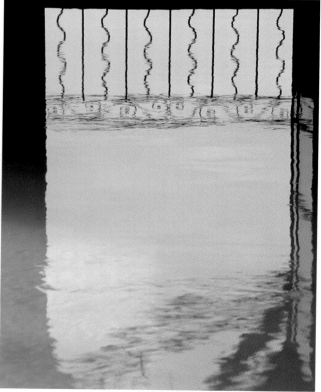

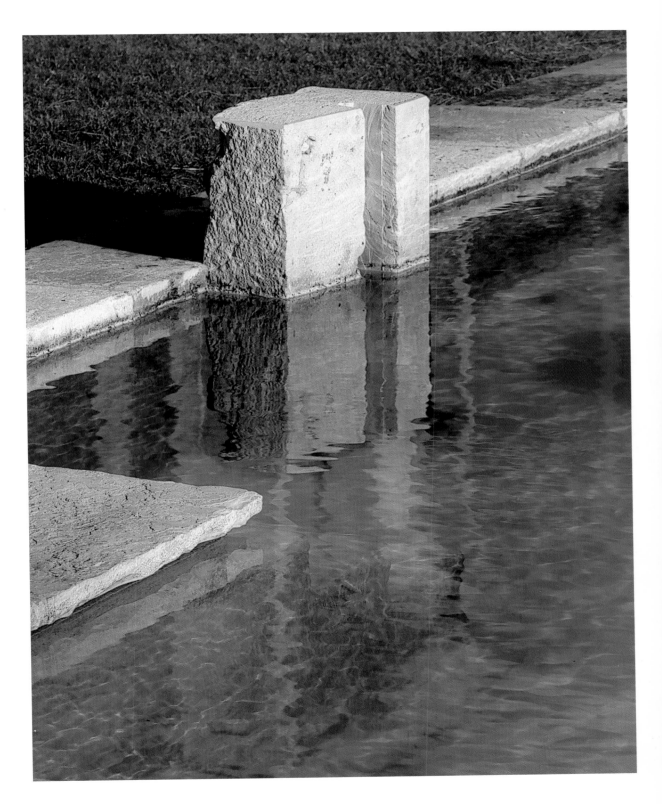

This unique overflowing pool is hidden away in the rocky wall of an old quarry high on a hill. To obtain the perfect fusion of the project and its natural setting, a recess in the rocky wall was used. The result is spectacular: an imposing wall of rock, eroded on one side by water from an artificial waterfall and covered on the other side by a blanket of plant life that softens the roughness of the stone.

The pool was treated like a sheet of water, although it resembles the small, deep, natural rock ponds in the eastern part of the Alps, where the water stays frozen even at the height of summer. The rocky wall was kept practically intact, even the submerged area, respecting its formal structure and unmistakable texture. The main entrance reveals the merging of the rocky wall with the volume of the pool.

Levels and gradients structure the placement of two extensive terraces paved with fired clay flagstones whose reddish color adds a note of warmth while creating a contrast with the light color of the rock. The simplicity of the natural materials enhances the rustic effect of the grouping, although it is softened by the sophisticated iron chaise lounges and the elegant color of the upholstered cushions.

Barcelona, Spain

In the Heart of a Quarry

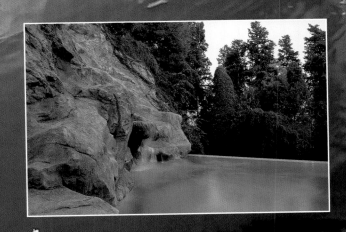

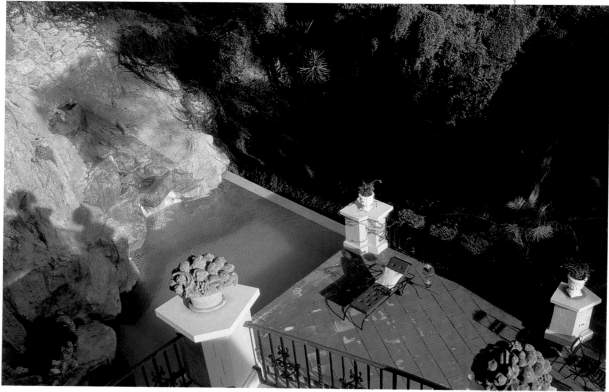

A spectacular view of
the pool and lower
terrace. The shape of
the old stone quarry,
now a luxuriant garden,
can still be seen amid
the thick vegetation.

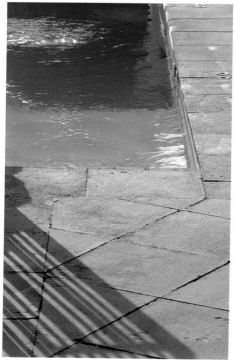

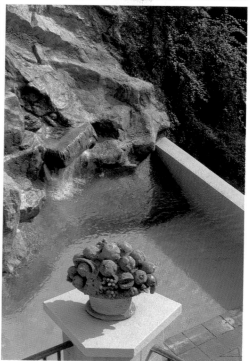

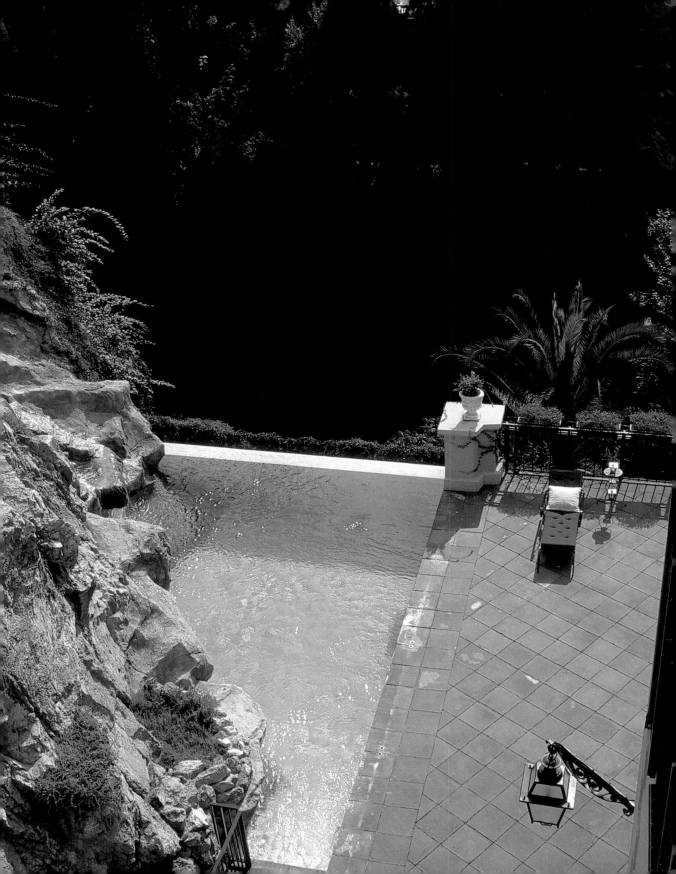

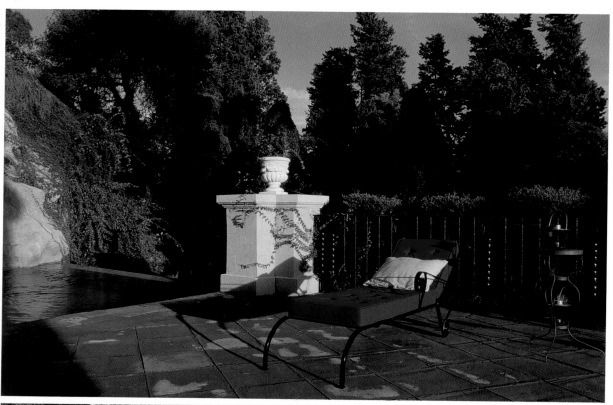

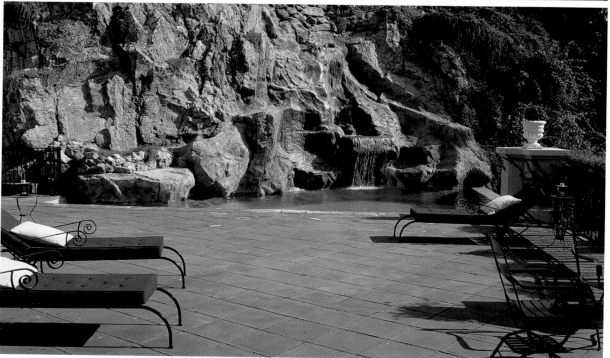

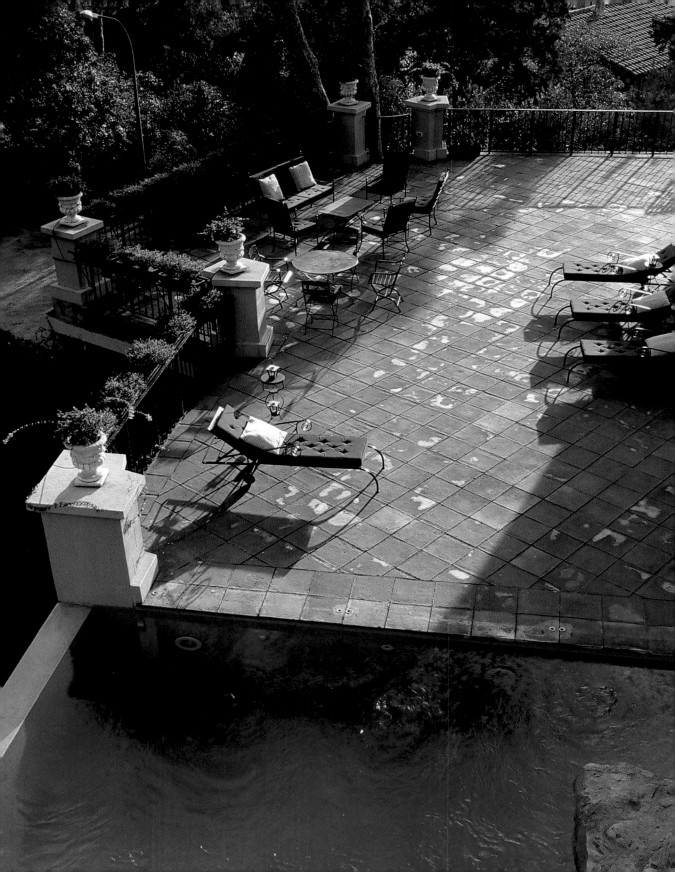

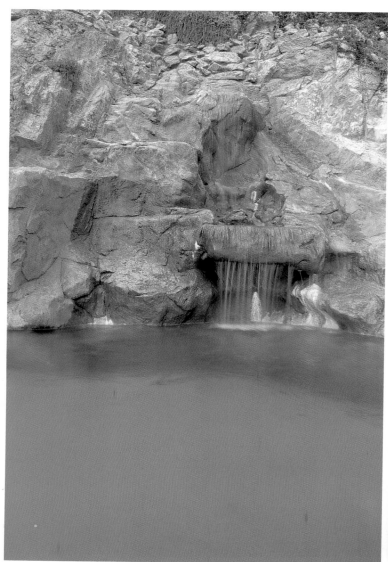

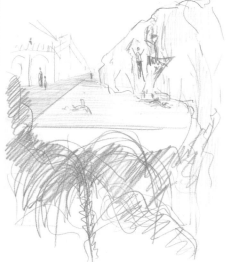

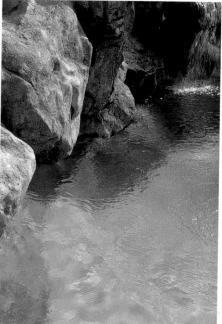

The rocky wall's structure and
unmistakable texture were preserved.
The fusion of this wall with the volume of
the pool is visible at the main entrance.

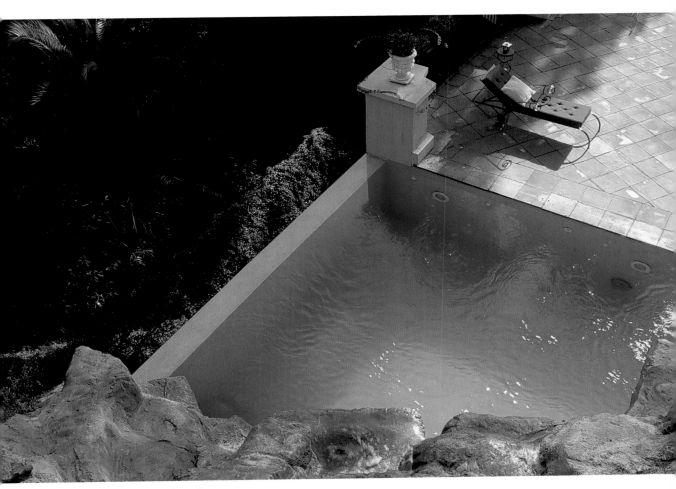

The pool was dealt with as a sheet of water, although it is similar to the natural rock ponds that remain frozen year-round.

This pool is surrounded by straight forms—like the walls of a house—that protect and define it. It was placed far from the main entrance to the house—an old, renovated garage—sheltered from the wind and from the gaze of passersby.

In fact, the pool is in the most isolated part of the garden, behind the house. So the space is open but pleasantly private.

Hidden behind geometric shapes, the rectangular lines of this pool are framed by polished concrete flagstones surrounded by soft grass—also enclosed by straight lines—alternating with stone pavement.

The contrast of textures, materials, and colors creates a space with a unique aesthetic, something between a Zen garden and the traditional gardens more representative of Mediterranean settings.

The linearity and tension produced by the upright figures is balanced by the colors used—ranging from green to purple, with white and dark blue—the plant life, the roughness of the stone wall, and the minimal furnishings.

The deliberate play of exaggerated, conspicuous structures creates an overwhelming visual spectacle. Irresistibly simple and restrained, the effect is generated by contrast, in order to define a corner with an aesthetic and stylistic mix seemingly separate from the reality of the grouping. The corner serves as one more illusion, since the pool is wholly integrated into its surroundings.

Nimes, France

Play of Shapes

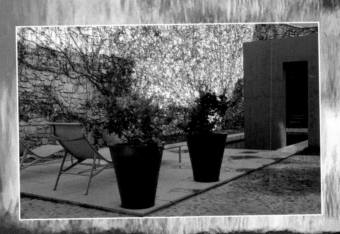

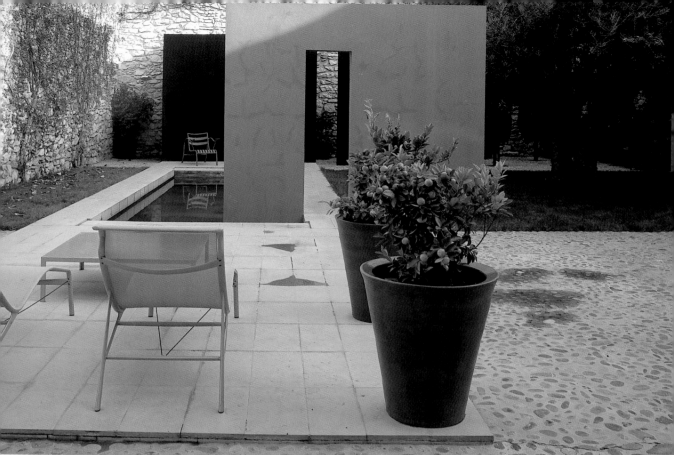

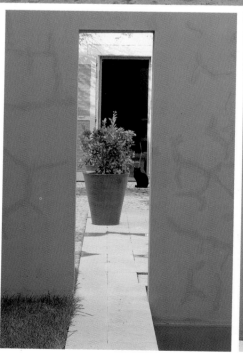

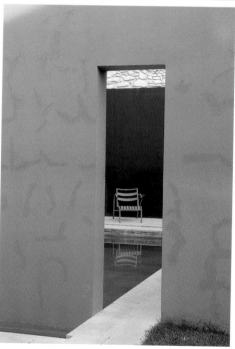

The geometric shapes define the space like a picture frame. An exaggerated theatricality is accentuated by the contrasts of the rough, natural stone wall, the straight geometric structures, and the grass and stone ground cover.

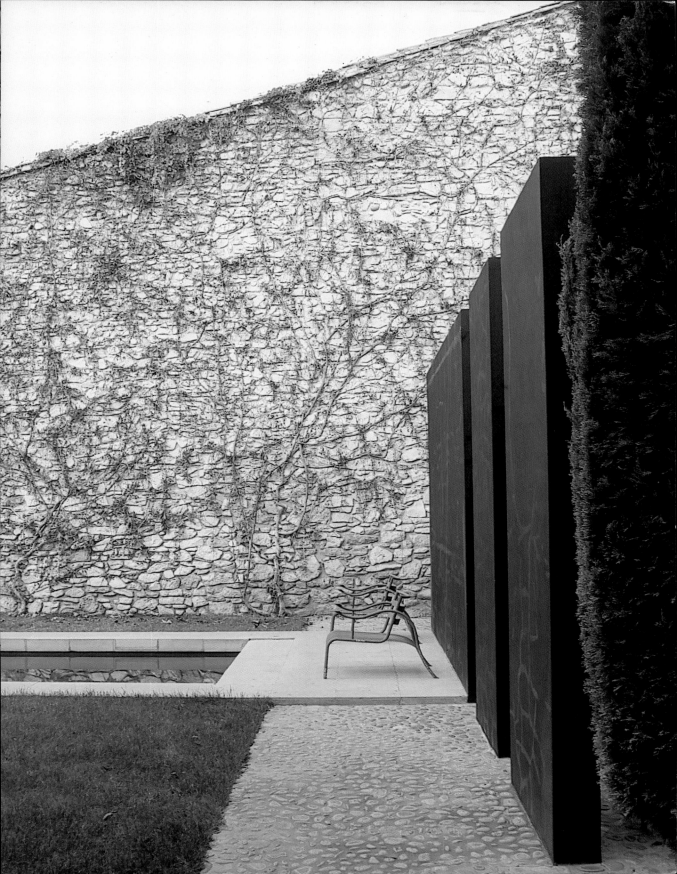

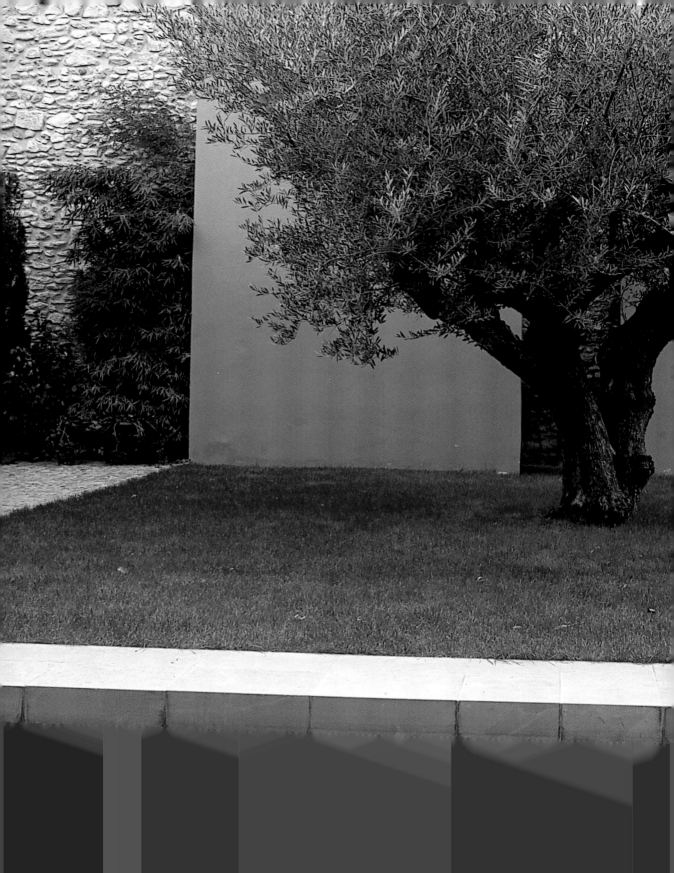

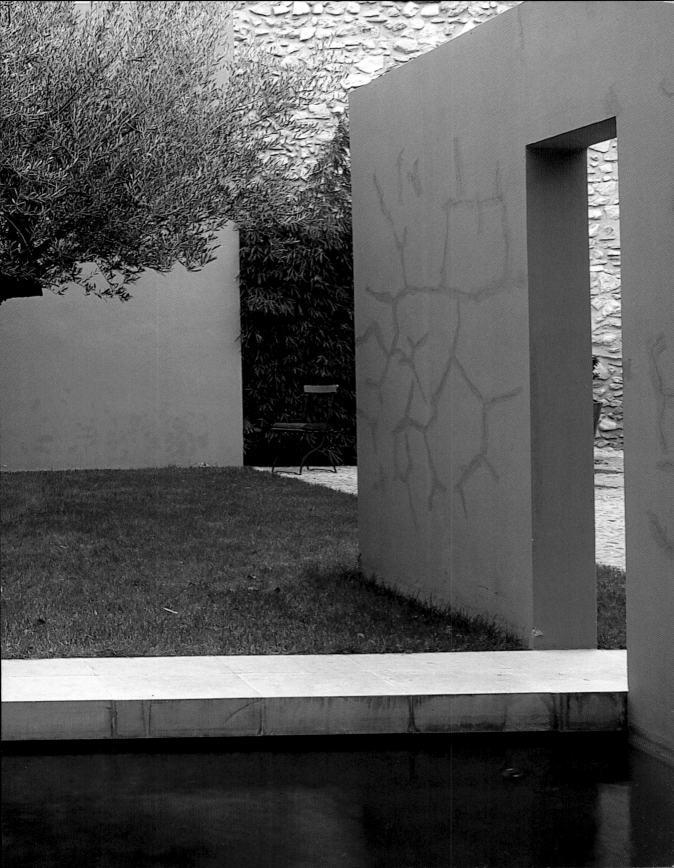

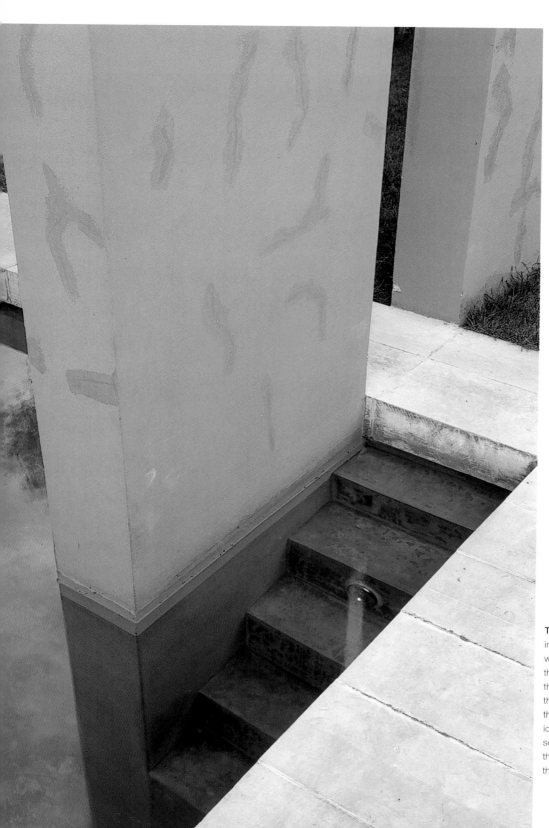

The solution of sinking the stairs into the water and hiding them behind one of the walls standing in the pool emphasizes the minimalist aesthetic that pervades the setting. The color of the water comes from the gray cement.

The formal hardness of the rectilinear outline stands out even more against the ivy-covered natural stone wall that protects the pool.

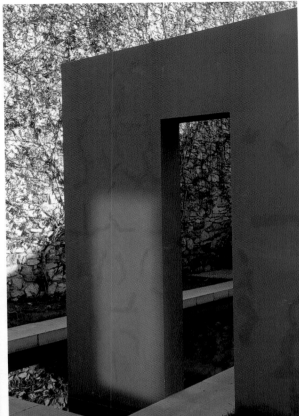

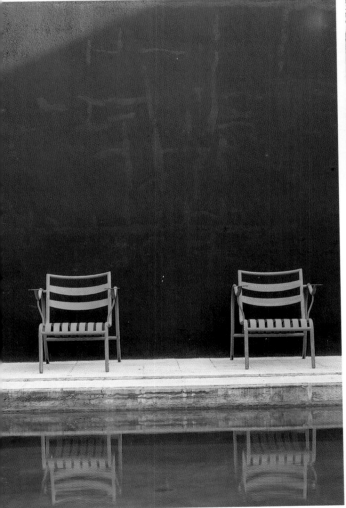

At the end of the pool, two lone purple iron chairs seem to be projected against a dark wall that also defines the space.

This pool is situated in an old restored Mexican ranch and framed by multiple visual perspectives. Located on the house's semi-covered patio, it was conceived as a small, cistern-like trough, inspired by old-fashioned washhouses. Symmetrically aligned above the pool, six spouts circulate the water and create a smooth, natural melody that can be heard from any corner.

In this project, space, color, and the texture of a single material, concrete, merge and complement each other to create a setting rich in nuances, where the light participates directly in creating volumes and perspective. In fact, the forcefulness of the color serves a dual purpose here: to soften the sober quality of the area and to visually lower the height of the room, creating a cool refuge from the summer heat. An intense earth color, a warm orangish tone that stands out in clear contrast, was chosen for the floor.

For decoration, both the furnishings and ornamental elements were carefully chosen to serve as sculptures. A collection of little bronze statues at strategic locations around the pool, a painting subtly placed at one end, the old swinging bench on the upper level, or even the group of ferns, acquire a special prominence enhanced by the presence of color. Finally, a delicate white dove crowns this beautiful composition, a symbol of peace that conveys the character of this room.

Jalisco, Mexico

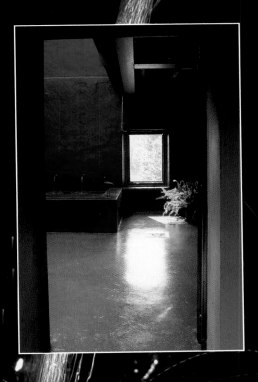

Chromatic
Personality

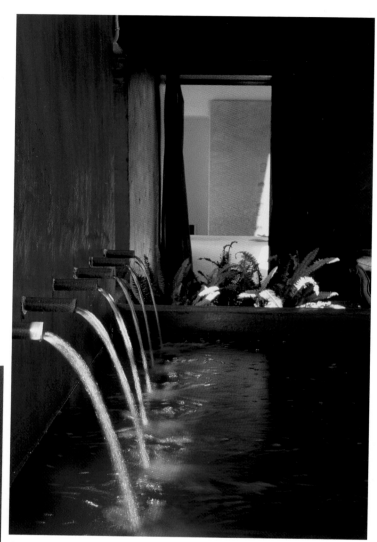

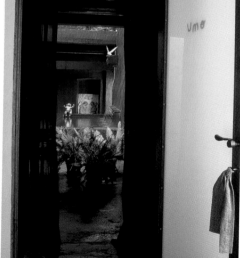

An etched glass door separates the water area, located on the semi-covered central patio, from the luminous interior of the house. The chromatic contrasts and informal balance can be appreciated from the threshold of the entryway.

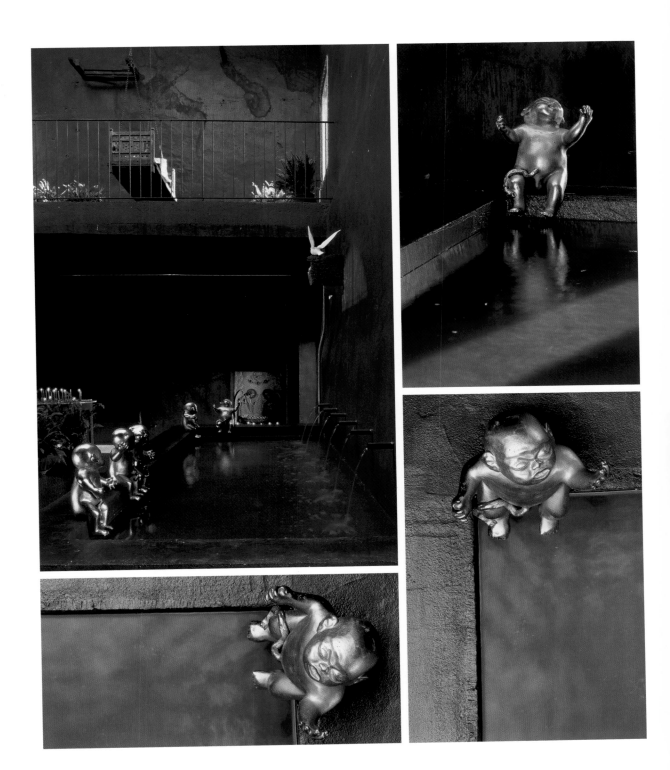

Symmetrically aligned, six slender jets
circulate the water in the pool, creating
an orderly but bright and colorful
cascade, which can be heard almost
anywhere in the house.

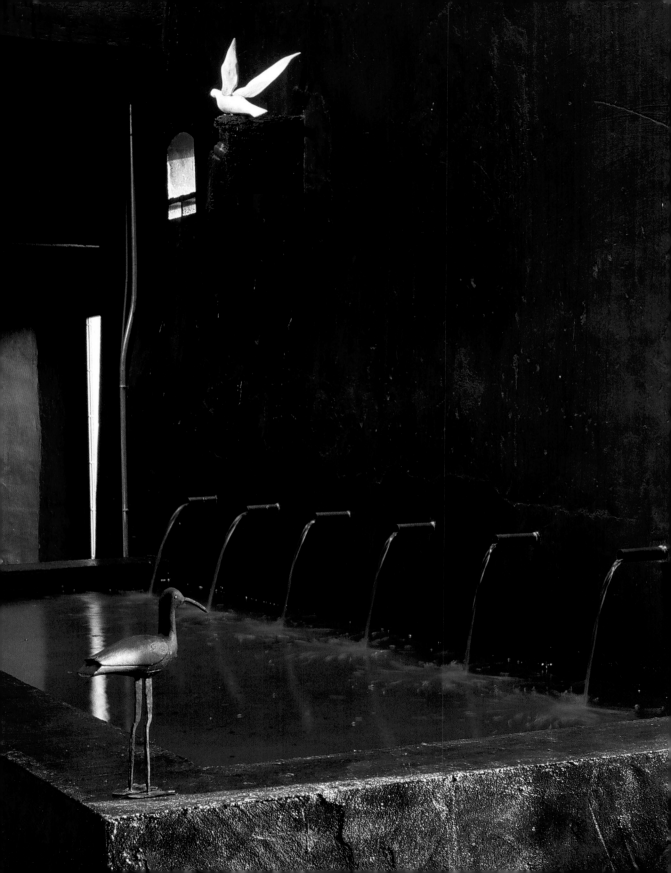

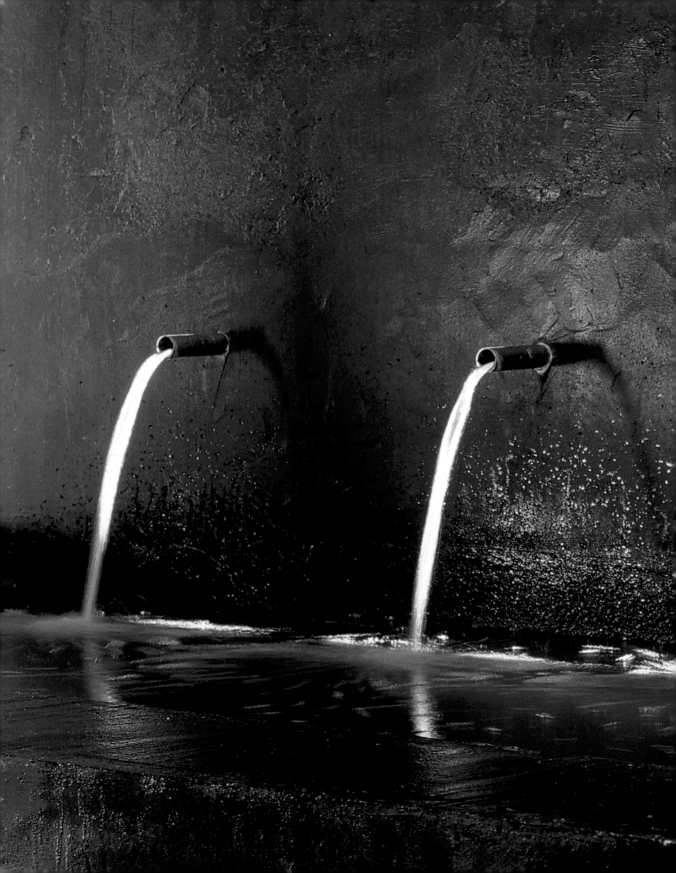

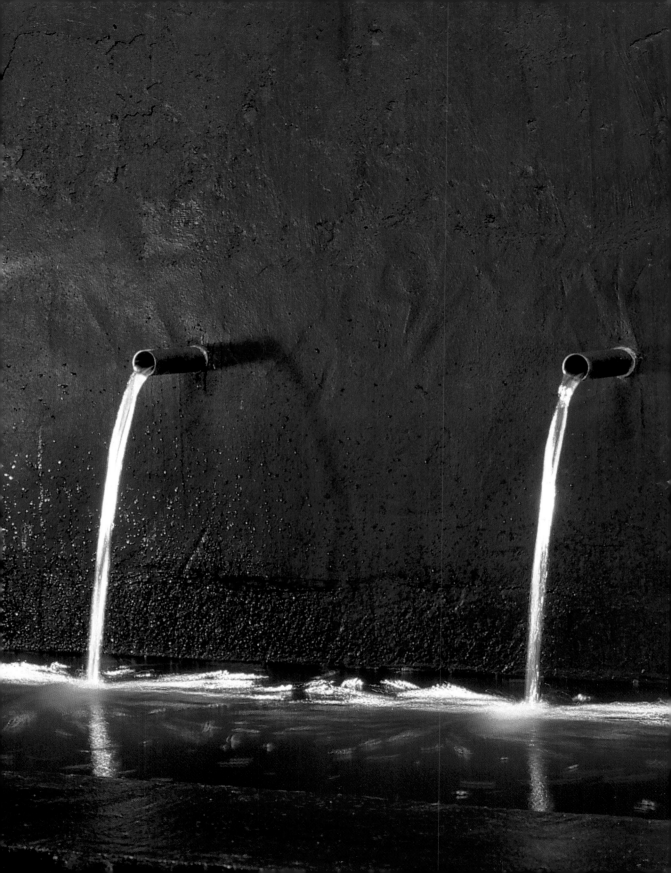

The eye is irresistibly drawn to this pool in its luxuriant Ibiza setting. From here, one can gaze at the island's spectacular scenery while enjoying a sunbath or a swim.

Rather than act an insurmountable barrier, the steep slope of the land has become an asset. Taking advantage of the topographical features, the pool was conceived as an extension of the two principal structures: the house and a small annex. An elegant rectangle, its interior has been painted white. The garden surrounding it was planned so that every element is perfectly integrated, from the shape of the pool to the colors of the furnishings, which blend with the setting. A refined, austere style pays homage to and enhances the surroundings.

Light, an essential and inescapable element in Mediterranean architecture, also has a crucial role. It plays with the water, the plant life, and the structures, creating surprising, unforgettable images.

This grouping, designed to take full advantage of the view, affords an attractive place from which to relax and enjoy the natural wonders that surround it.

Ibiza, Spain

Perfect Blend

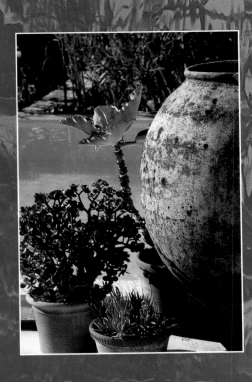

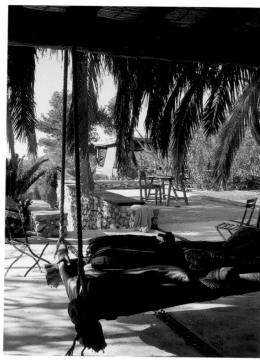

The placement of the pool took advantage of the sloping terrain. The loungers face the exquisite landscape, a total luxury for the senses.

The pool was designed as an extension of the house and can be accessed directly from the living room. The two spaces—separated only by a few steps—flow into each other.

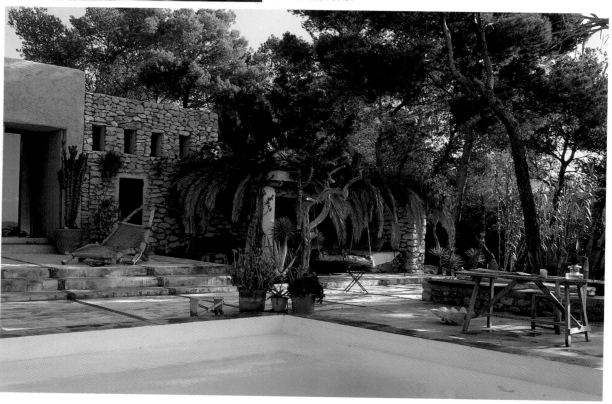

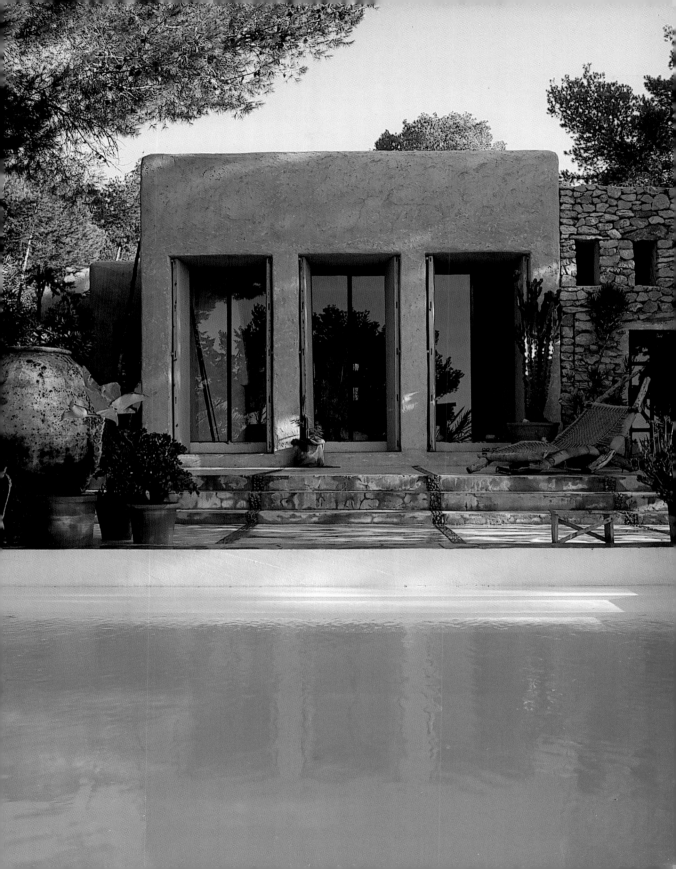

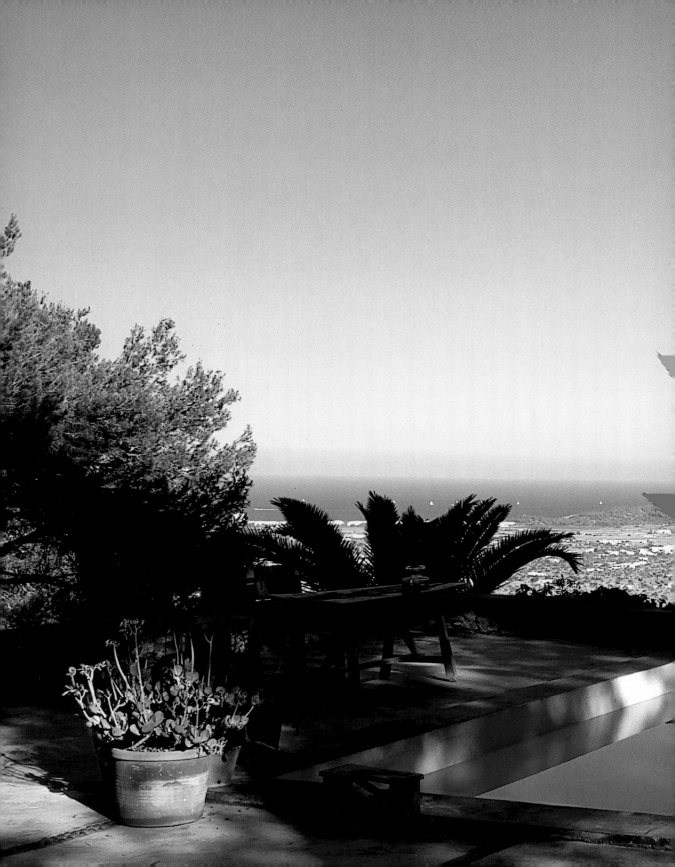

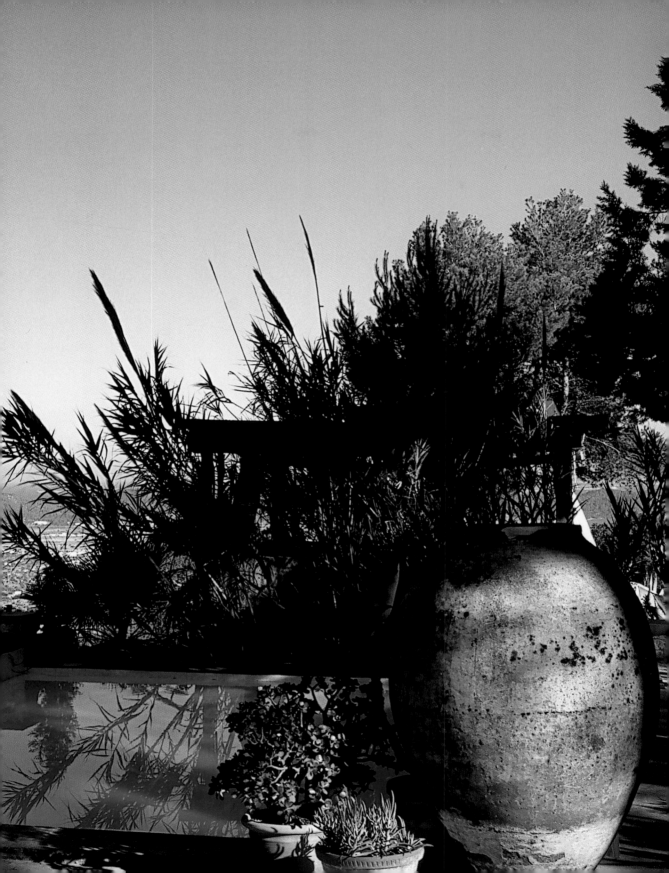

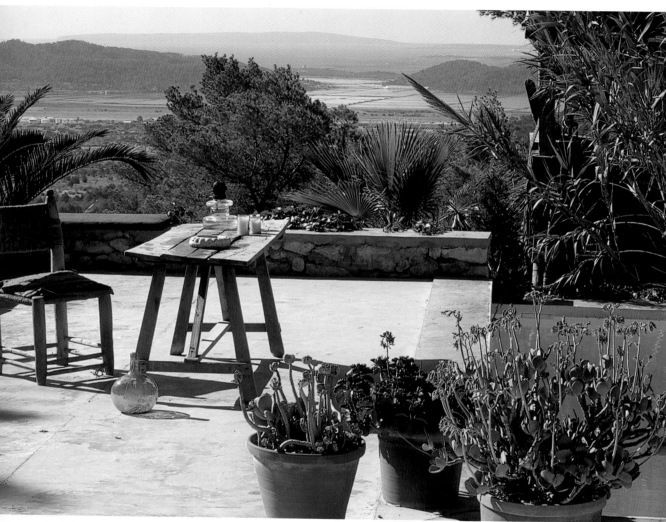

The furnishings and decorative elements exude simplicity and tradition. They have been strategically placed, almost merging with the surroundings, making the plant life a dominant force.

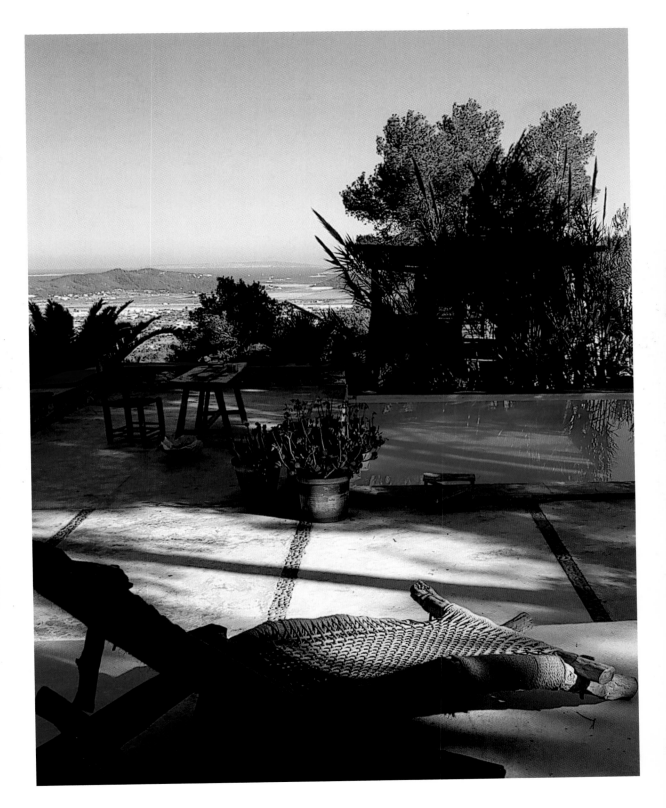

On the edge of a small thicket, this pool, in the shape of a Hispano-Arab irrigation channel, emerges like a placid mountain river. The quiet murmur of a fountain, placed strategically between two rows of stairs leading to the water, completes this balanced, mature landscape whose reminders of the past fade as the grouping as a whole is studied.

The visual center of this project is the low sculptured wall that encloses the pool and also provides a means of entering the water. In addition to visually isolating the pool from the more wooded areas of the garden, the pool's texture and chromatic streaks, together with the flat fountain between the two areas, constitute an original technique to formally balance a narrow, long pool.

This visual element, together with the studied landscaping, has softened the pool's strict linearity. In fact, just a glance away from the center of attention are two soft patches of grass serenely surrounding the pool, countering its formal hardness. The different tones of the nearby vegetation and the colorful presence of a magnificent bougainvillea, which covers the porch of the house, are the elements that visually order the natural setting, making it a self-contained, easily-maintained garden.

Mallorca, Spain

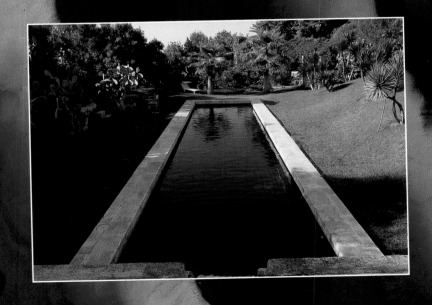

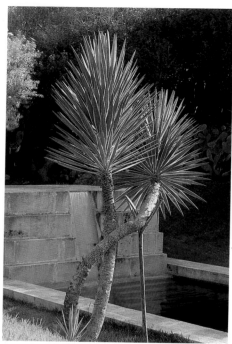

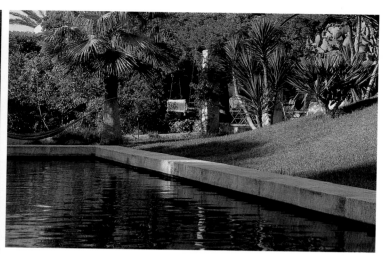

The linearity of this pool, shaped like an irrigation channel, is softened by two grassy slopes covered with easily-maintained vegetation. As the only note of color, a magnificent bougainvillea graces the porch adjacent to the pool.

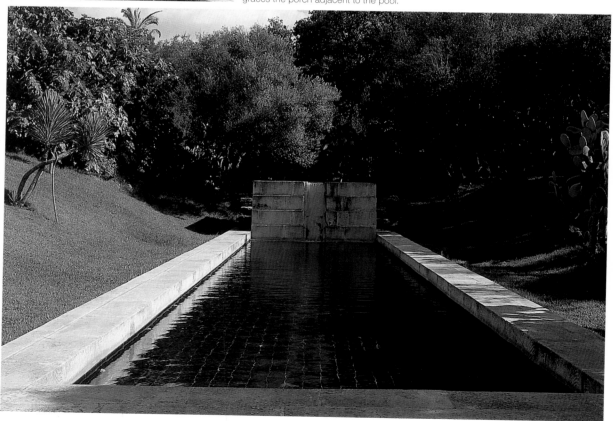

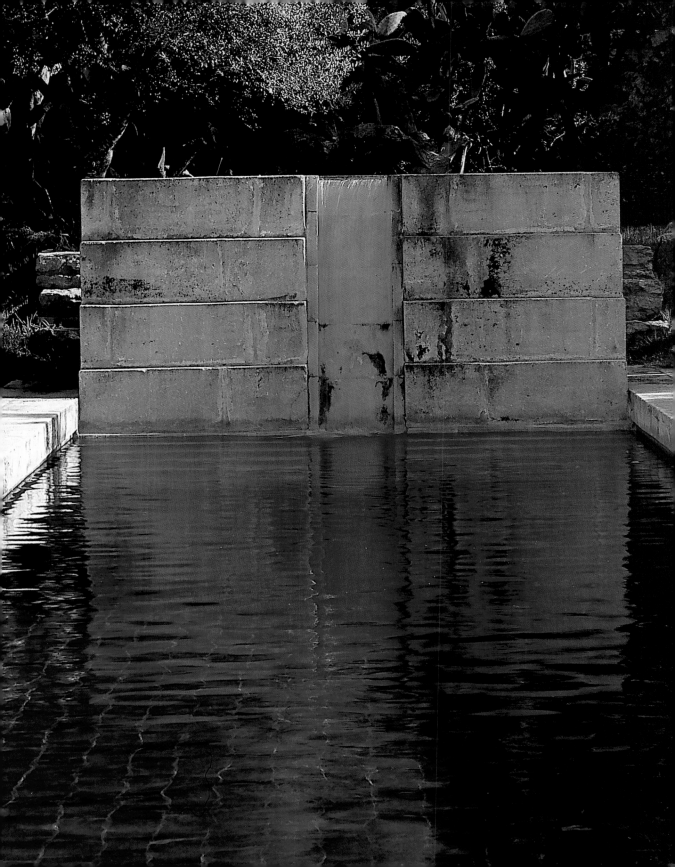

This pool invites the visitor to contemplate its depths and swim. Situated at one side of the house, on a wooded hill, under the blue of an infinite sky and with the sea in the background, it enjoys an attractive visual connection with the interior of the home. The pool's design makes excellent use of the available space. A large glass wall extends the entire length of the pool, making for a fluid relationship between exterior and interior. Theatrical curtains protect privacy when required.

Supported by concrete posts, the pool is striking in its length and narrowness, emphasized by the rest of the grouping's architectural elements, such as the façade of the house, the wooden planks that cover it, and the delicate, plain railings of the terraces. Vantage points placed at different levels, parallel to the house take advantage of the irregular terrain. Spatial limitations imposed by the site and the building are overcome by employing solutions that combine aesthetics and functionality.

The rectangular lines, finished in white and highlighted by a floor of appropriately treated wooden planks, frame the pool, which echoes the lines of the building. This cutting-edge style and minimalist aesthetic dominate the entire grouping. The deep blue of the water contrasts with the formal and stylistic simplicity of the rooms. This project does an excellent job of unifying the architecture of the house with its immediate surroundings.

Marseille, France

Bordering on the Theatrical

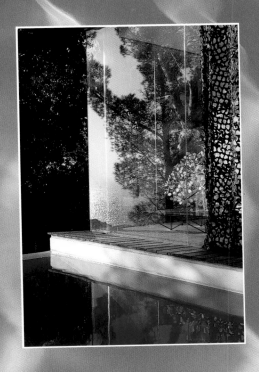

The wooden planks alongside the pool, as well as the suggestive texture of the generous curtain, give the grouping an exquisite warmth, in pleasant contrast to the austere interior décor, the cold glass walls, and the plain railings.

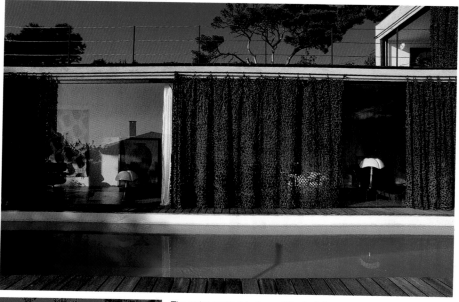

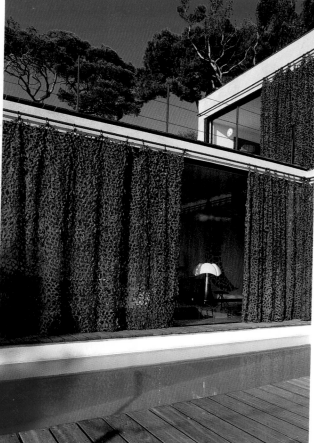

The strict geometric lines of the building are echoed by three elements: the roof terrace, the pool, and the other terrace, a vantage point which is near the water and supported by wooden columns. The grouping makes no concessions to luxurious decor or unnecessary ornamentation. Purity and clarity of line define the spaces.

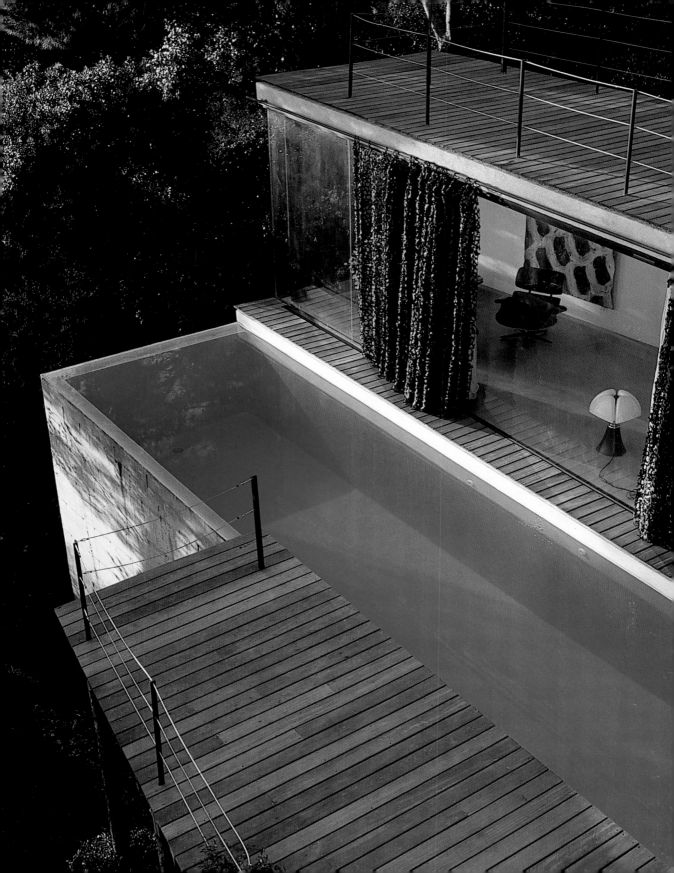

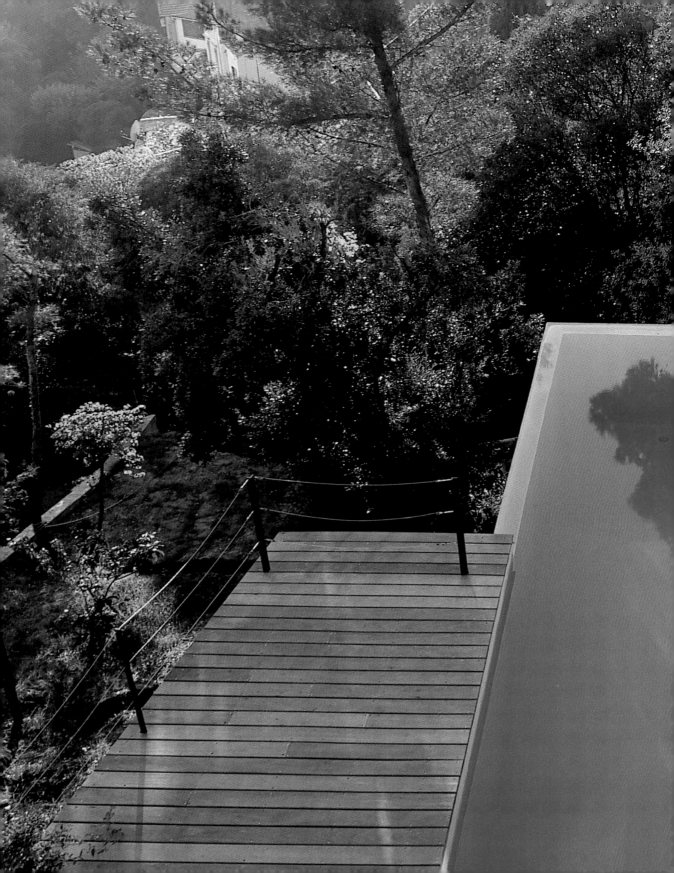

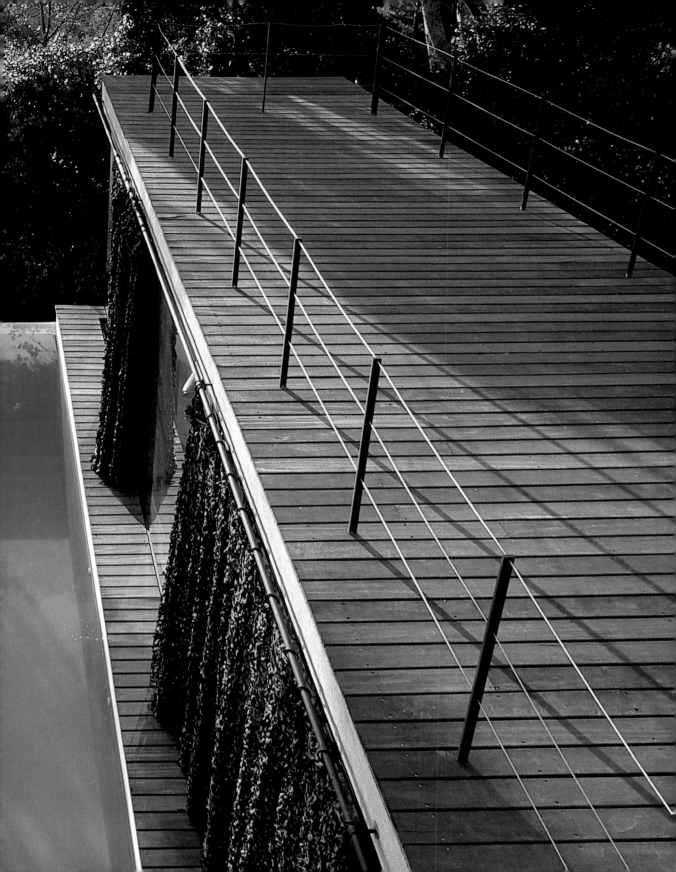

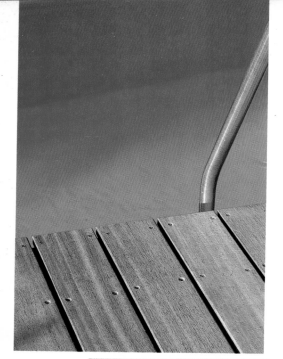

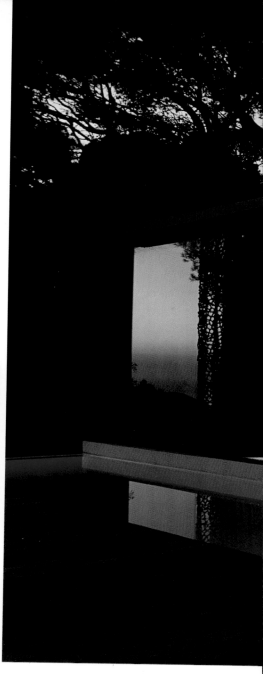

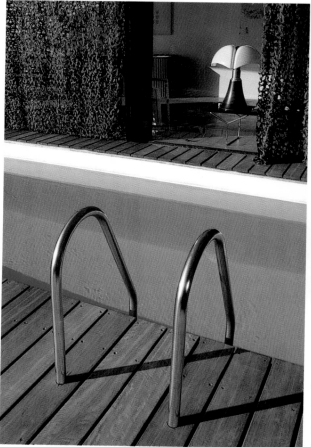

The wooden planks alongside the pool
have been treated to withstand the rain,
wind, strong summer sun, and constant
humidity. The color of the water was
achieved by painting the lining white.

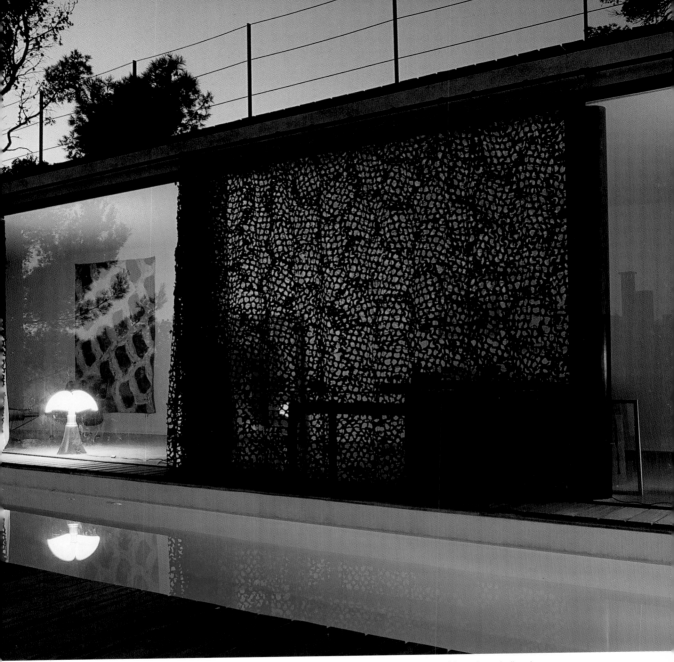

At night, lighting makes it possible to enjoy the spectacular beauty of this extremely severe composition, whose hallmarks are simplicity and austerity.

The emerald water of this pool engages in a dialogue with the geometric shapes and the natural, rugged stone. This pool, whose waters flow among the rocks, breathing the essence of the past, silently and graciously occupies its assigned niche amidst the house and garden. At the foot of an old building's spectacular stone wall, the water in this unique pool lies hidden away in the heart of the complex, and the wall gives way to subtler shapes.

Overwhelmed by the vegetation and the surroundings, the pool becomes a part of that evocative setting: a stately old renovated Mallorcan house.

Its very simple profile contrasts with the square shapes where it meets the flower-strewn stone of the original building, which has been restored and expanded. This is precisely where its beauty lies.

The intention was to create a private, relaxing, peaceful space in which to enjoy idle hours. A covered, glass-enclosed porch, slightly elevated and accessed by stairs, joins the home and garden. In front of the porch rests a small pond, filled with water lilies, that flows through a narrow, white Moorish channel into the pool.

Preserving the site's special features, making only the necessary changes, was a basic requirement in the design of this pool, whose external perimeter has been covered with a plain, wide band of gray cement.

The intent was for the pool to be an additional element in the grouping, in which the setting plays the leading role, and where absolute respect for nature and a deep love for simplicity and austerity prevail.

Mallorca, Spain

A Small Oasis

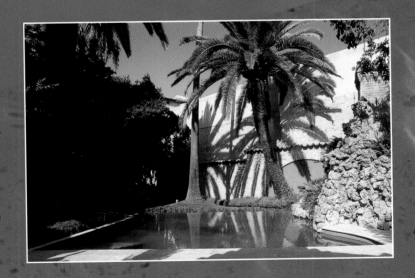

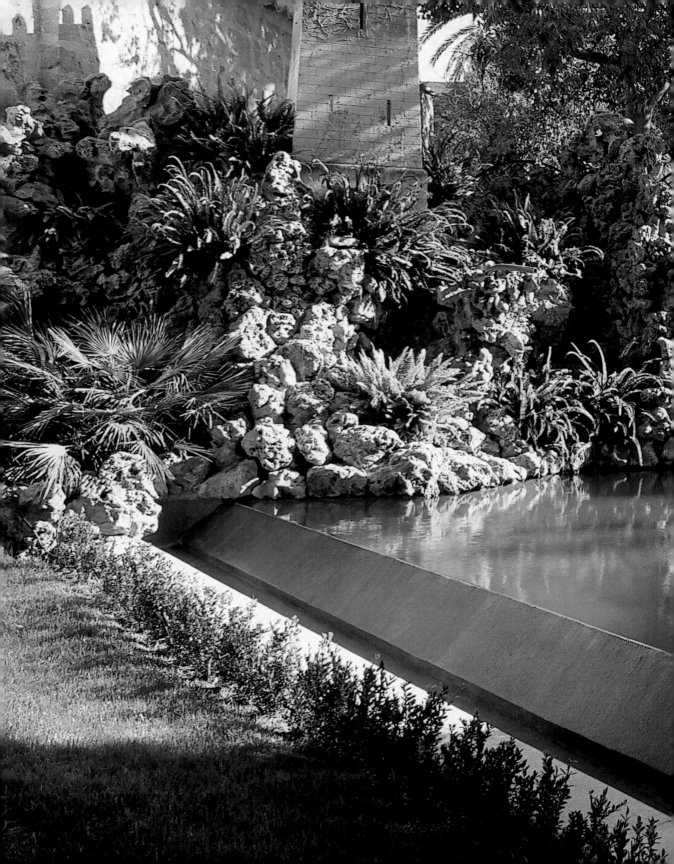

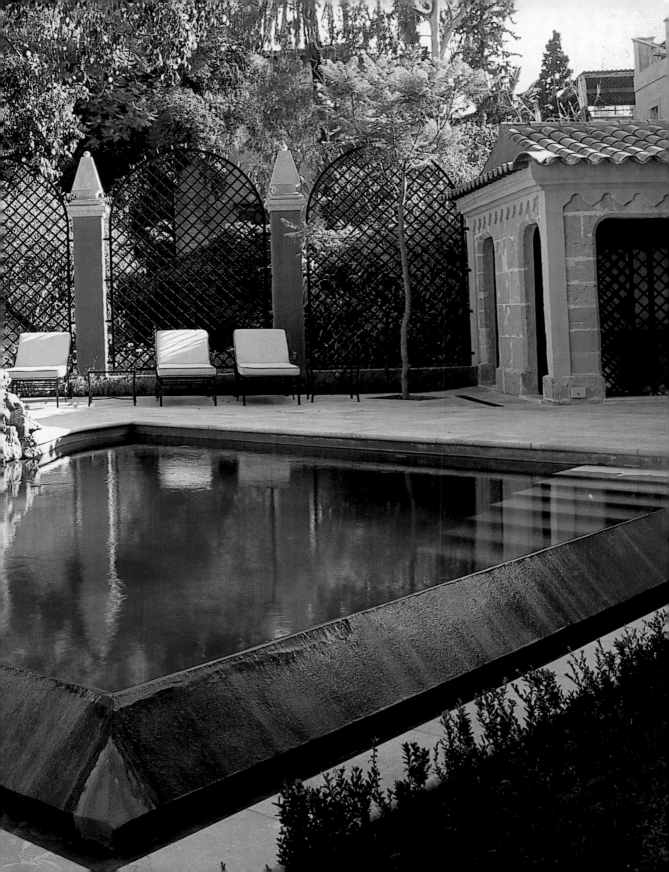

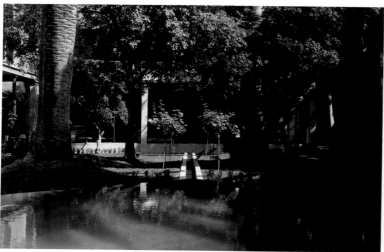

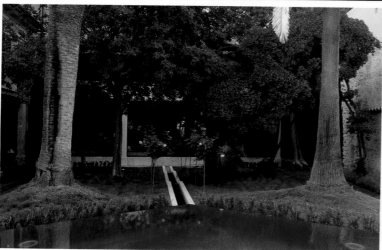

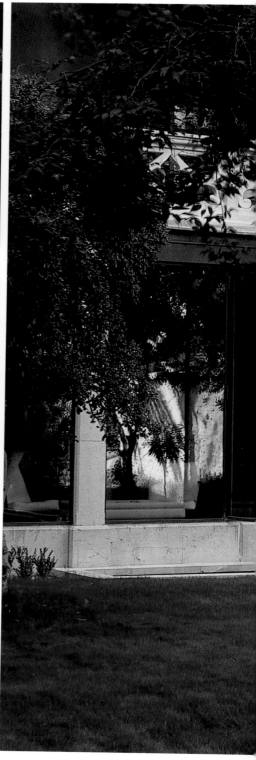

Classical features with a touch of modernity and Moorish elements give the composition an aesthetic as unique as it is inviting. The architectural solutions that were employed achieved a continuous connection between the garden and the interior of one of the structures.

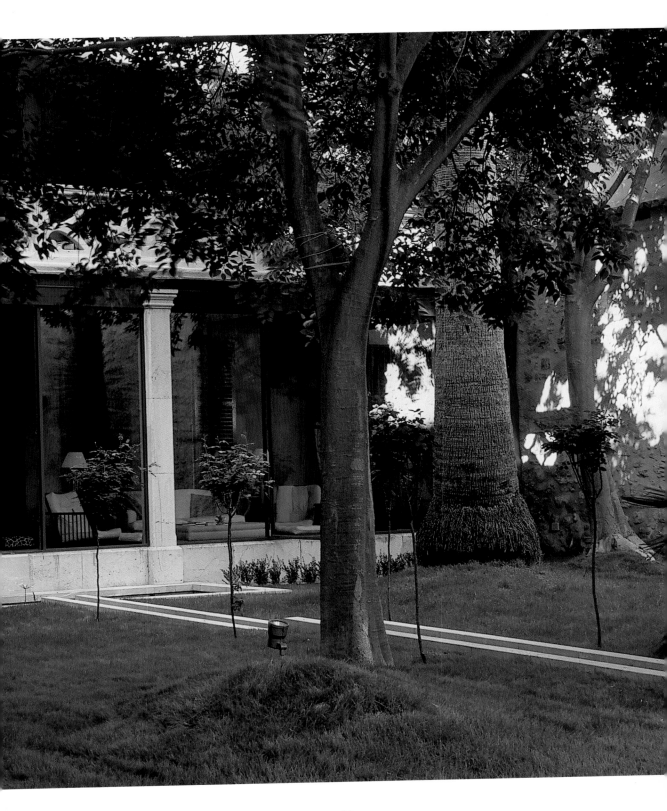

The simplicity of the materials contrasts with the luxuriant vegetation that surrounds the grouping. The exterior space is divided into two well-defined areas: one is more private and fresh, protected from the elements and sheltered from the sun. The other, on the opposite end, is more open, accented by the iron chaise lounges and white cushions, perfect for sunbathing

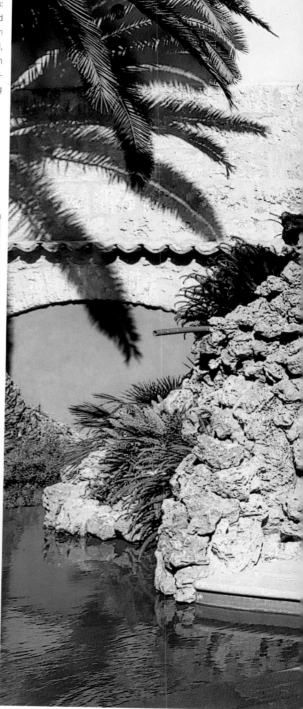

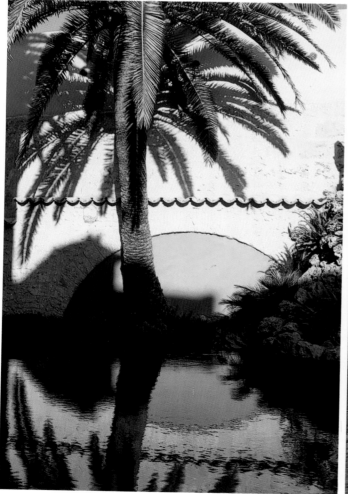

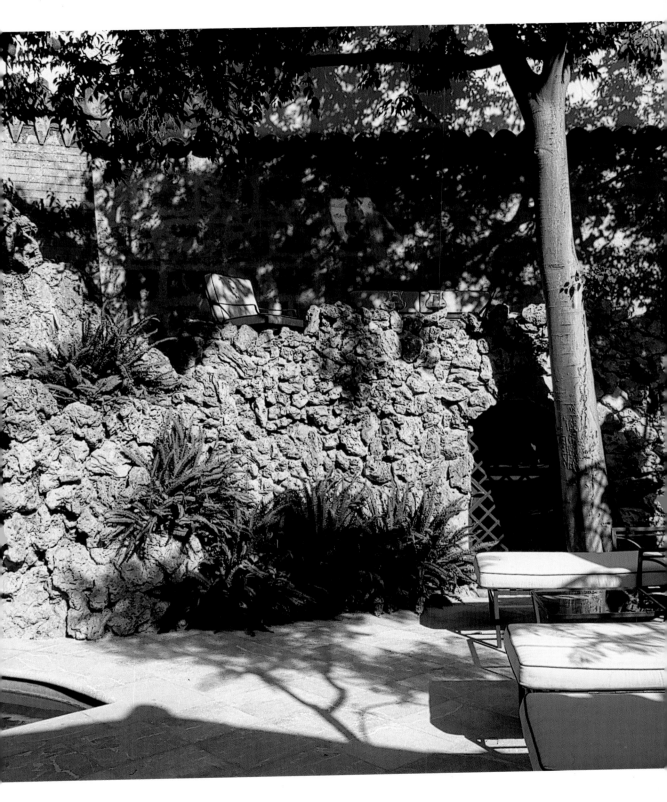

Ensconced behind the century-old walls of an ancient Seville palace, this pool lies at one end of the courtyard, which overflows with freshness and life and the distinct Andalusian flavor that pervades the complex.

The garden surrounding this composition has a firm geometry and linearity that are softened by the vegetation. Laid out in an orderly fashion, it is an exquisitely beautiful place for peaceful relaxation and reflection.

The pool is slightly higher than the rest of the objects in the courtyard. At the end of a set of stairs, one of the building's rear walls—made of stone and dotted with balconies—defines the pool's rectangular outline. These balconies belong to the palace rooms that look out on the courtyard and open onto the pool, gazing at it in all its beauty. Stairs and an iron railing separate the garden from the pool. The remarkable wall behind it features a mural of colored stone and gravel, an imitation of Roman mosaics. Finishing off the mosaic is a frieze, also classically inspired, depicting the signs of the Zodiac. In the center of this wall is an ancient, restored metal spout in the shape of a human face, which constantly pours water into the pool. The spout is situated below an arch flanked by representations of the sun and moon, both enclosed in a circle that makes them stand out against the colored gravel. Additional ornamental and symbolic motifs include inscriptions and seashells.

The area around the pool, between the stone wall and the access stairs, is paved with terra-cotta tiles alternating with colored glazed ceramic tiles in floral motifs, creating an attractive frieze. The same tiles extend throughout the rest of the courtyard, on the other side of the railing. In the center of this garden, at the intersection of the four paths, is a stone fountain in an octagonal recess finished with these same tiles. In the four corners around this centerpiece, abundant plant life thrives, lending visual dynamism and color to a typical Andalusian composition. Here is a truly Sevillano design, filled with charm and personality.

Seville, Spain

Passion for the Traditional

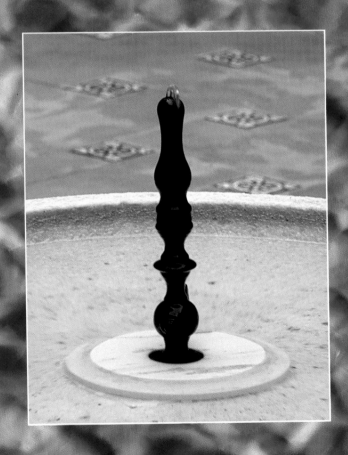

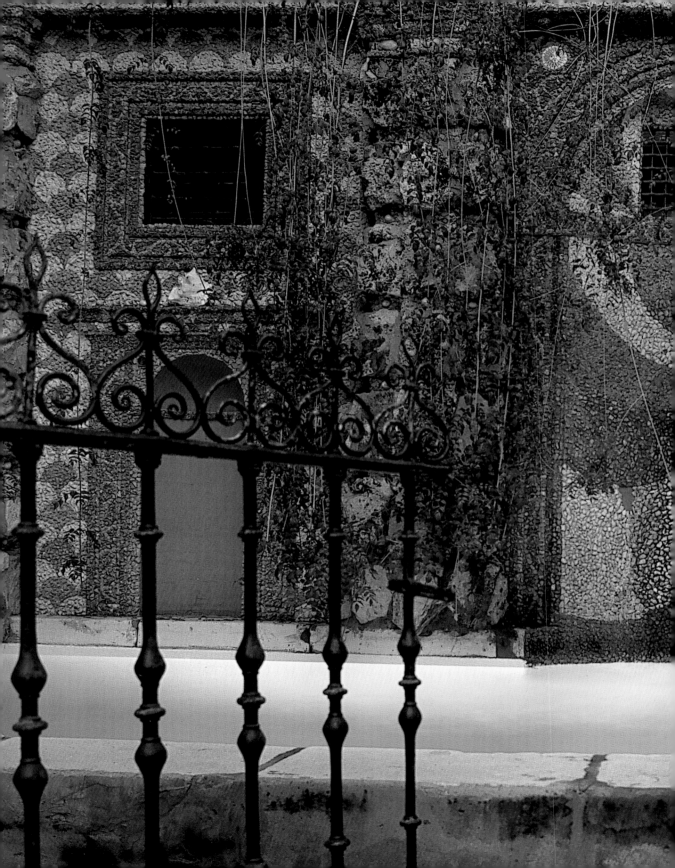

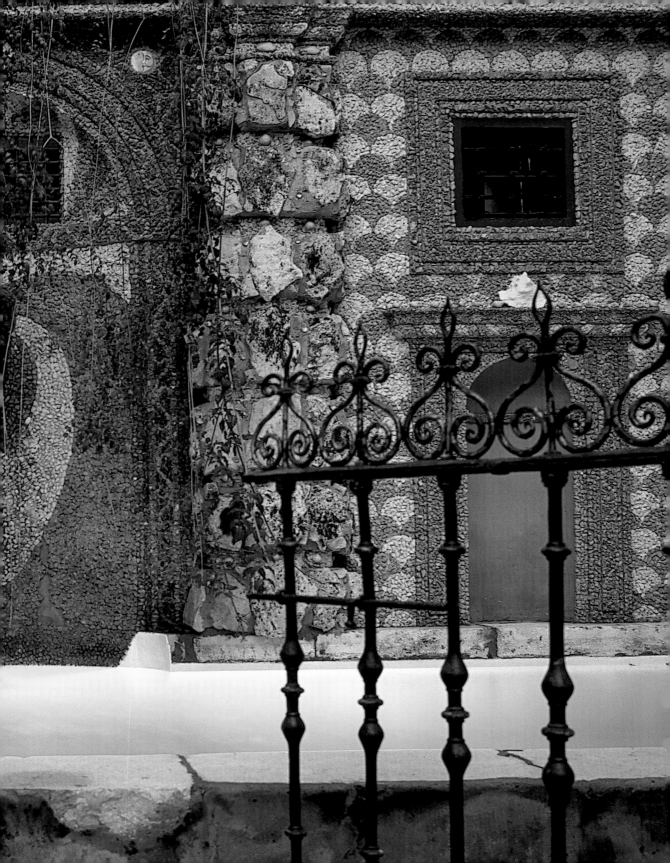

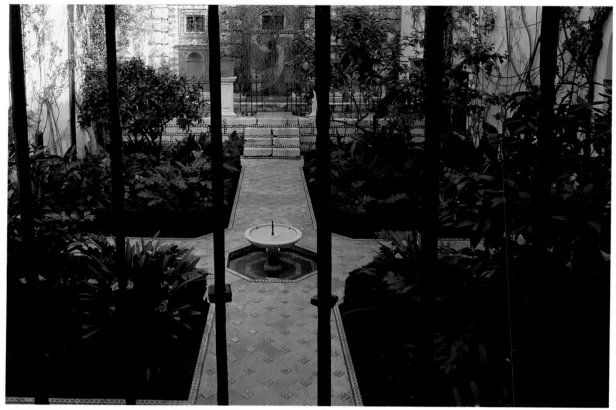

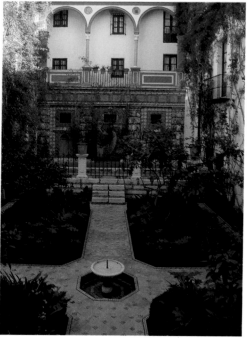

Andalusian flavor dominates, but classical and Moorish elements influence the composition as well. Different inspirations and a subtle mixture of reinterpreted styles are the key to this evocative, suggestive, and enchanting hideaway.

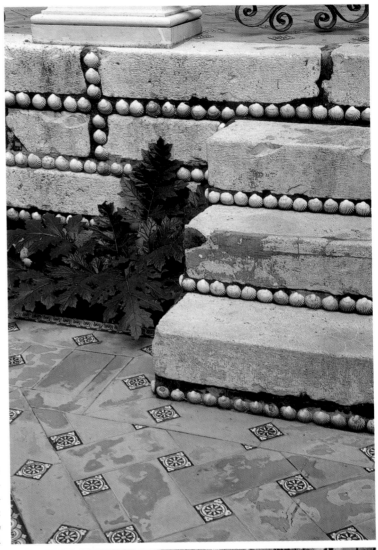

The sturdy stone stairs leading to the pool and the front strip of the raised section containing the pool repeat a decorative element used in the mosaic's frieze: seashells in the mortar joints of the stairs and in the wall.

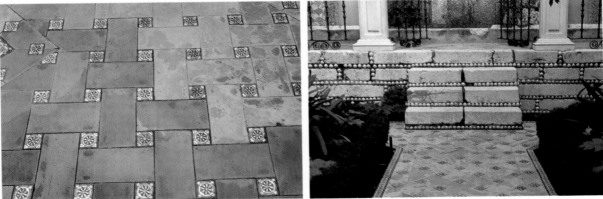

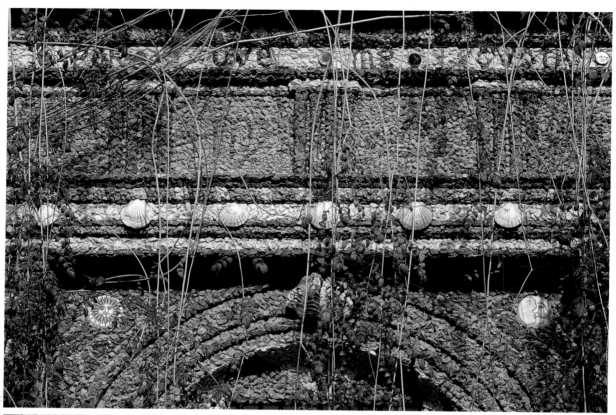

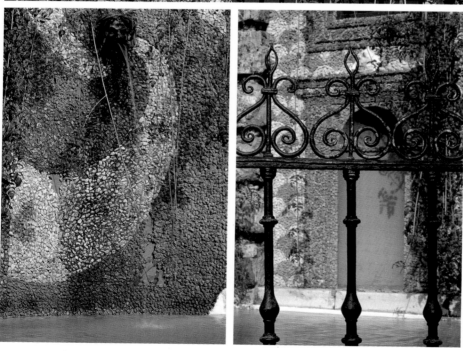

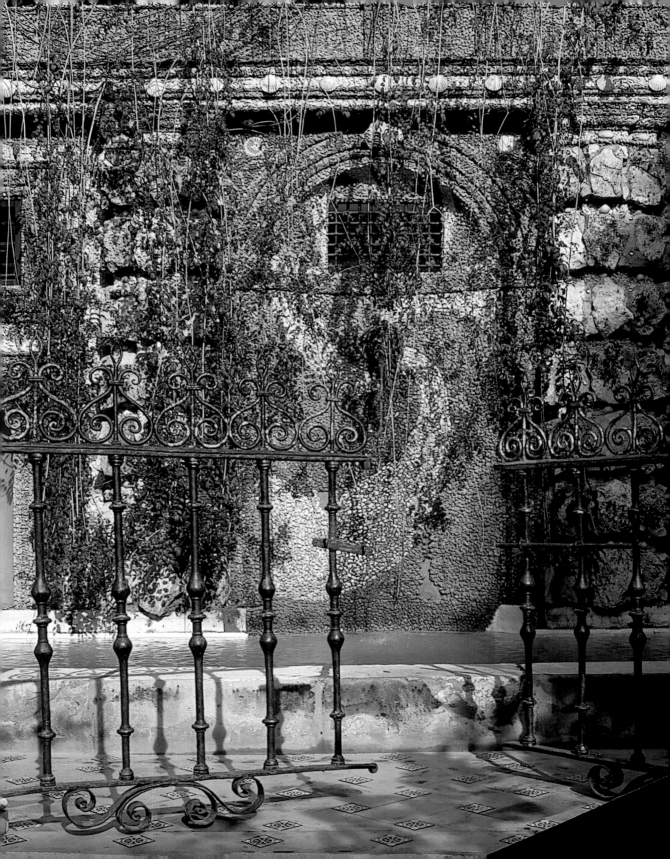

nspired by Versailles, this swimming pool imitates the soft shapes of the lush gardens at the French royal palace. However, it has a trait all its own: an ingenious system of channels surrounding a small island where six symbolic olive trees grow. There is a continuous movement of water, since this area is connected to a pond on a lower level. This keeps the pool clean, converts a retaining wall into a charming waterfall, and adds the relaxing sound of running water. At night, an arbor that serves as an informal porch is a magical area for dining, enjoying a drink, or just chatting.

The pool is perfectly symmetrical, its symmetry broken only by two semicircles. The first forms the island and the second, directly across from the first, contains underwater steps.

The immensity of the garden has been strictly respected, both on the upper and lower levels. The olive and palm trees, freely spreading their fans of exotic beauty, are the stars of this orchard.

This project attempted to integrate the entire grouping, respecting the setting by employing a refined, almost stark style, which brings out, on one hand, the central axis created by the pool, and on the other, the setting itself, creating many perspectives, such as the one framed by the columns of the arbor. The counterbalancing of pool and setting is quite an exercise in visual style.

Mallorca, Spain

The Eternal Cycle of Water

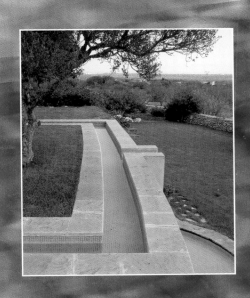

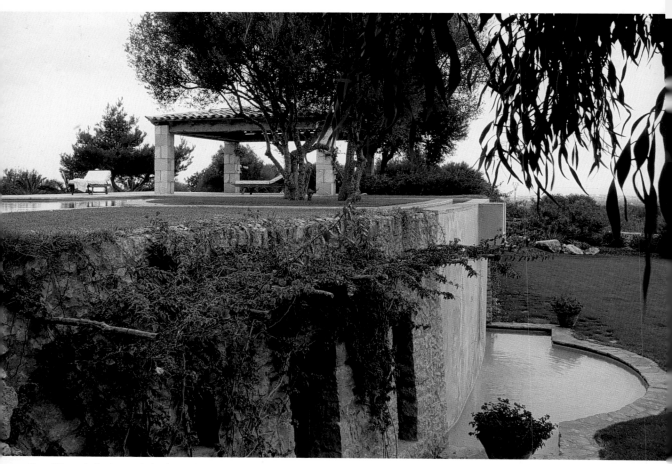

From this angle the two main levels can be seen, and the water is the link between them. Bougainvillea dots the immense garden in a variety of warm colors.

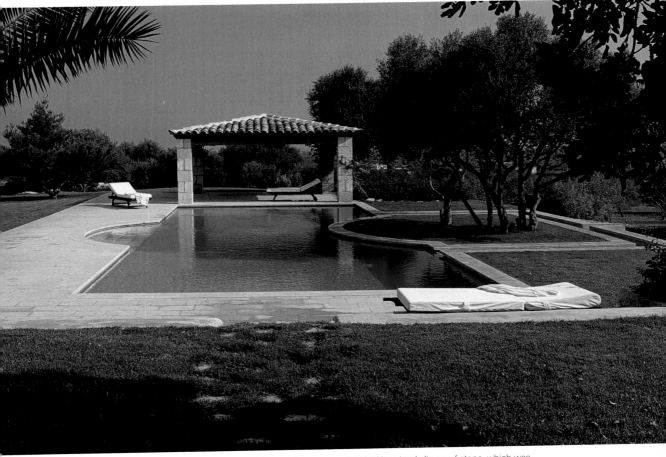

The location of the arbor provides a placid, shady area. The pool was surrounded with natural slip-proof stone, which was also used for the columns supporting the arbor.

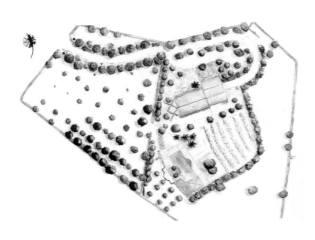

This drawing of the development's design for the garden and the water area gives an aerial view of the entire property.

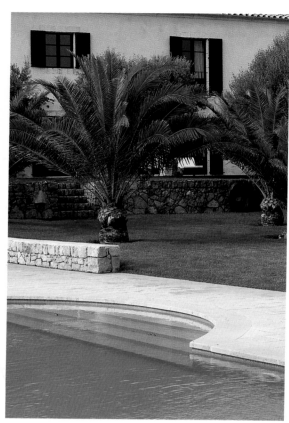

Five wide steps invite swimmers into the water. Low, natural stone walls define the pool and house areas.

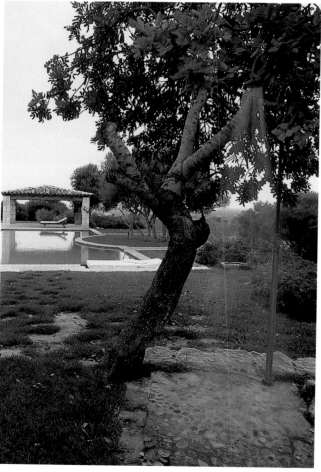

A rustic shower emerges from the foliage of an indigenous tree.

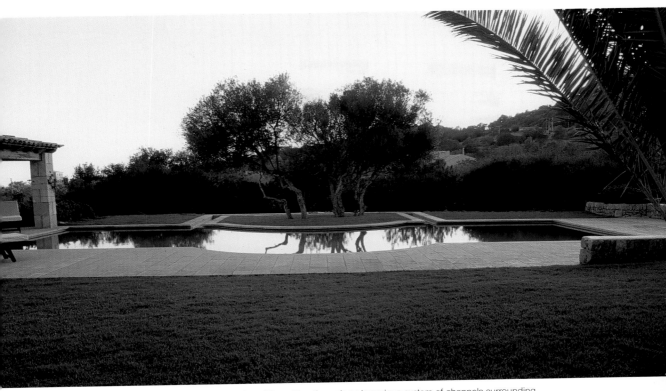

The olive trees are perfectly integrated with the pool and the setting through an ingenious system of channels surrounding this island of vegetation. The visual continuity between the group of trees and the landscape that softly envelops it can be appreciated from any angle.

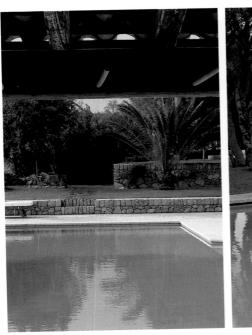

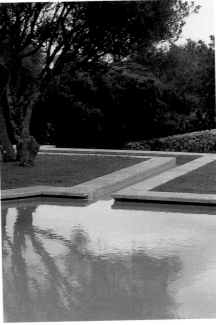

High and low walls mark the different levels as well as the various landscaped areas surrounding the house and pool. A combination of open and secluded spaces was chosen to enhance enjoyment of the natural beauty.

T his magnificent, colorful pool, surrounded by a dense wall of vegetation, blends perfectly with its surroundings yet also emerges from the natural setting. A spectacular stepped entrance invites the visitor to slip into the therapeutic pleasure of the water and enjoy the beauty of the landscape from a wide underwater bench.

The chromatic intensity of this pool, bright and cheerful, combined with the complex geometry of the fired clay that finishes off the edges, is a sampling of the craftsmanship still practiced today in Marrakech, where the property is located. The excellent glazed mosaic work on the central band of small channel that divides the edging and the various geometric finishes located both inside and outside the pool, are small examples of the ornamental richness that has characterized this country for centuries.

At one end of the pool, aligned at ground level, are ten slender jets of water directly connected with the highest part of the pool, forming a fountain, which is an integral part of the project.

Details, sounds, colors, and textures merge here to create their own world, with the strength and personality of a thousand-year-old architectural culture.

On the grass, beneath the thick foliage of the trees, two contemporary white butterfly chairs invite us to contemplate this mysterious and magical place.

Marrakech, Morocco

The Reinterpretation of Water

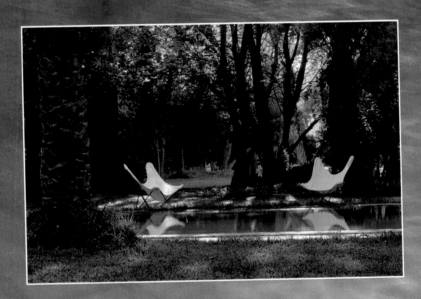

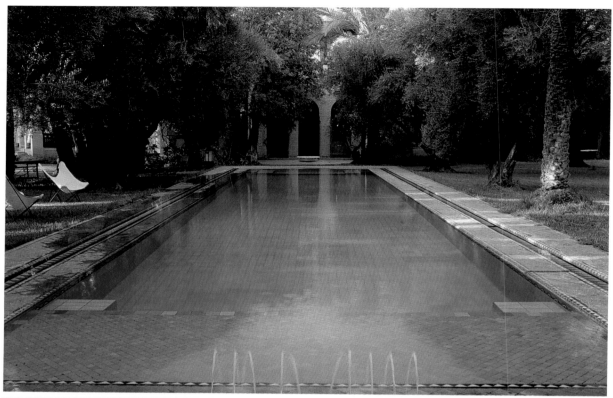

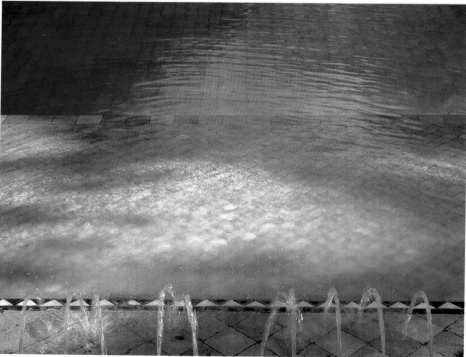

Behind the water fountain, on the carpet of grass, there is a glimpse of the past in the form of an ancient fired-clay vessel. The entire pool is surrounded by grass that comes right up to the edge.

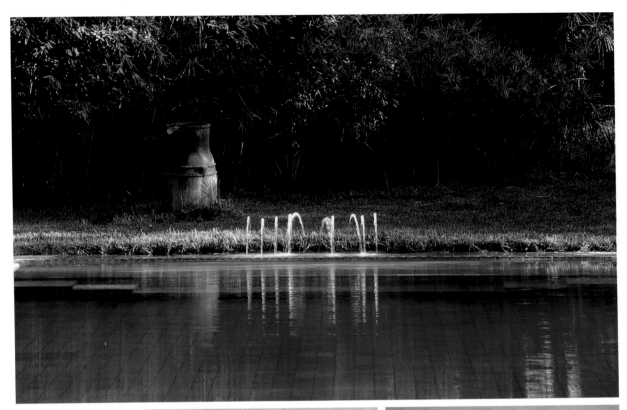

The water jets at ground level are integrated with the rest of the pool. Under the water, the special treatment applied to the ceramic floor tiles separates the fountain area from the pool area.

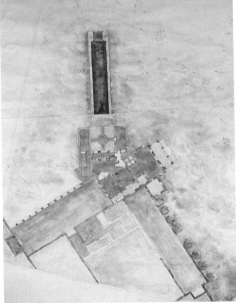

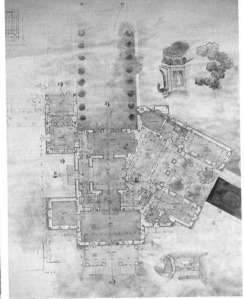

Two drawings show the landscape architect's original design for the project.

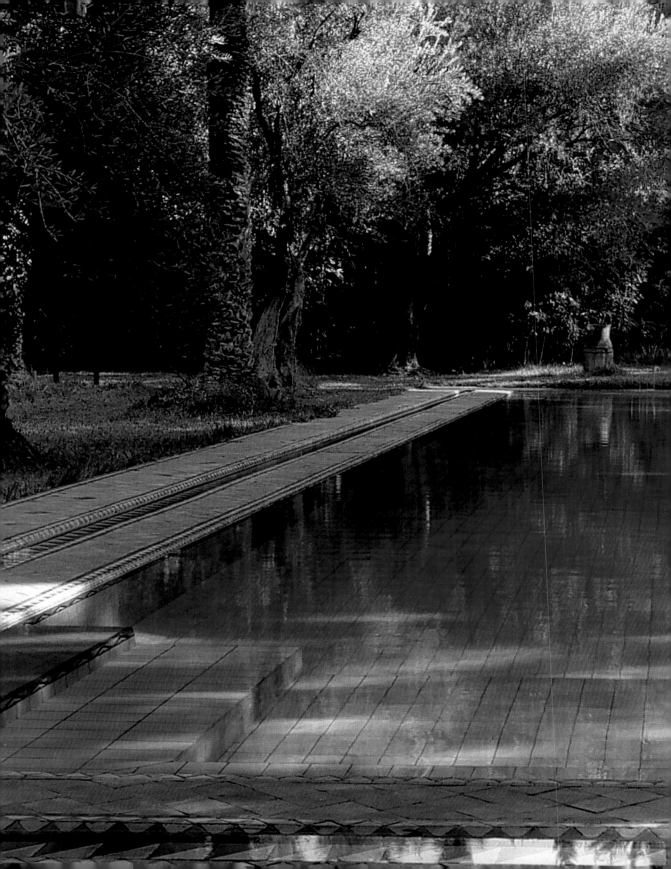

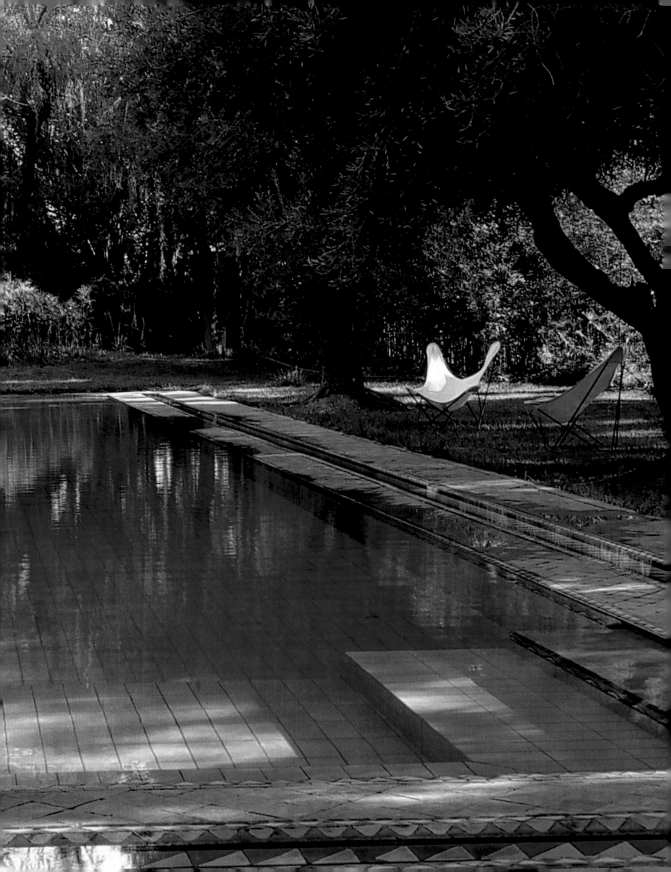

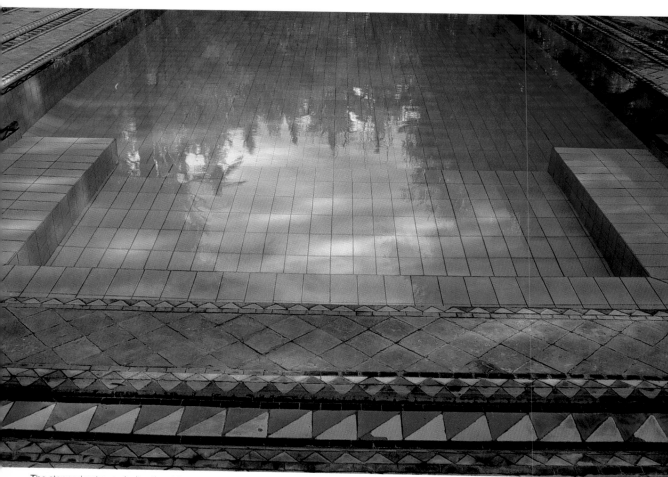

The stepped entrance invites the visitor
to slip into the water and enjoy the beauty of the landscape from an underwater
bench.

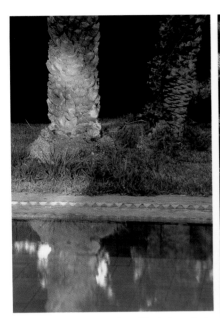

The double edging of fired clay reflects a geometric exercise that is characteristic of this country's tradition.

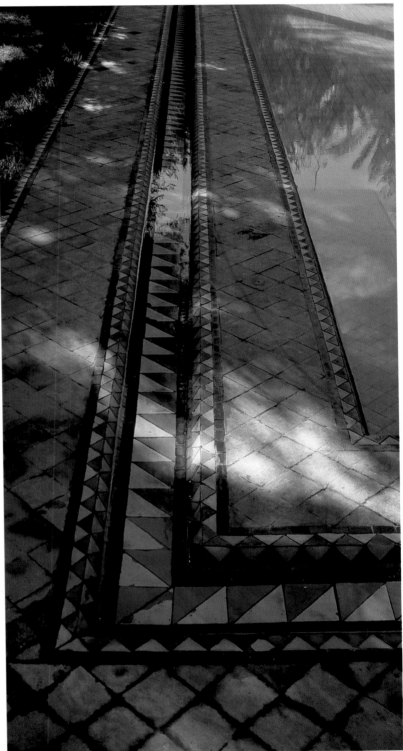

Nostalgia, part of the love of nature, often brings to mind an idealized image. This space evokes that idealized image of the past. Like a mirror, the turquoise water in this old, classically-inspired pool reflects the façade of the house and its setting: a splendid garden conceived as a succession of spaces, chromatically different but united by an imaginary path.

Born at the foot of a restored rustic building characterized by simple lines, this pool was originally an irrigation pond. Now, transformed into a small pool thanks to the installation of a motor that circulates the water, it is the focal point of the grouping of the house and its natural setting.

It is defined by austere, simple, severe lines traced by a frame of thick, unpolished stone. The combination of colors, textures, and materials achieves surprising results.

The white color, echoed in the façade's window and door frames, stands out against the green overwhelming scenery drawn by nature, and contrasts with the stone. In the center of all this beauty, the discreet pool draws all eyes upon itself. Stone sculptures dot the garden and break the chromatic hegemony of nature's green tones. The result is an attractive grouping that drinks from the past without rejecting the advances offered by the present.

A dirt path marks the pool's entire perimeter and leads to other corners of the evocative garden, tracing peaceful trails through the natural setting. A tranquil haven where time seems to have stood still, it is a world of its own in which to escape from humdrum everyday life.

Provence, France

In the Garden of
the Imaginary

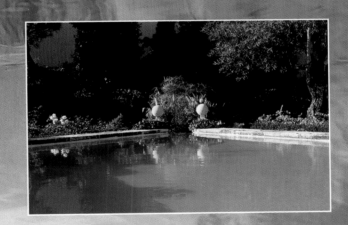

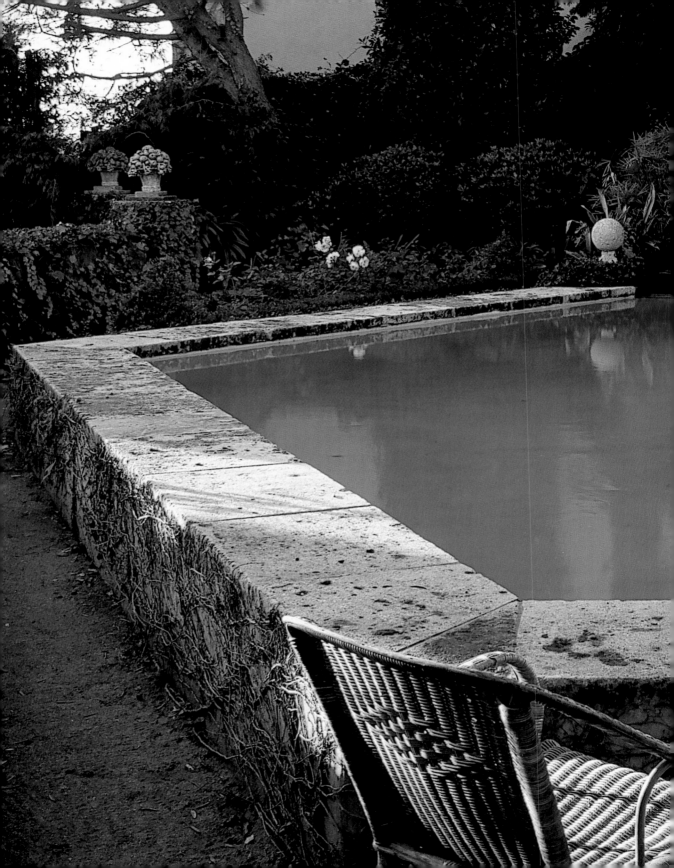

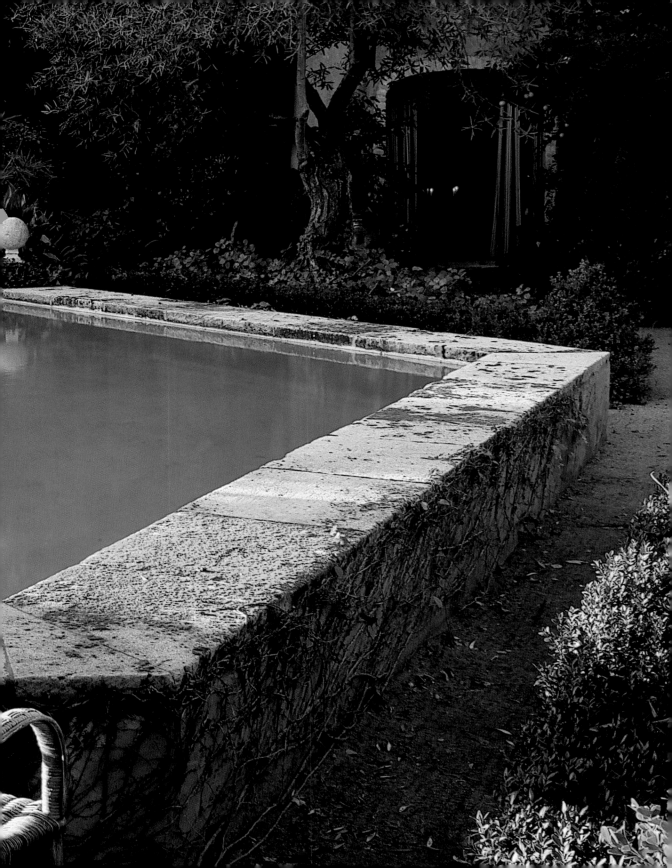

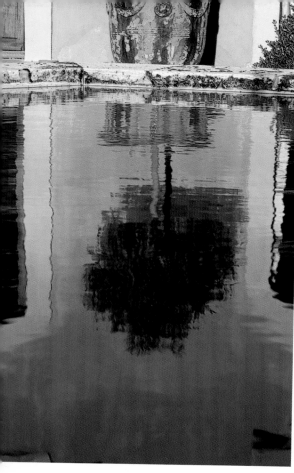

The generous proportions of the house, an old, renovated building, and the annexed units are overshadowed by the pool, situated in the heart of this restored garden, which retains all the flavor of the past.

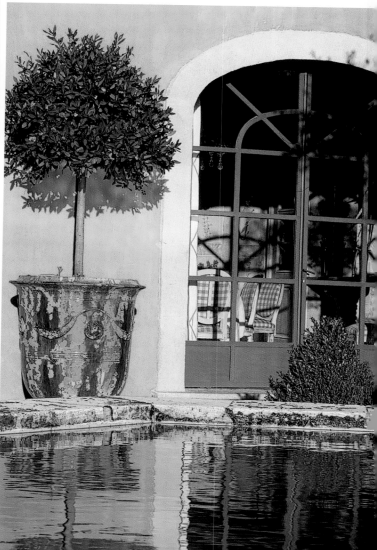

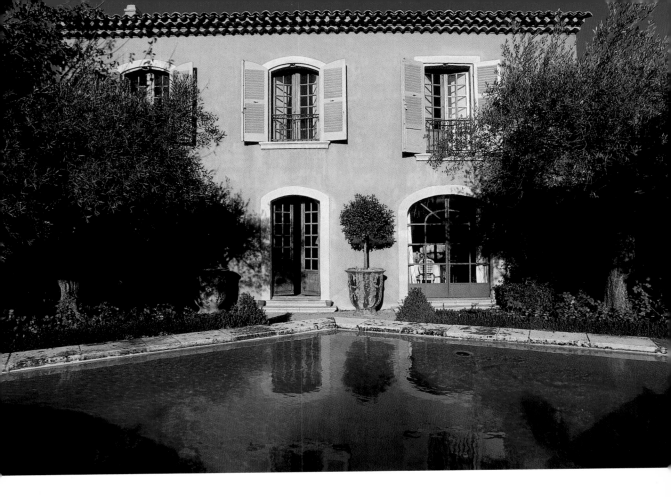

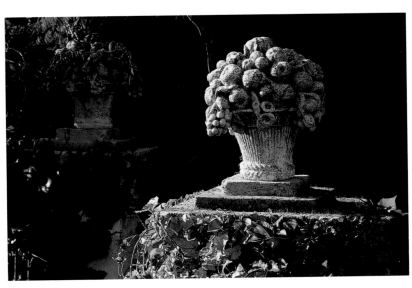

The decorative stone sculptures, inspired by early twentieth-century gardens, delimit and mark a path around the pool.

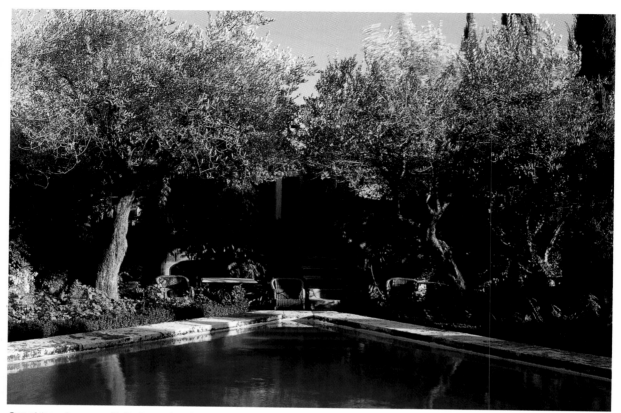

One of the units annexed to the house has direct access to the pool. The small difference in elevation was overcome with stone steps. Abundant vegetation camouflages the building and shades the ends of the pool from the heat of the sun.

What was once an irrigation pond is now a small pool. From the right angle, it seems to be an immense mirror of water surrounded by a stone frame. The sense of tranquility and isolation is always present.

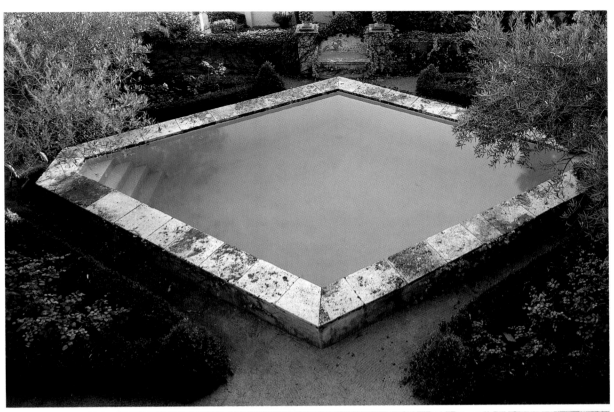

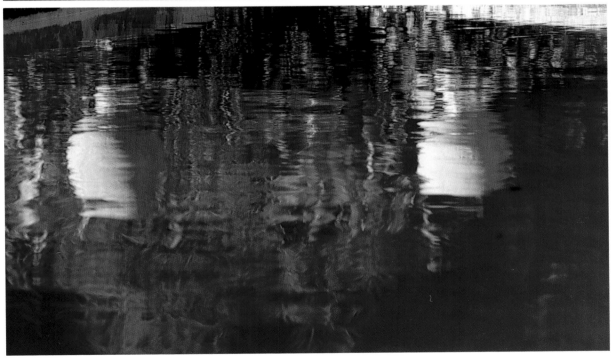

Between a small plot of cropland and an orchard of young fruit trees, this swimming pool, located in Palma de Mallorca, Spain, is framed by a row of rocks on which the patina of time has left its mark. Three mysterious steps invite the onlooker to enter the transparent fluidity of its water.

The swimming pool is associated with contemplation, a fresh pool flanked by a soft grassy area in deliberate contrast to the arid land surrounding it.

This project wisely used the elements of the country house to visually shape the space on different levels, in a manner similar to a three-dimensional picture. The original stones from the country home were used to divide the principal space into three areas: the swimming pool, the ancient watermill, and a sunbathing area on the upper level.

The old Z-shaped retaining wall becomes a path and shelters the pool, originally a reservoir that collected water to irrigate the field. On the second level, the small, tidy orchard still stretches to the foot of the pool, along with the remains of a small watermill, recycled as a sculpture for contemplation, a silent witness to the past.

Mallorca, Spain

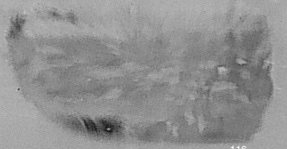

Recovering the Past

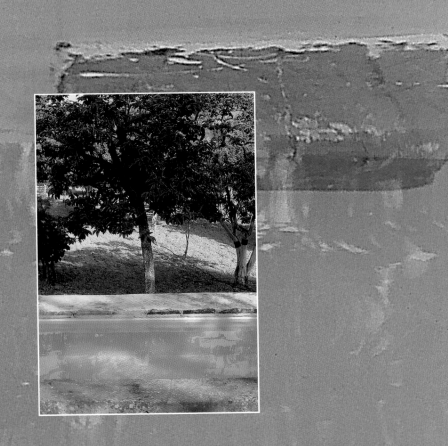

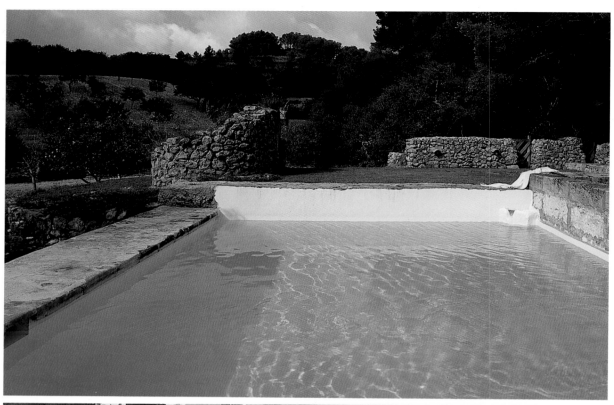

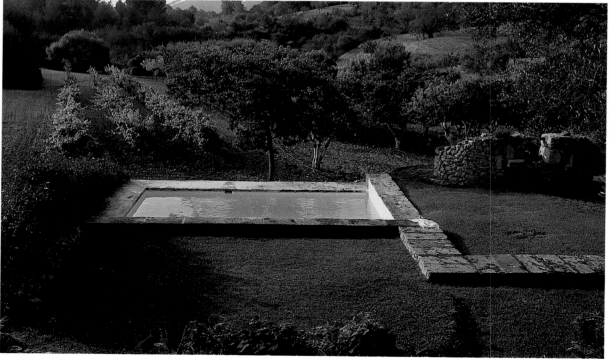

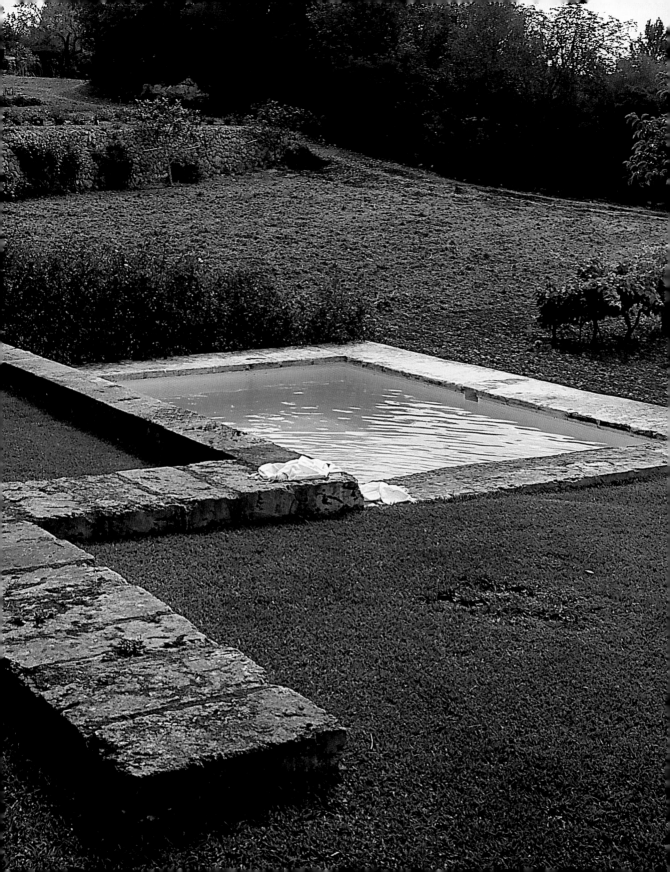

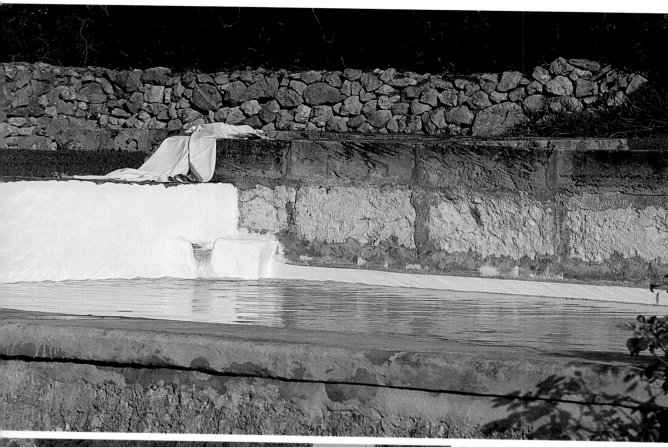

This renovation converted a water depository into a pool enhanced by the charm that emanates from the fruit of the crops.

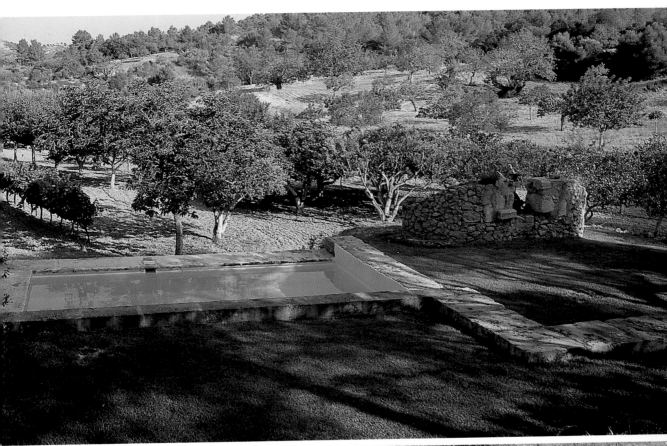

A panorama offers a view of the three areas that comprise the main level: the swimming pool, the old watermill, and a living area. On a second level, we see the orchard of young fruit trees.

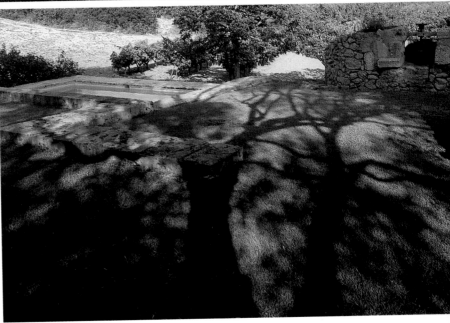

121

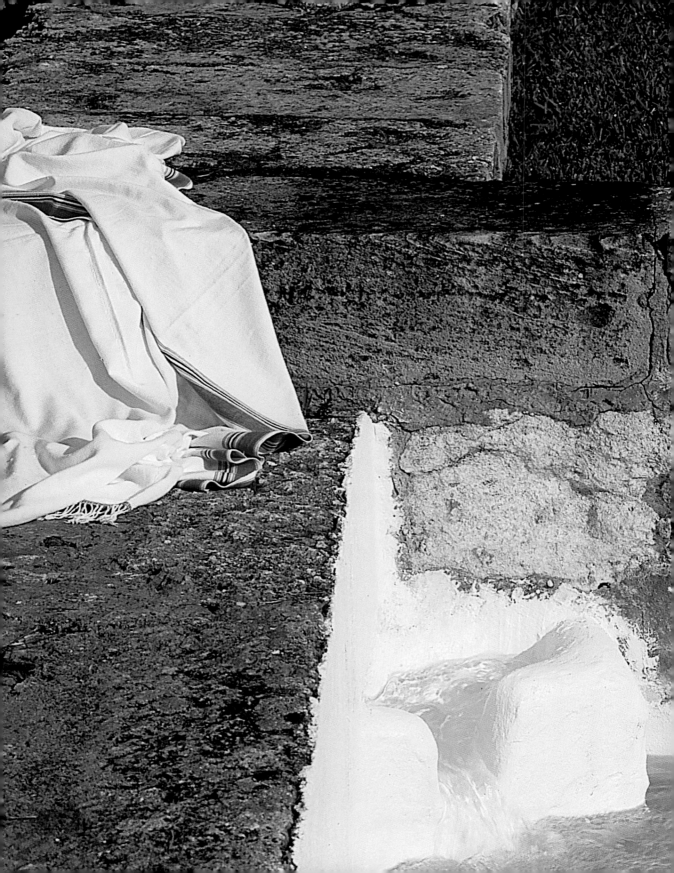

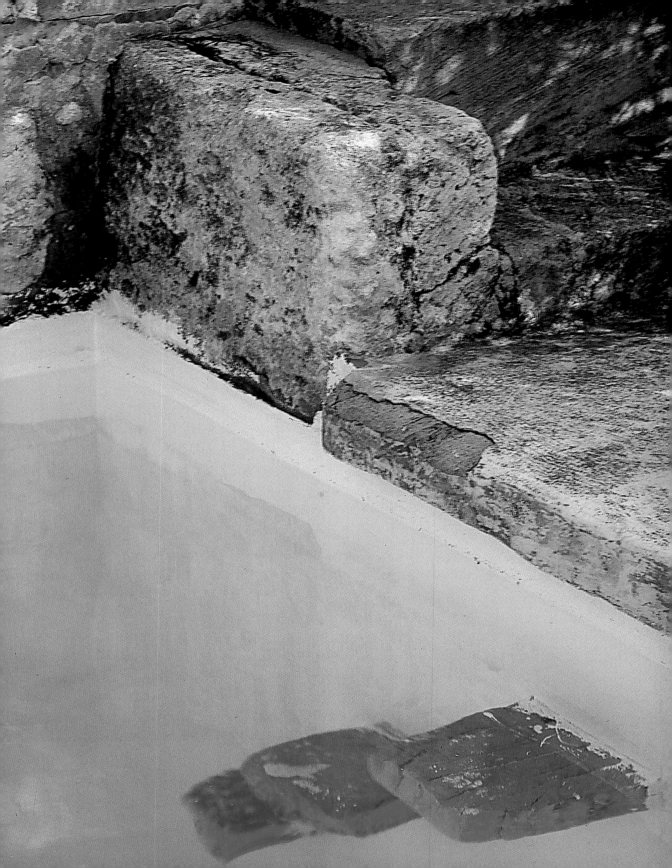

Amid rocks cracked by the sun, rural fragrances, and the buzz of the grasshoppers, a smooth slope shelters low stone walls which were once used for terrace farming, a traditional system of agriculture. At its feet, as if in a stream bed, lies the emerald water of this pool, which combines artificial curves and rough shapes.

This project applied architectural criteria to the natural setting and achieved a perfect blending of both. All landscaping around the pool was rejected in order to maintain the strength of the earth and rock, in stark contrast to the colorful luminosity of the water. In accordance with this principle, the land needed for the pool was cleared, and the exterior perimeter was covered with a simple, wide stone strip.

The rocky side of the pool has a small platform that evokes the feel of a stream and serves as a lounging area and natural diving board. A small, completely whitewashed well that provides fresh water is prominent. The mountainous slope serves as an informal entrance to the pool, which seems to be reinforced by the presence of steps in the shape of waves submerged in the water.

In this place of light and contrast, the priority was to preserve the authentic appearance of the landscape without changing it; the setting had to remain the star player, without sacrificing the magnificent advantages of modern conveniences.

Ibiza, Spain

A Stream Amid the Rocks

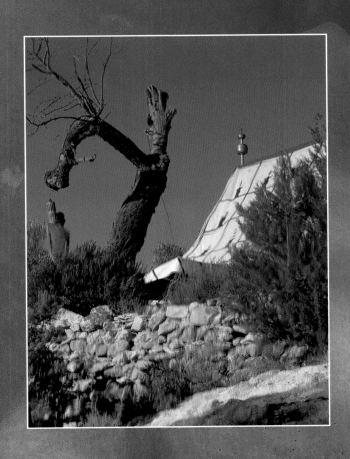

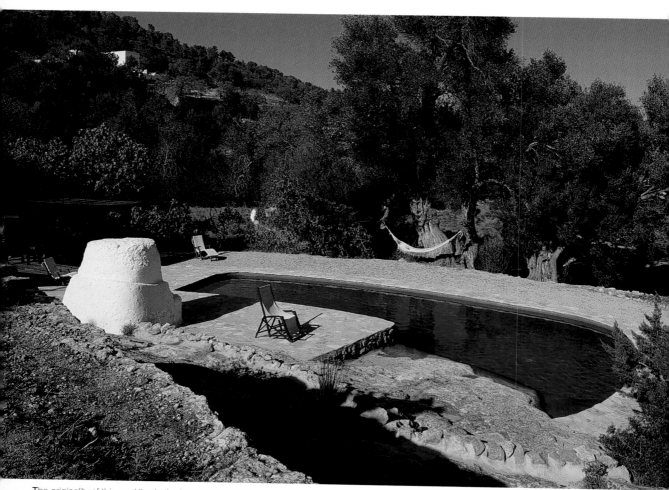

The originality of this pool lies in the incorporation of the rugged terrain as an integral part of the project. The construction criteria were blended with the setting, creating a pool shaped like a natural pond in the new grouping. A whitewashed well that provides fresh water overlooks the setting.

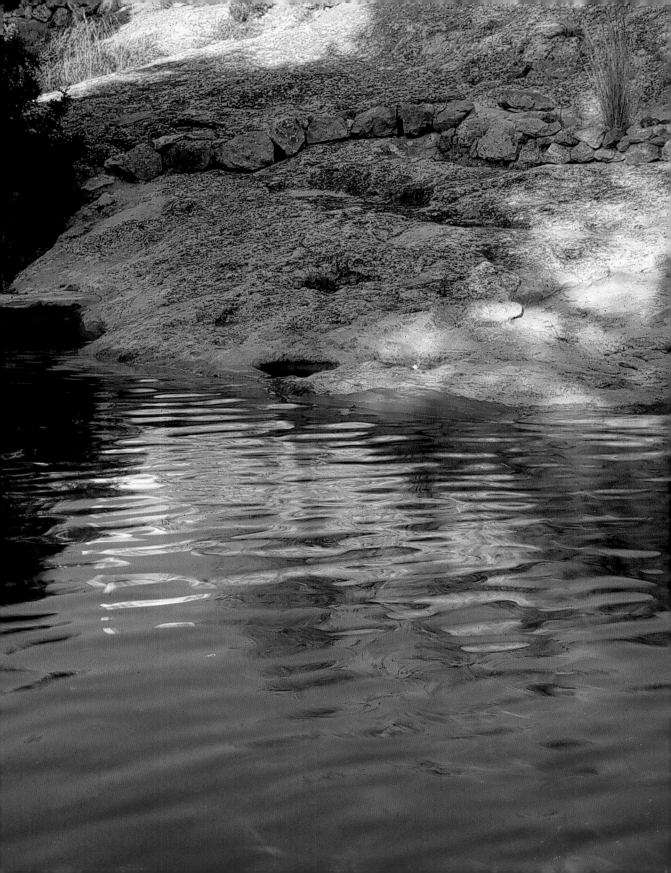

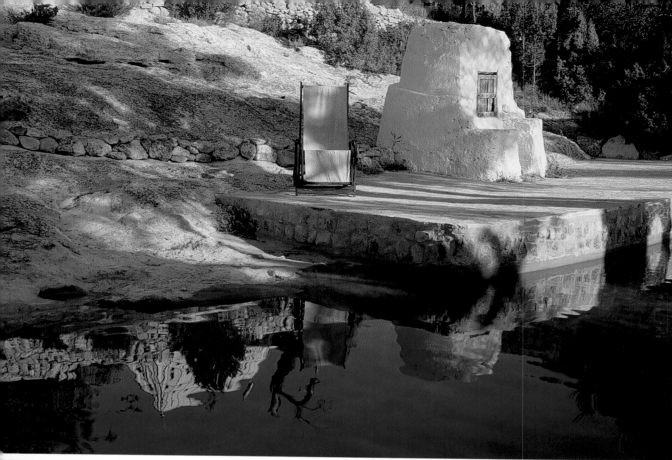

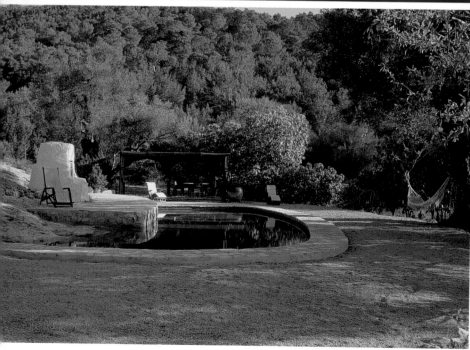

The contrast between the emerald color of the water and the ochre of the rock reinforces the sensation of being at a stream bed. The incorporation of a rocky skirt into the pool keeps the water at the proper temperature all summer long.

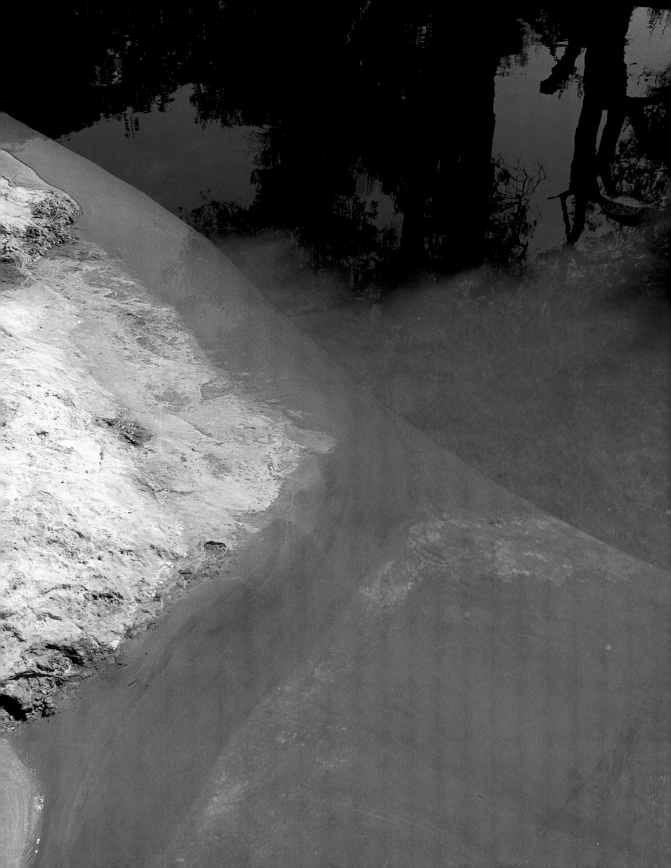

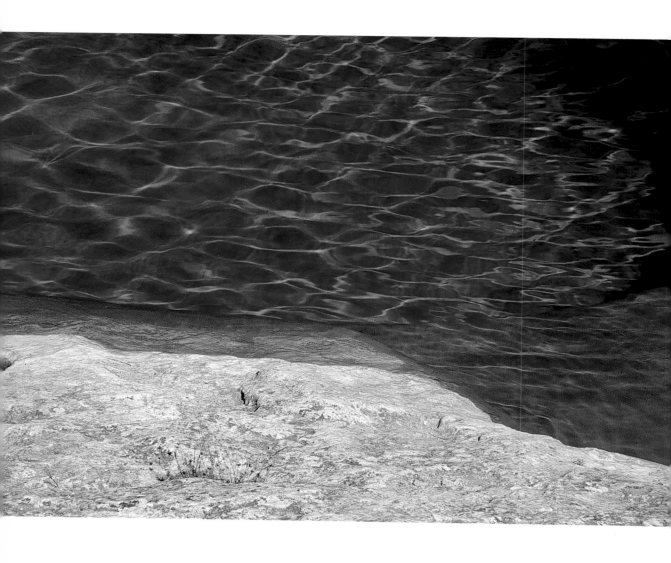

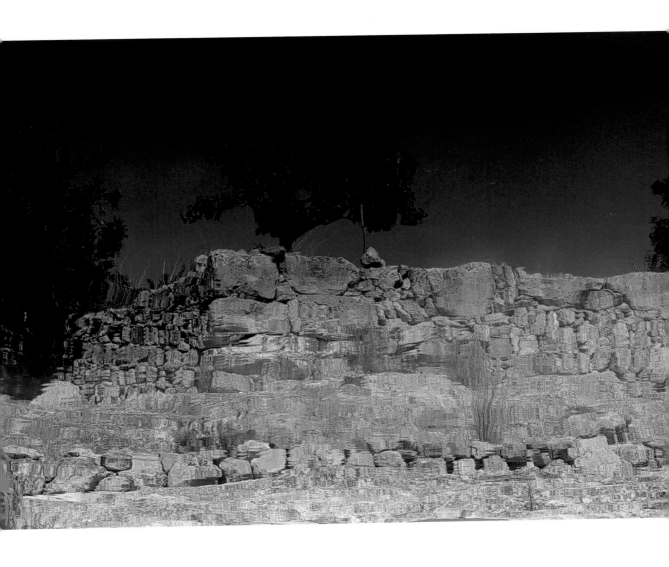

A cool, peaceful refuge, this small oasis emerges from the arid land that surrounds it. The geometric balance comes from the perfect relationship of its three volumes: the swimming pool—rectilinear and with a smooth surface of water—and the semi-open porch and main building, both just one story high. A perfectly restored stone wall joins the two structures and at the same time surrounds and defines the entire property, creating a dividing line between it and the setting, based on color and a single texture, the roughness of the stone.

The visual perspectives from this line exist at any point, since the property and the adjacent land are at the same level. The intent was to bring out the play of contrasts resulting from the juxtaposition of the dry land and the lawn that surround the blue surface of the water.

The sense of continuity comes from the homogeneity of the colors and from the materials used to restore the property and build the pool. The stone and the sand color become the chromatic base of the grouping, heightening awareness of the intense blue of the water and green of the vegetation.

The only vertical elements, two regal palm trees, stand between the two main buildings, dominating the pool and breaking the immensity of the sky. The evocative presence of these palms, as in a desert oasis, acts as a guide from the road.

Mallorca, Spain

Color
Contrasts

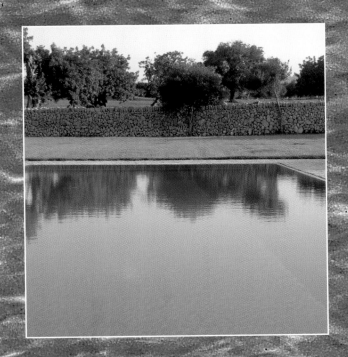

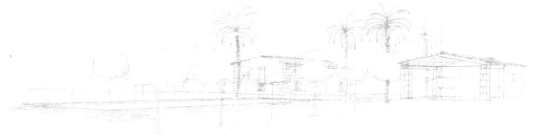

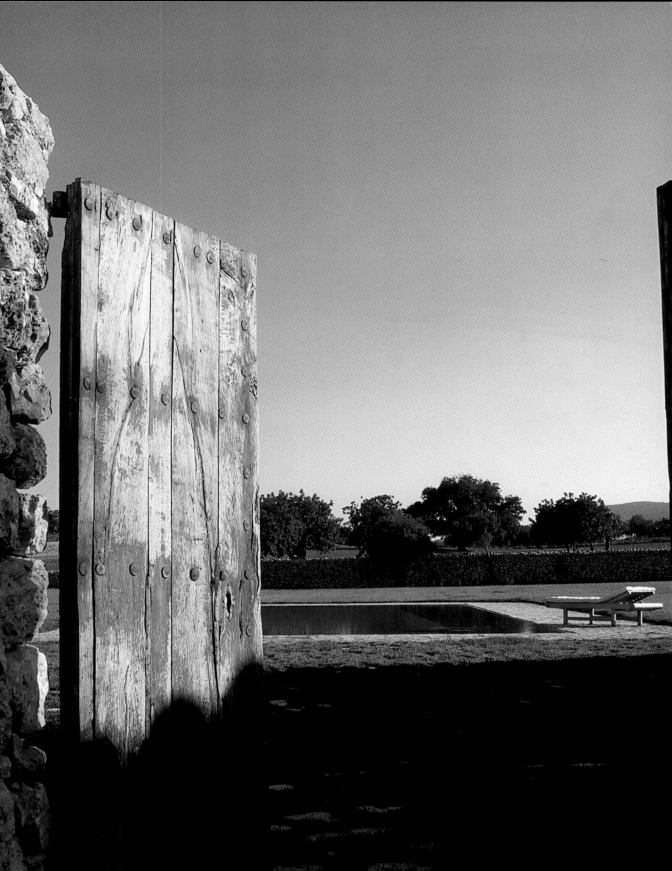

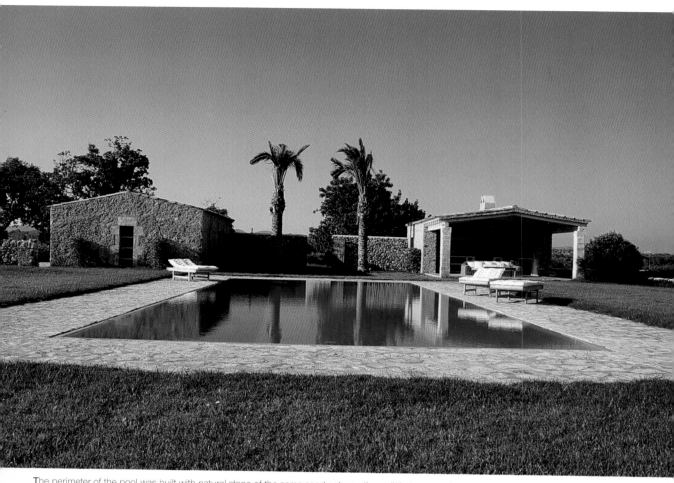

The perimeter of the pool was built with natural stone of the same sand color as the wall that surrounds the property. The predominance of straight lines enhances the contrasting colors while making the pool a fluid mirror, perfectly integrated with the surroundings.

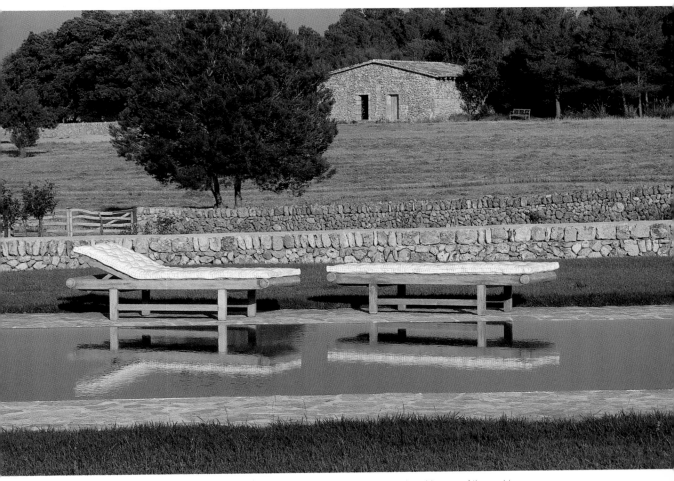

The only decorative elements are wooden chaise lounges whose refined style heightens the whiteness of the cushions.

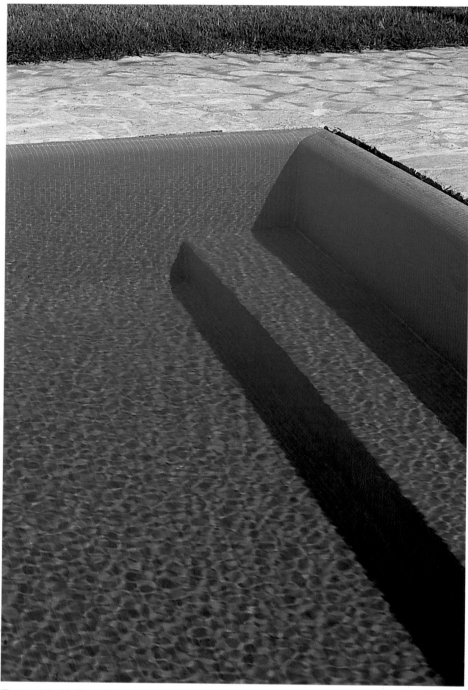

The porch, where the granary originally stood, opens up onto the pool at the same level as the rest of the construction. The barbecue area can be seen next to the sofa.

The bench inside the pool extends from side to side.

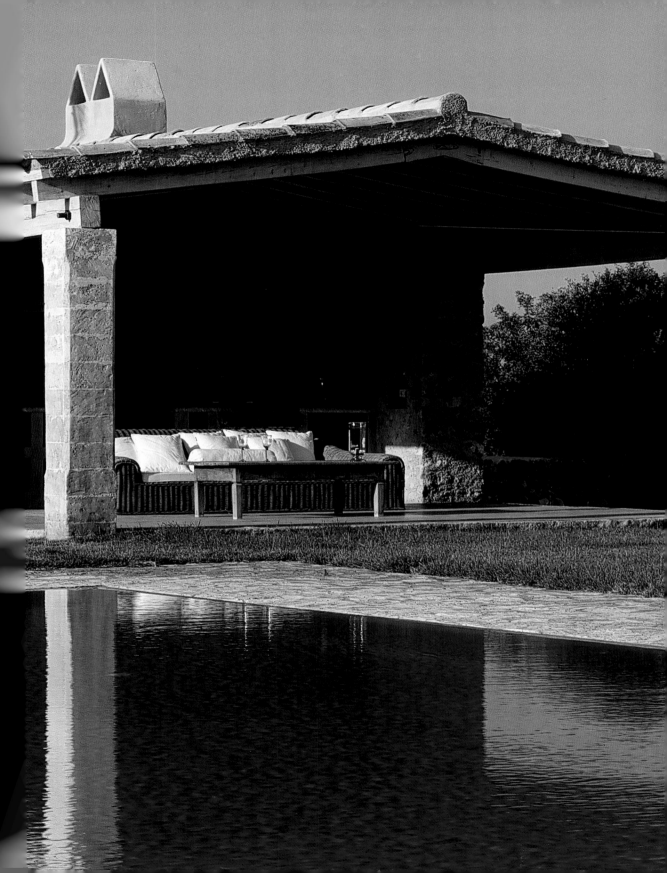

This silent, landscaped pool is unquestionably the focus of attention. From the midst of the abundant natural elements projects the pool's curved silhouette, defined by a discrete yet subtle white outline—the only thing separating it from the surrounding vegetation.

Perfectly integrated into its setting, the pool occupies the physical center of this typically Mediterranean garden. Facing it is a small porch that provides access to the pool from the interior of the residence.

The two sets of masonry steps, which face each other, descend into the pool. They were placed under water to avoid breaking the composition's sinuous shapes and to achieve the effect of a calm beach with inviting turquoise water that extends the color palette. Every shade of green, dotted with an explosion of color from the flowering plants, merges with the blues with which the light regales the water throughout the day. The bottom is painted blue, and the edge is concrete, except for the area intended for sunbathing, which is decorated with blue Moorish mosaics.

The studied landscaping, with its definite Moorish inspiration, invites the visitor to relax and forget everything except what is inside that private universe. The construction materials, textures, shapes, and colors combine perfectly, creating a magnificent, peaceful atmosphere dominated by a lush garden.

Marrakech, Morocco

Hidden in a Garden

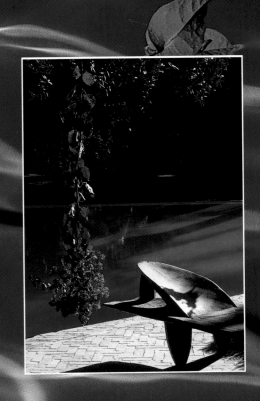

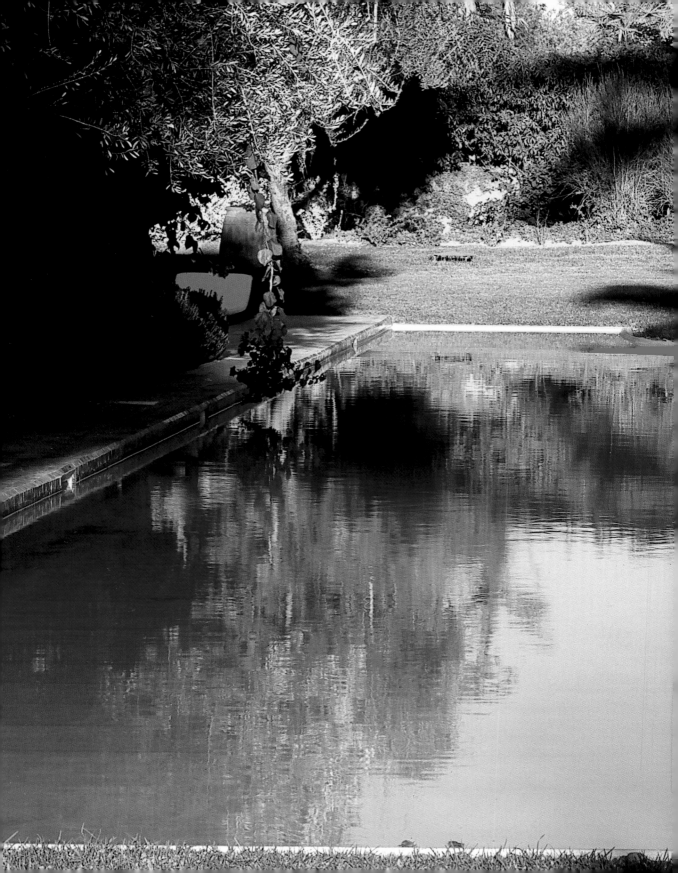

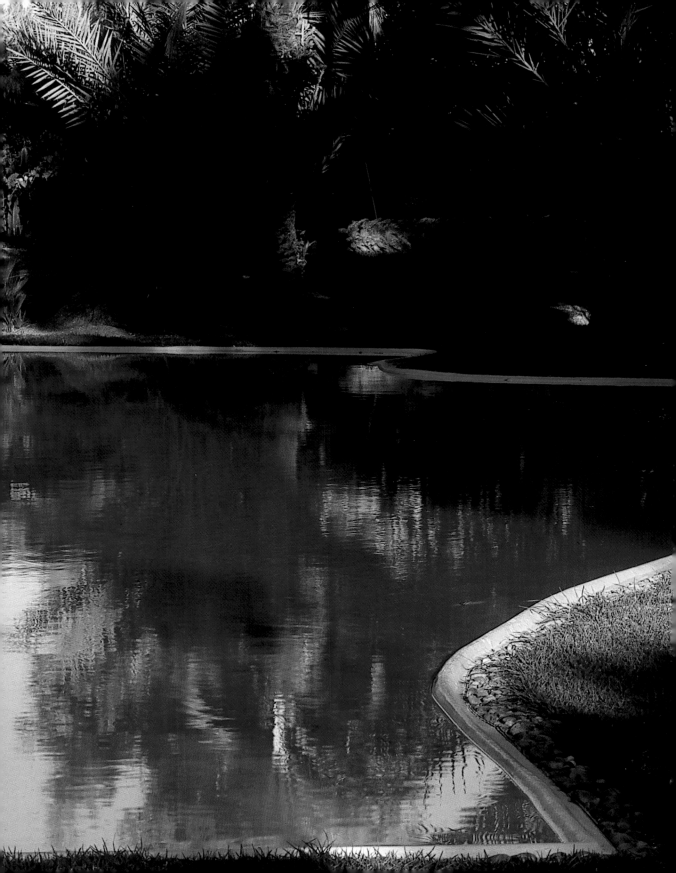

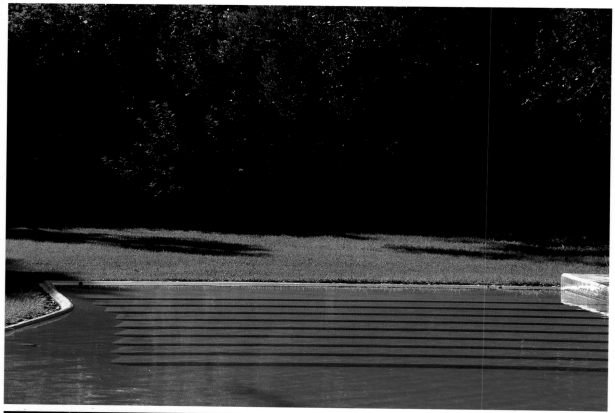

To avoid breaking the continuity of the shape and to extend the visual connection between the natural elements and the pool, the masonry steps are submerged. They are practically invisible from outside the pool.

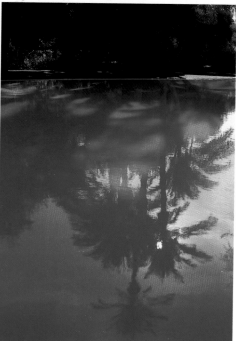

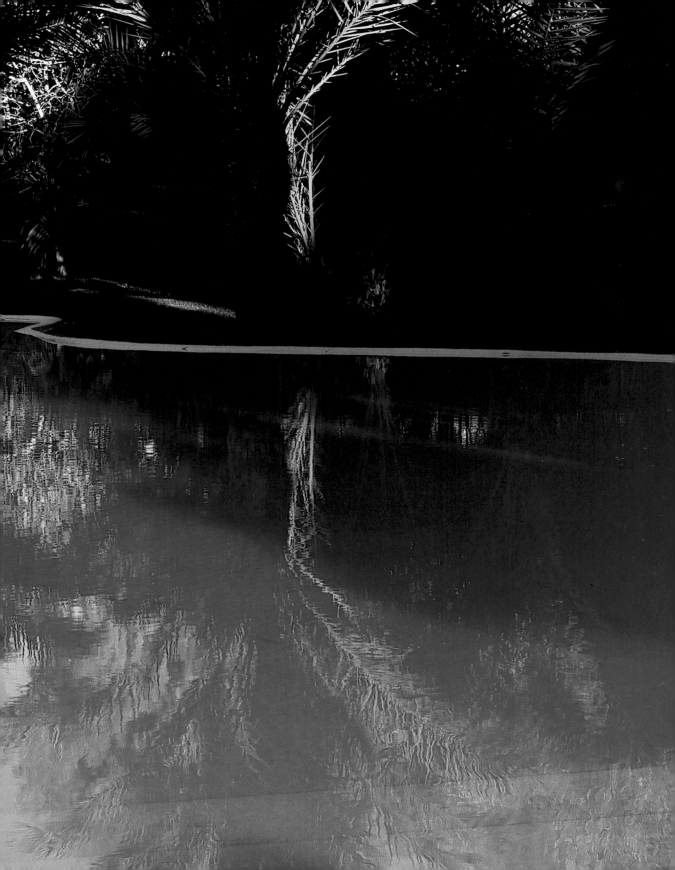

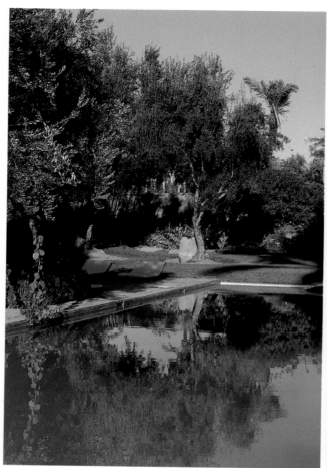

The light constantly plays with the water and plant life in this lush garden, creating attractive contrasts.

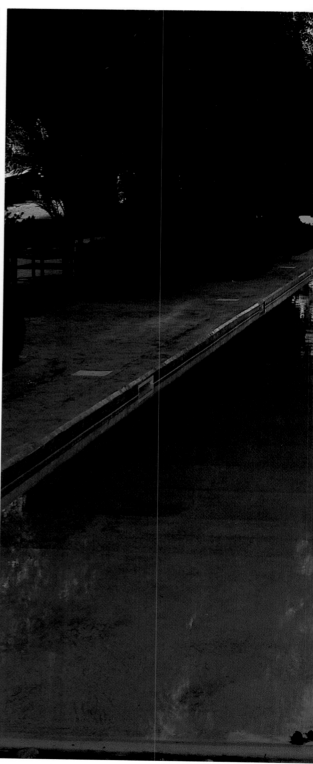

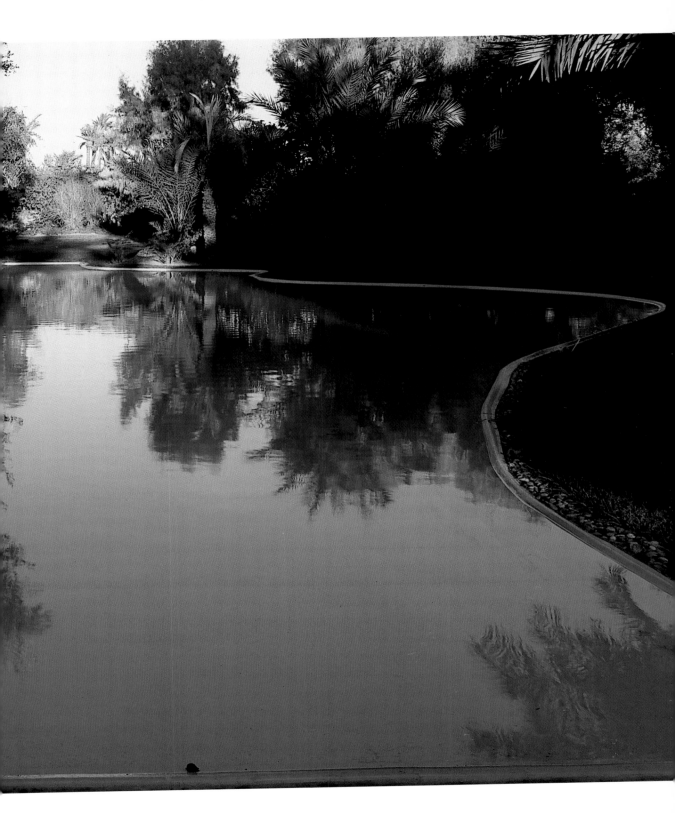

The placement and magnificent orientation of this swimming pool were the determining factors in this project. It is treated as a sheet of still water that creates a dialogue with the surroundings. The overall effect is like an infinite mirror between the earth and sky.

The irregularly-shaped swimming pool, dotted with small peninsulas of rock, resembles a calm natural lake, a niche where one can find peace and primordial silence. In one of the angles, which melts into the landscape, one can see a tree trunk, twisted by the passage of time, placed strategically for contemplation, in accordance with the tenets of Zen philosophy. In this respect, the designers wanted to avoid overloading the space around the swimming pool, preferring to give prominence to the splendid natural surroundings.

This pool is edged with the same type of rock used for the small artificial peninsulas. This accentuates the natural, integrated feeling by creating a discontinuous, undefined edge. The swimming pool was not intended to change the landscape, but to be a continuation of it. So the materials for the pool and the various living areas surrounding the sheet of water are unified. These are at the same level as the water's surface, strengthening the visual continuity and the spectacular character of the landscape, which blends seamlessly with the main level of the swimming pool.

Mallorca, Spain

A Mirror Between the Earth and Sky

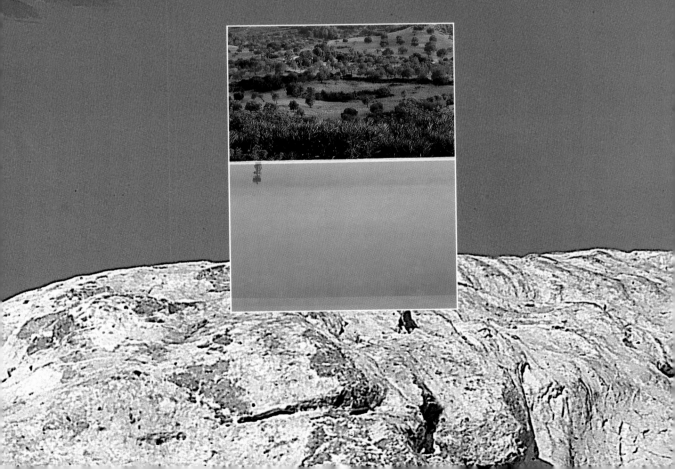

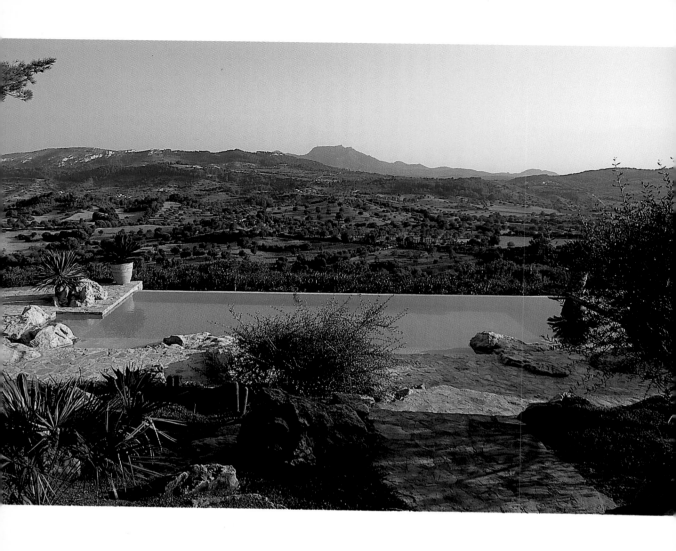

The twisted trunk of a tree that shows the passage of time is situated in a strategic position where it merges with the landscape. The tree obliges the onlooker to stop and contemplate it, in accordance with the guidelines of Zen philosophy.

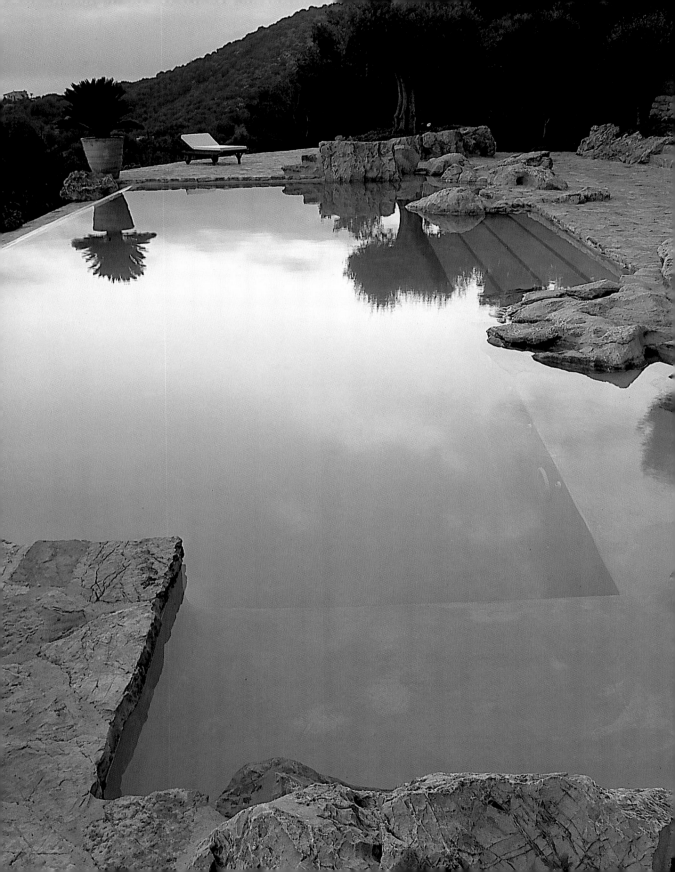

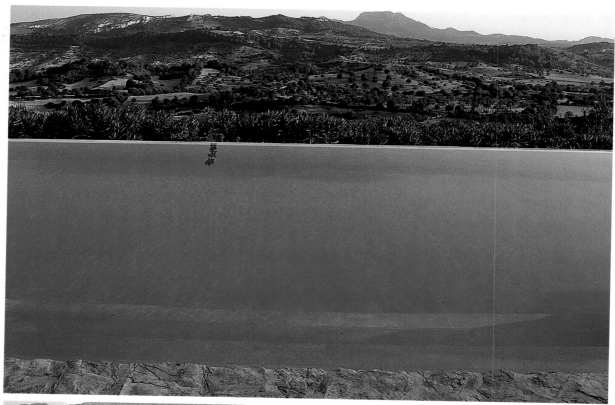

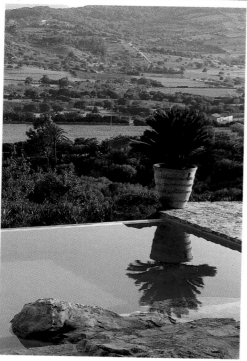

A key factor in integrating the
pool naturally into its surroundings was
unifying the materials and the different
zones that surround the sheet of water.

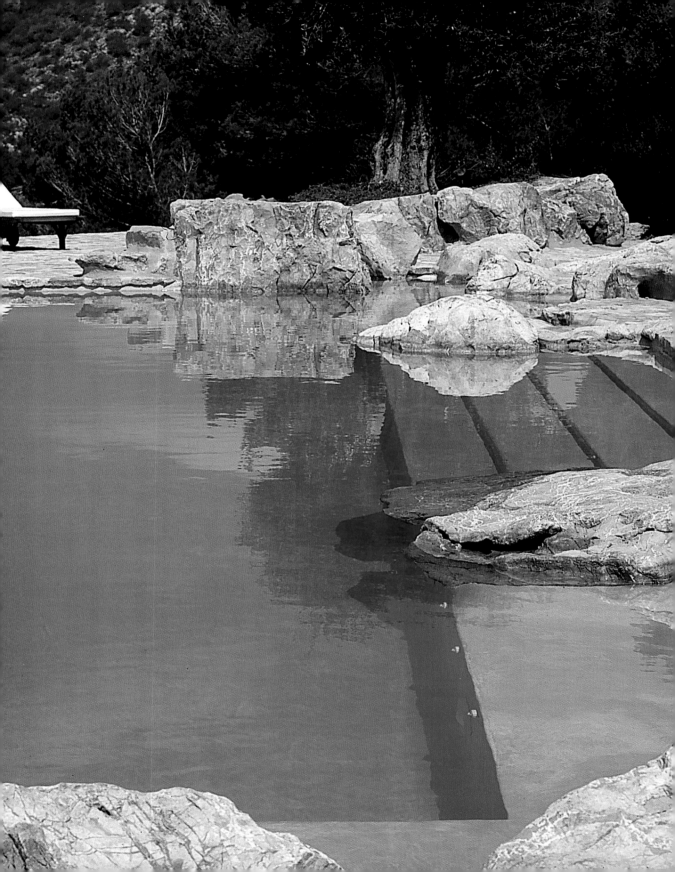

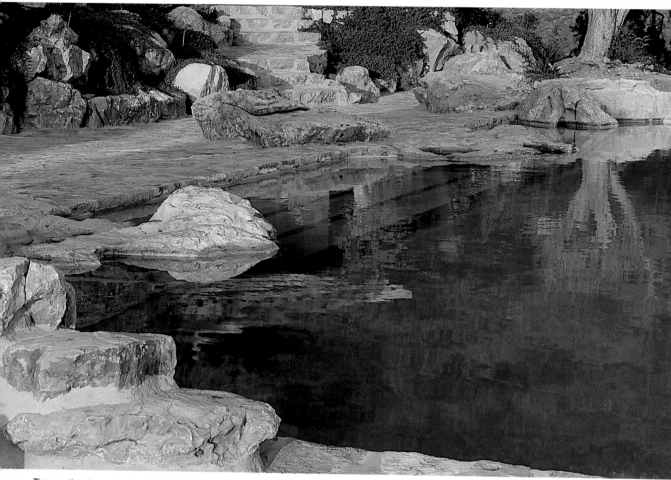

The small rock peninsulas and the use of unified materials in the surrounding area give this pool the sensation of being a natural pond.

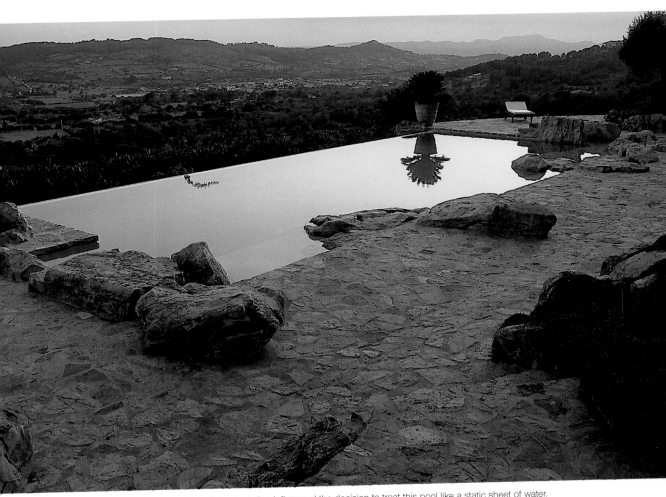

The beautiful perspective offered by the site's orientation influenced the decision to treat this pool like a static sheet of water.

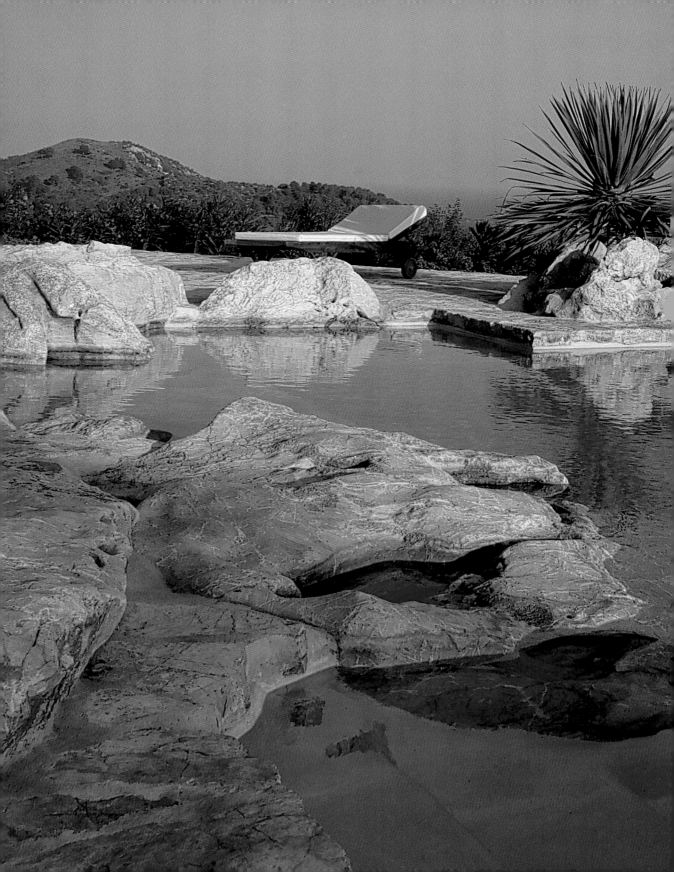

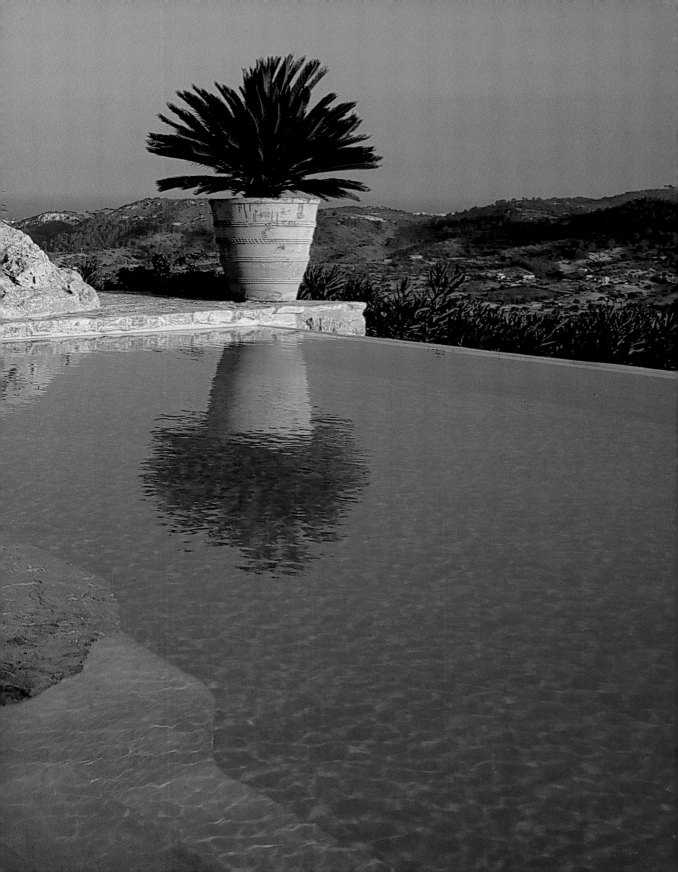

This long, narrow crescent-shaped pool has an air of secrecy and grandeur in its lush setting. Its placement and orientation were two of the factors that determined its structure. It sits in the shadow of a single-family home, and its curvy shape offers a lesson in how to make the most of the available space and achieve optimal results. Topographical limitations and its dimensions notwithstanding, it is clearly the star of the show.

The green grass, which blankets the entire garden, gives way to a pavement of terra-cotta tiles that outlines the semi-circular pool. Alongside them is a strip of embossed marble that provides a non-slip surface, and next to this is another strip of terra-cotta, closest to the water. With the polished cement coating the inside of the pool white, the water reflects the surrounding plant life and displays every shade of blue. The water overflows when it reaches the rounded side and the ends, making advantageous use of the terrain and the shade of the century-old trees, which are framed by an iron rail. Comfortable chaise lounges invite the visitor to stay and enjoy the landscape. More trees, shrubs, and flowerpots, as well as a vast carpet of grass, complete the delightful setting.

The combination of colors and the play of contrasts surrounding the blue surface of the water makes this a cool, peaceful refuge where it is easy to forget everything except how to enjoy the fine weather and the idle hours.

Cádiz, Spain

Hymn to Sensuality

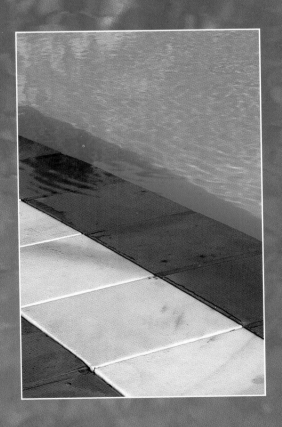

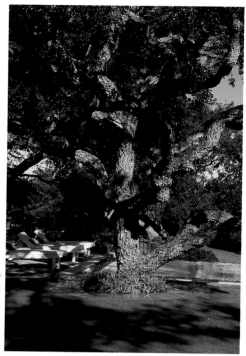

The spatial continuity is broken by the contrasting textures, materials, and colors. Even so, the overall effect is harmonious because everything is deliberately and perfectly laid out to achieve the desired effect.

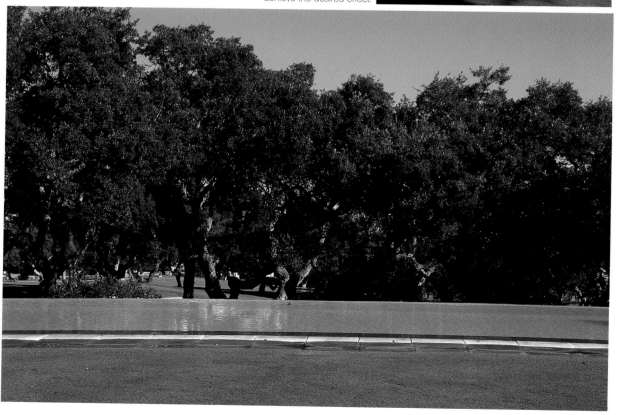

The chaise lounges at the water's edge take advantage of the shade and face the garden for an unobstructed view.

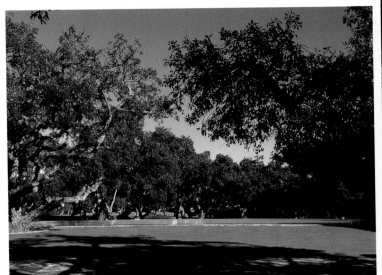

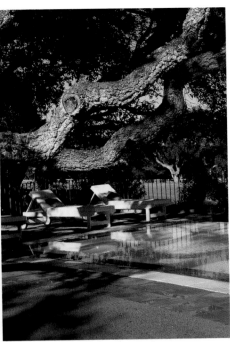

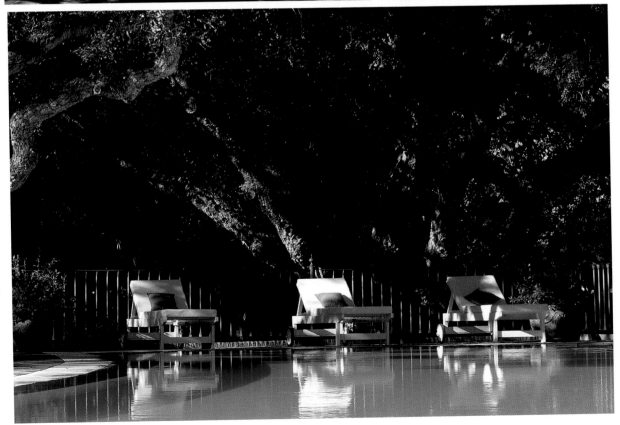

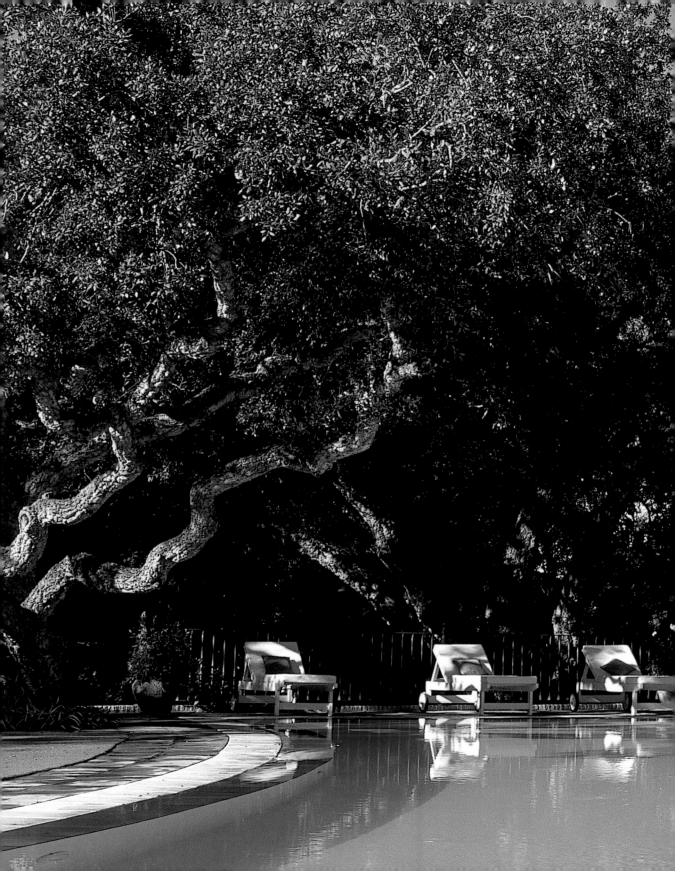

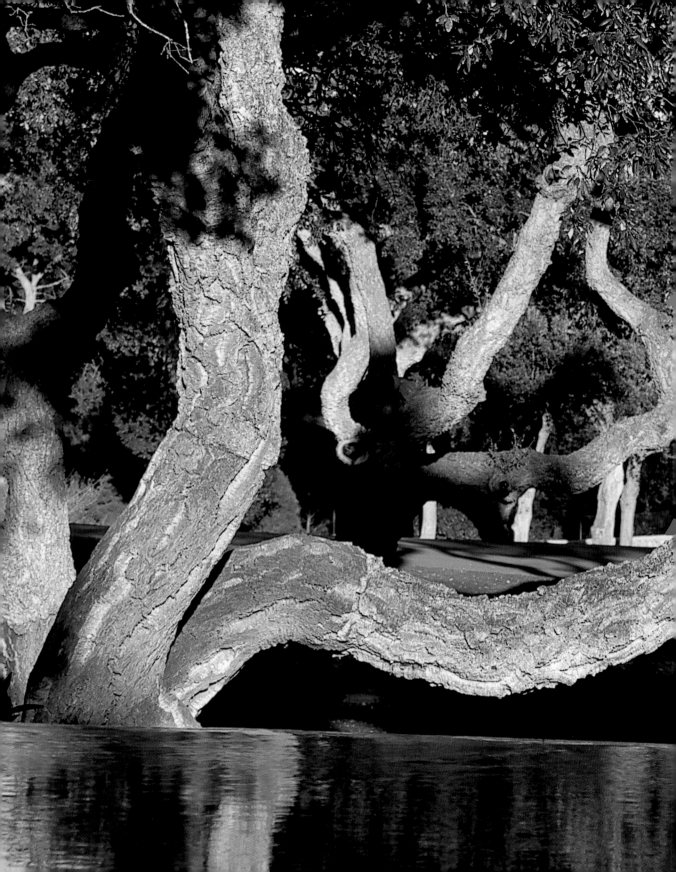

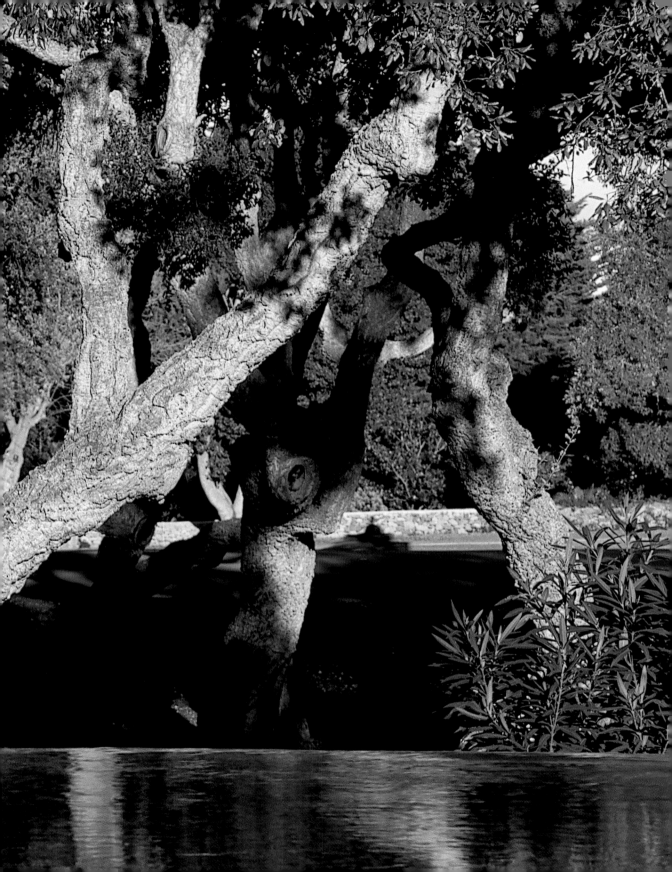

A small pond in the exotic intimacy of an interior Moroccan patio, this shallow pool is another example of how mosaics are still used in Morocco.

An elaborate, bright turquoise finish that derives all its splendor from the sun's reflection crowns a bright border which extends around the interior perimeter of the pool. A soft salmon color covers the structure, creating a chromatic axis between the pool and the principal and side façades, which also boast Moroccan floor tiles and two magnificent wooden chairs that preside over the pool like ritual carvings. At a higher level, steps covered with mosaic tiles the same color as the pool lead to a small terrace dominated by three arched windows. Wrought iron and wood furnishings decorate a breakfast/dinner nook with elegant simplicity.

This is a dynamic space, conceived for intimacy, based on Moroccan decorative tradition, in which even the simplicity of a border stands out as a complex geometric exercise. Color and textures merge here to create a unique, formal, balanced, aesthetically pleasing whole.

Douar Abiat, Morocco

Traditional
Inspiration

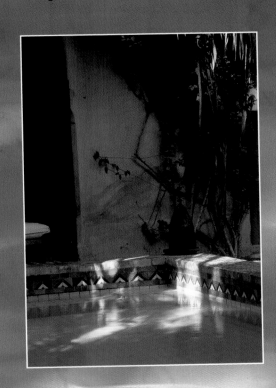

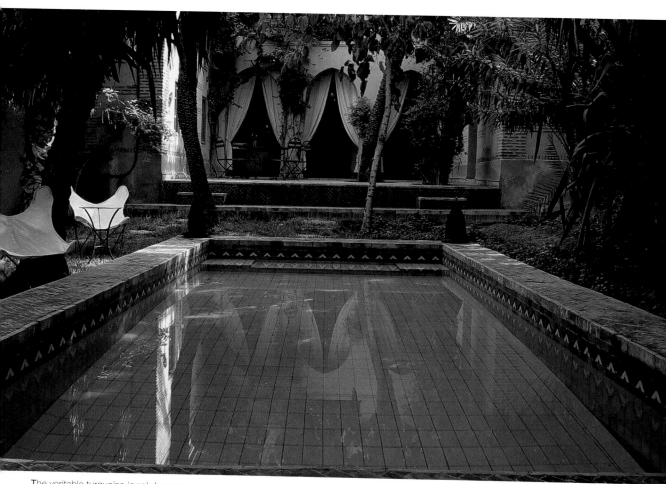

The veritable turquoise jewel draws a traditional Moroccan flavor from the geometrically simple border, which paradoxically gives the pool a more ornate appearance.

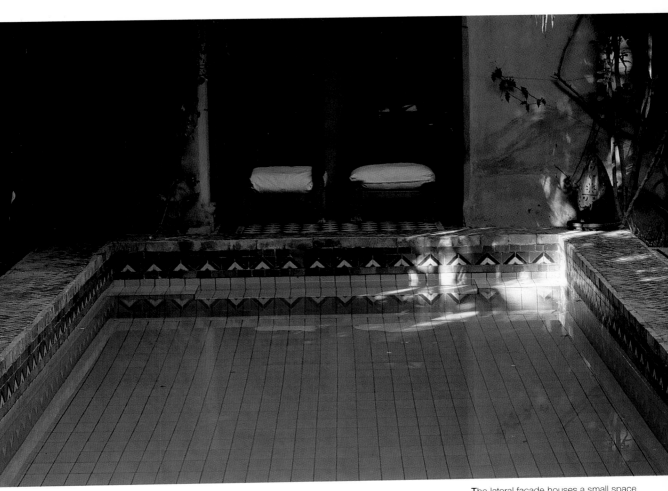

The lateral façade houses a small space paved with Moroccan tiles and is adorned with two stately wooden chairs that appear to govern the pool with regal authority.

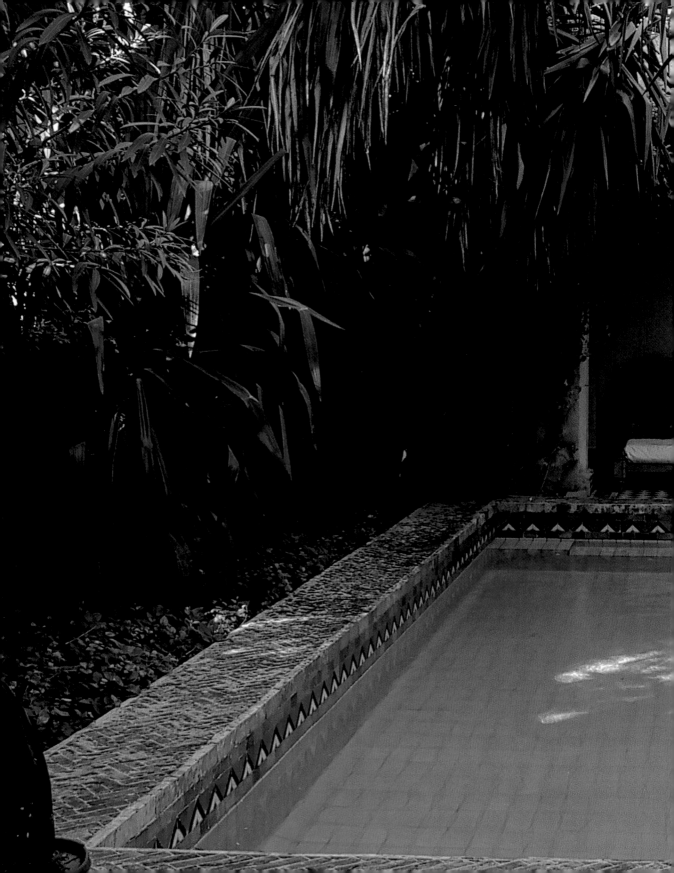

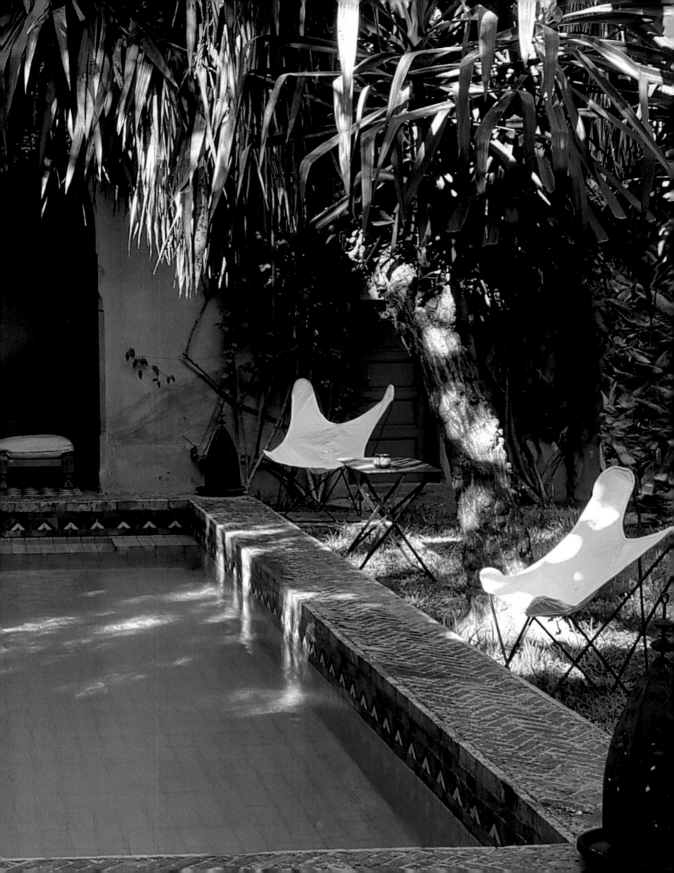

This magnificent trapezoidal pool is surrounded by a spectacular deck of tonka bean tree wood. Situated next to the main building—a country house—this area was designed and visually linked to the adjacent building with a tropical wood deck, colored an intense brown.

The restoration of the country house, the construction of the pool, and the reclamation of a secondary building as a water area occurred slowly in stages over a period of more than five years. The entire water area was planned in the last phase, when the owners bought the adjacent property, which now houses a complete leisure area with Finnish sauna, Turkish bath, and changing rooms situated under an impressive arch which reaches up to the ceiling of the old building. A jacuzzi, strategically placed to take advantage of views of the Ampurdan landscape, completes this formally balanced, oversized room whose refined style harmonizes the different textures: stone, etched glass, and tropical wood.

Outside, a wall of varying heights, perfectly restored and crowned with a bright, colorful tapestry of vegetation, isolates and protects the area and creates a cozy, intimate space. Moreover, the intelligent combination of colors and textures—including the green of the vegetation, the pale ochre of the stone, and the chromatic intensity of the tonka bean tree wood deck—enhances a blended set of natural contrasts that make the grouping a splendid exercise in integrating landscape and architecture.

Girona, Spain

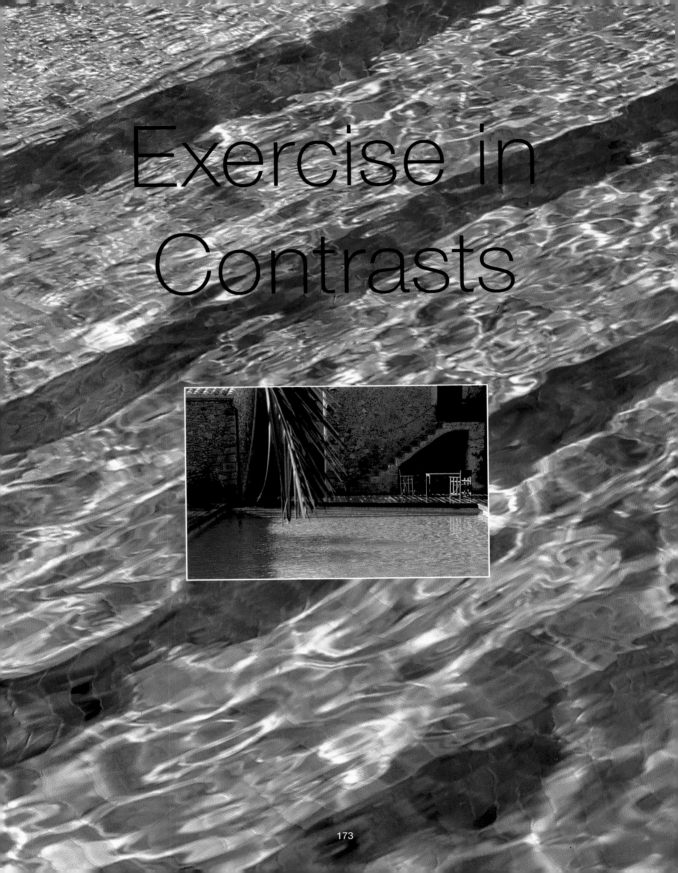

Exercise in Contrasts

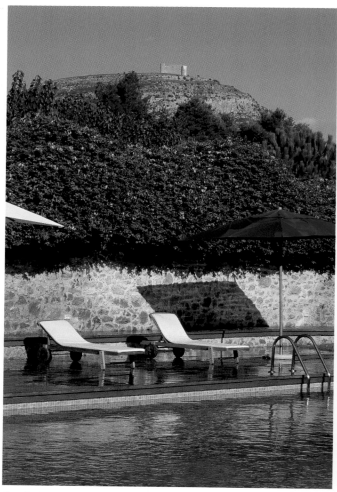

A wall of varying heights, in conjunction with a dense, colorful layer of vegetation, creates a cozy and intimate space.

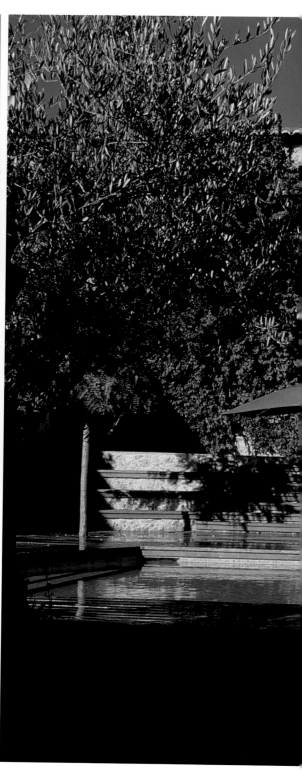

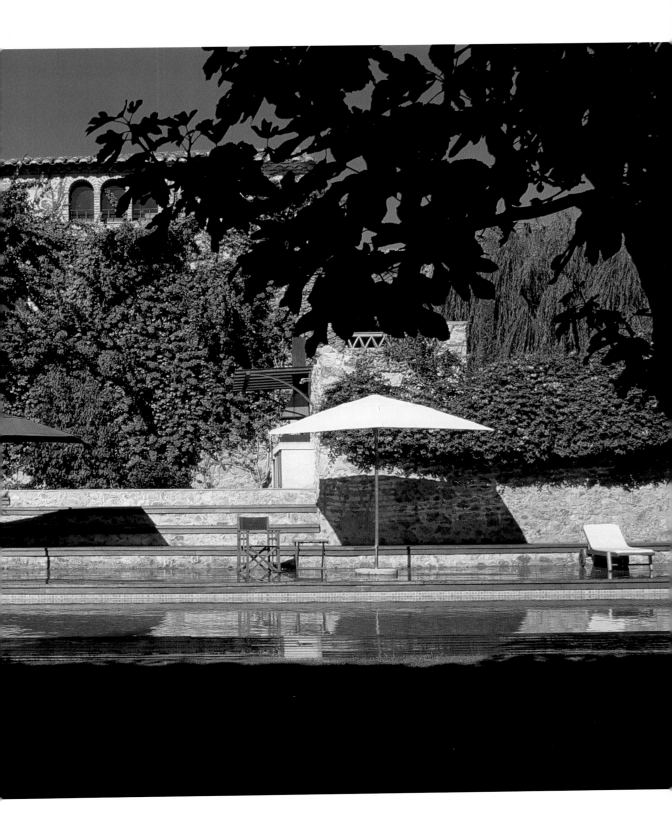

Tonka bean tree wood was chosen to cover the water area because of its great chromatic intensity. The wood enhances the blended set of contrasts.

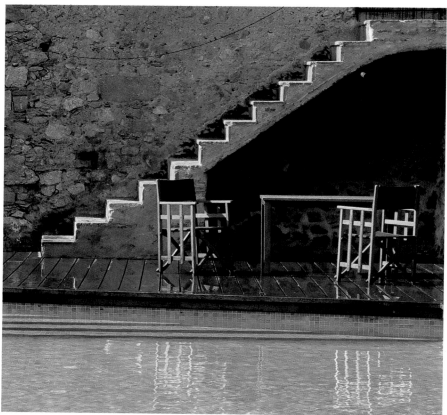

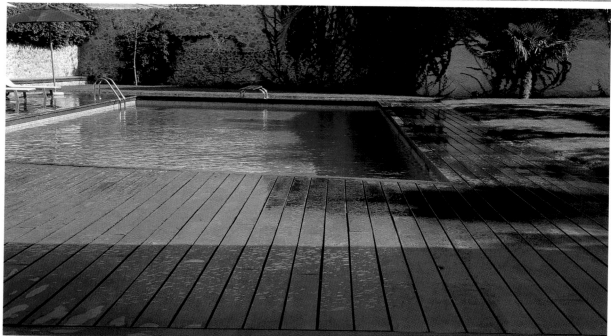

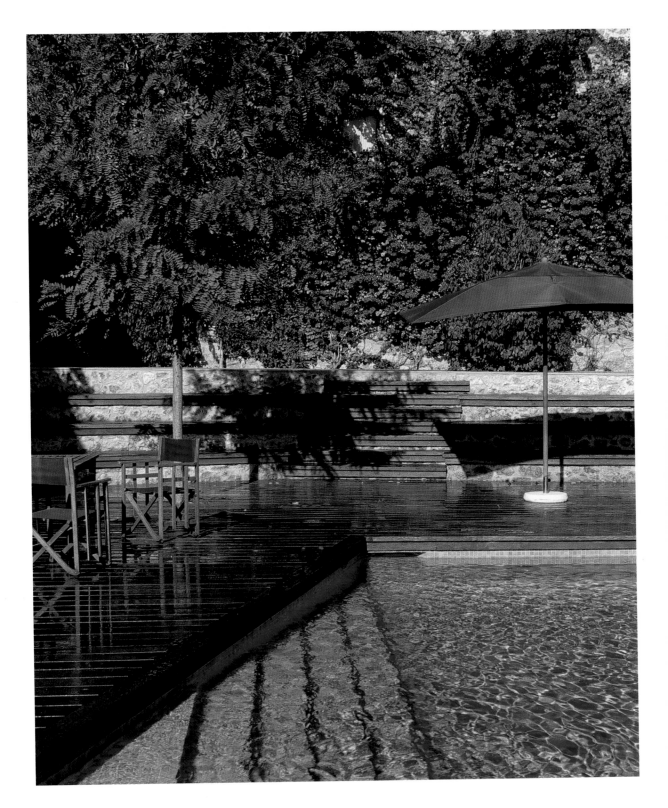

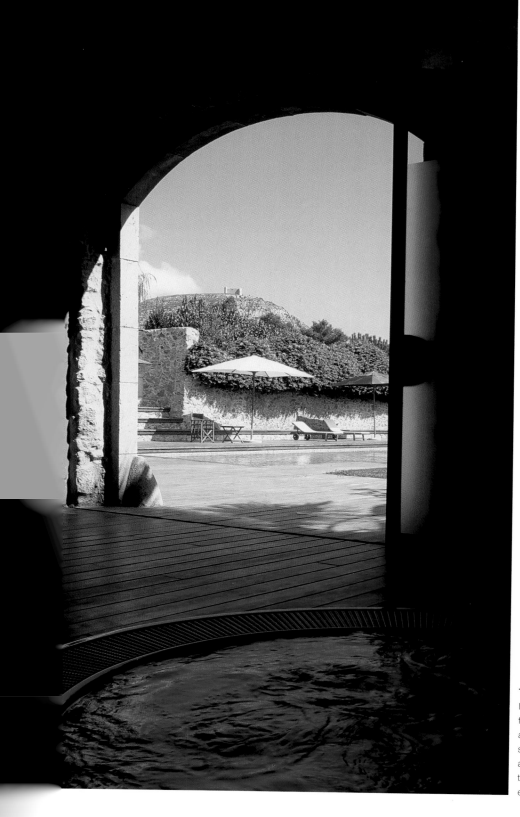

The beautiful Ampurdan landscape can be enjoyed from the jacuzzi. A sauna and Turkish bath are situated under an impressive arch which reaches up to the ceiling of the existing building.

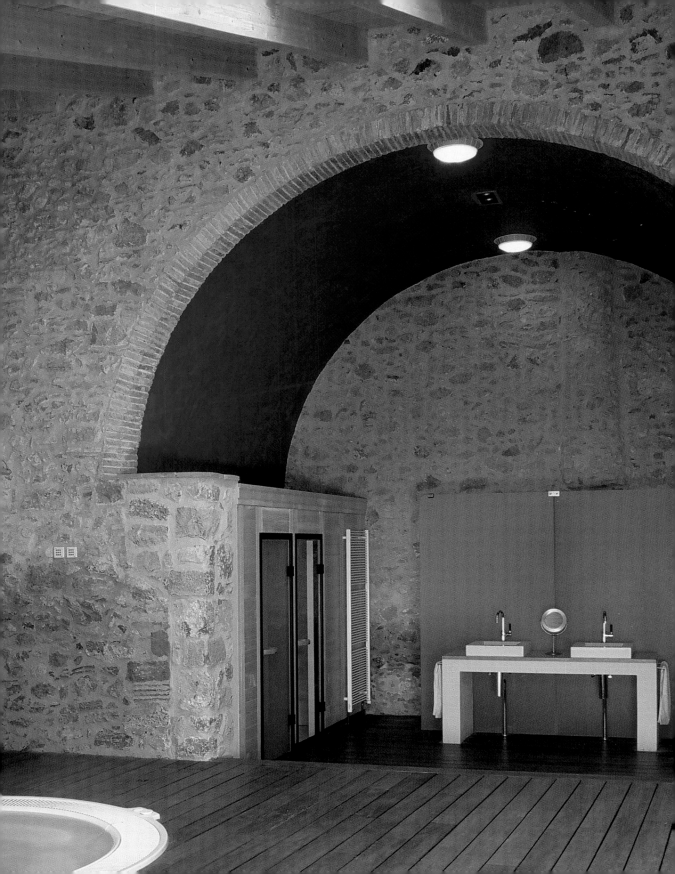

This serene pool rests in a deck of tropical wood which comes flush up against the rear façade of the house. The highly stylized, formally refined project, in which the pool is on the same level as the thick carpet of grass covering the entire garden, was built on a highly contrasted base of three intense colors: organic green, deep blue, and honey brown.

Constructed with Mediterranean-blue mosaic tiles and finished inside with the same wood that covers the area, the pool has an entrance which is visually separated from the composition and breaks the pool's rectangular line. The tropical wood deck that shelters the water and covers the entire outdoor lounging area imparts a sensation of visual dynamism and a touch of velvety warmth.

To unify materials and textures, the dividing wall between properties was designed with the same tropical wood used for the deck and the roof of the minimalist pavilion, which was built as an outdoor lounge. For this more protected and intimate space, stylized sofas and a central table made of iron were chosen, as well as tropical wood chaise lounges in a slightly more rustic style.

A thin steel rail visually unites the grouping with the interior bay window at the corner of the house and separates the outside lounging area from the façade.
Barcelona, Spain

Zen
Symmetry

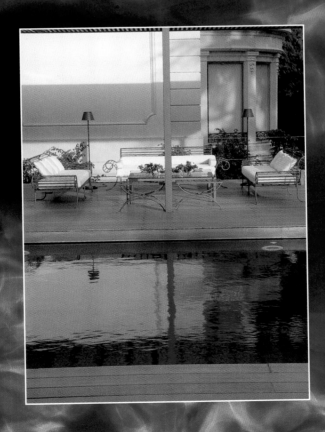

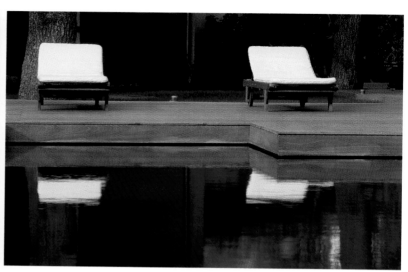

For this project, the typical edging was rejected in order to visually integrate the pool area with the tropical wood deck. From this angle, one can see the interior finish of the pool's edge.

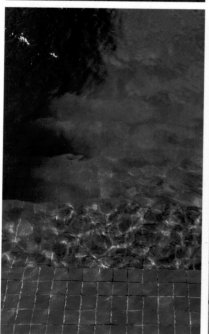

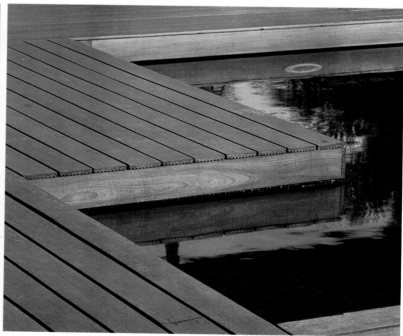

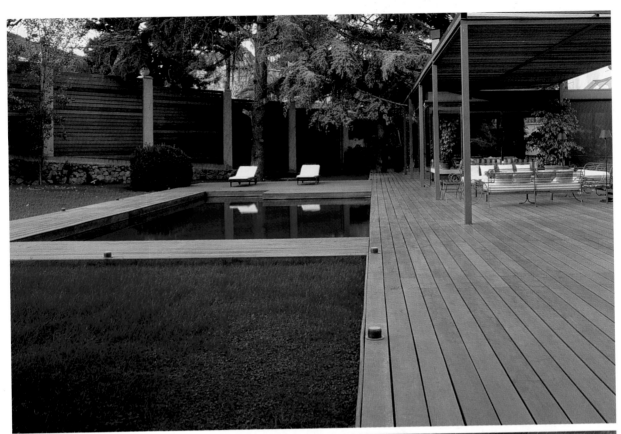

The outdoor lounging area is sheltered by a minimalist pavilion. The tropical wood surrounding the pool gives the setting a touch of visual dynamism and integrates the pool and lounging area on a single level.

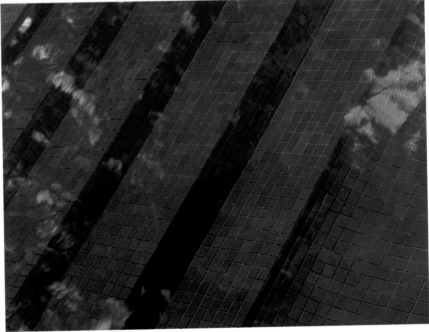

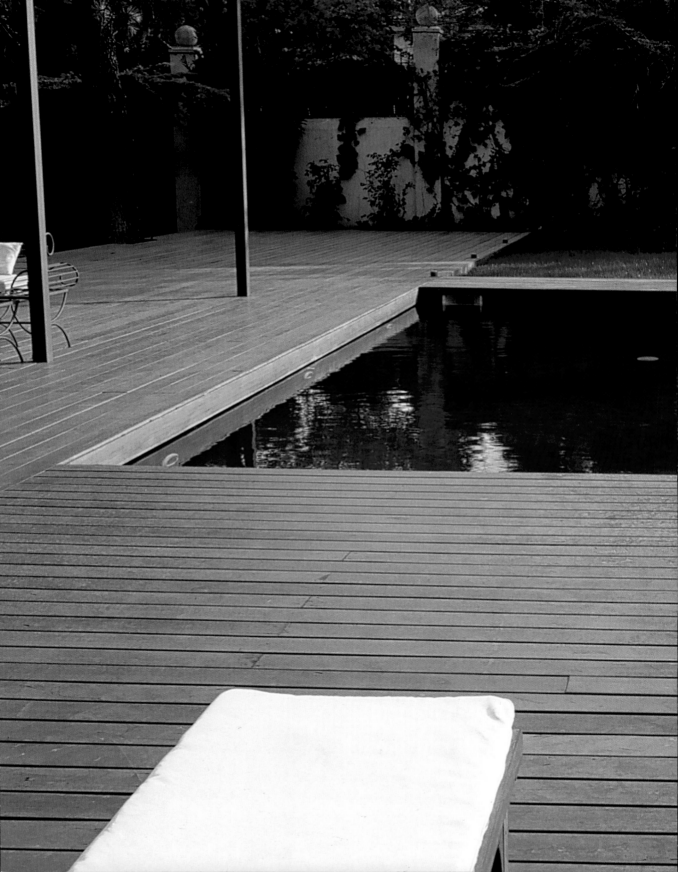

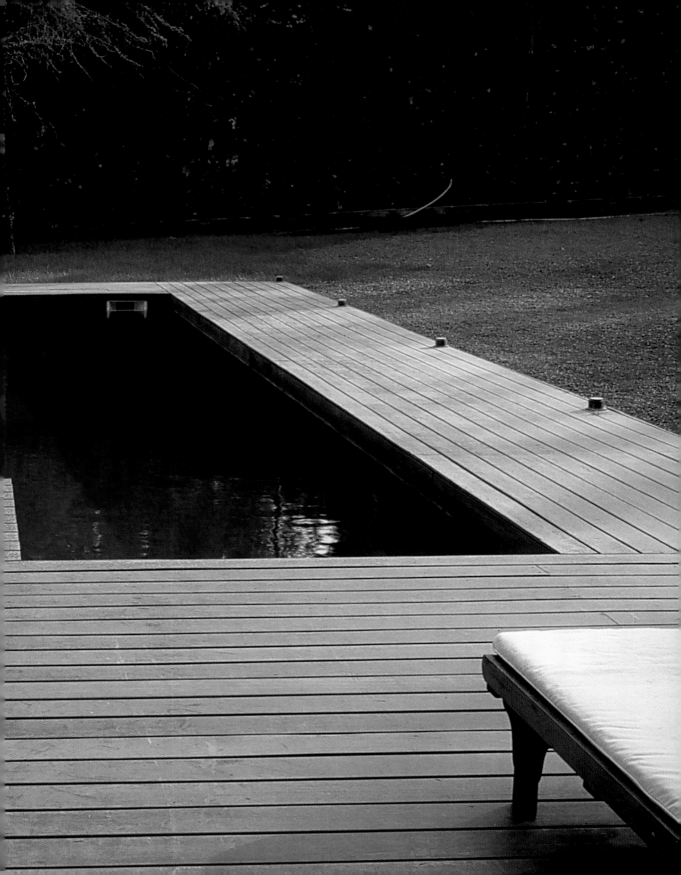

This pool's layout follows the model of the classic houses of France's Provence region, with two clearly differentiated exterior spaces. Situated opposite the house's rear façade, directly in front of the main rooms to facilitate direct access, this delicious water area is well defined and clearly organized, starting with the various hedges that stretch out in succession from the façade.

On one level is the pool, peaceful, welcoming and classic, with the subtle elegance that only the passage of time and the hand of an expert gardener can achieve. Formally, it is finished with a rustic crown of natural stone, and the inside is coated with blue mosaic tiles. Large slabs of unglazed fired clay pave this recreational area, adding a warm note and ensuring easy maintenance year round.

This pool's enchanting character is mainly a result of the deliberate French-style landscaping. The garden, conceived as a natural extension of the house, maintains a delicate symmetry of plant life. Boxwood hedges of different heights visually separate the various landscaped areas. A hammock, the only informal element in this composition, hangs from a refined, stylized, solid wooden structure, which also supports a thick, climbing rose bush, making it the focal point of the grouping.

Opposite the house, in the landscaped area, sits a small, ancient stone cistern for collecting rainwater. The presence of this beautiful cistern confirms the personality and style of the property.

Les Beaux de Provence, France

Classical
Personality

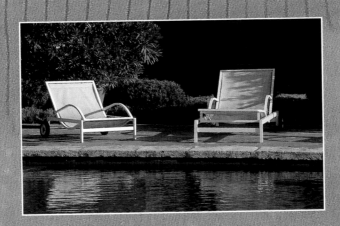

Opposite the main
entrance, a beautiful,
ancient solid stone water
fountain sits next to a
small cistern for collecting
rainwater.

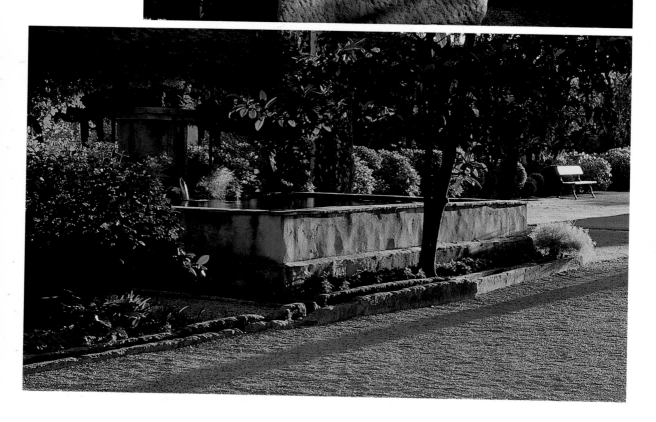

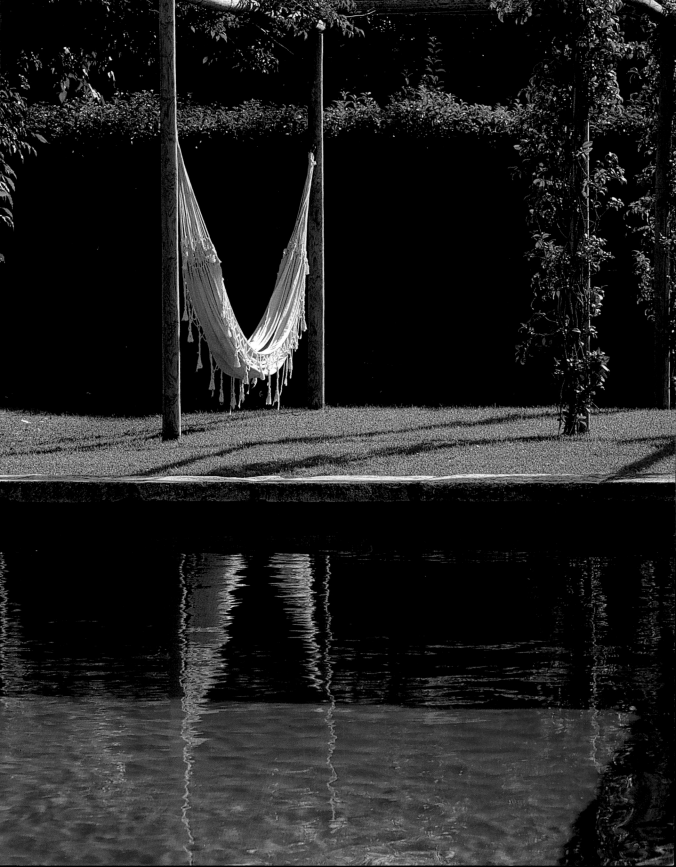

The pool can be accessed from the main rooms of the house through quaint landscaped parterres that form a path parallel to the rear façade.

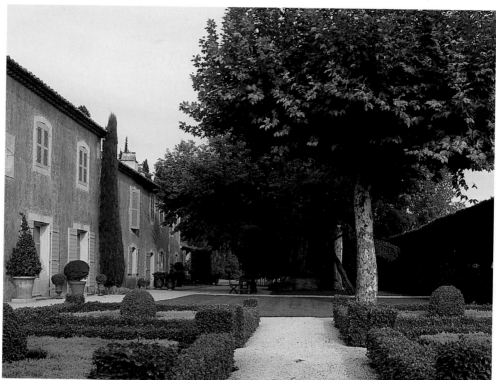

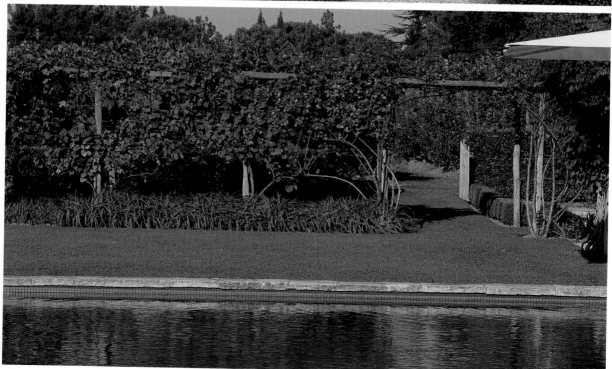

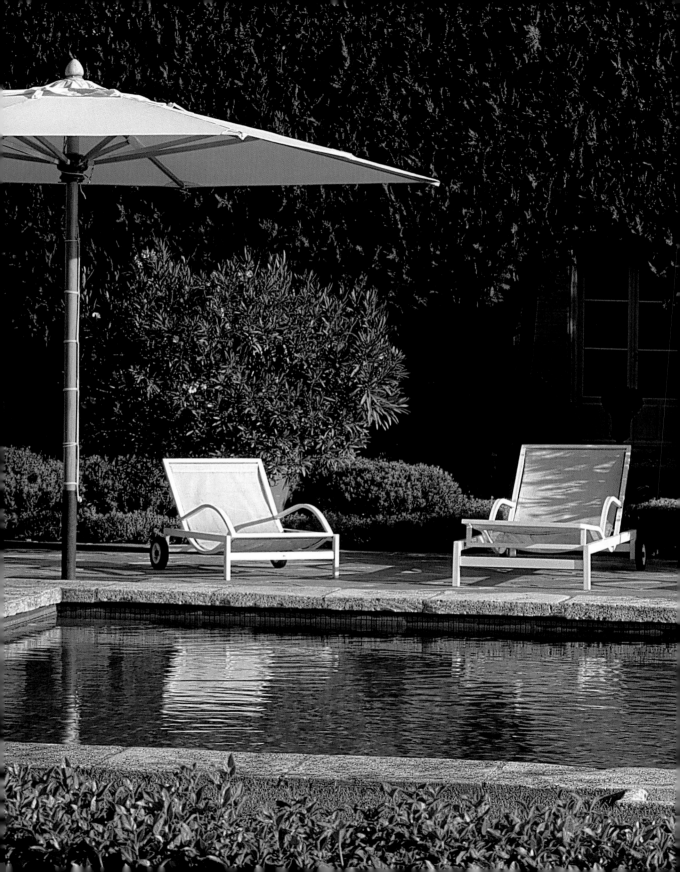

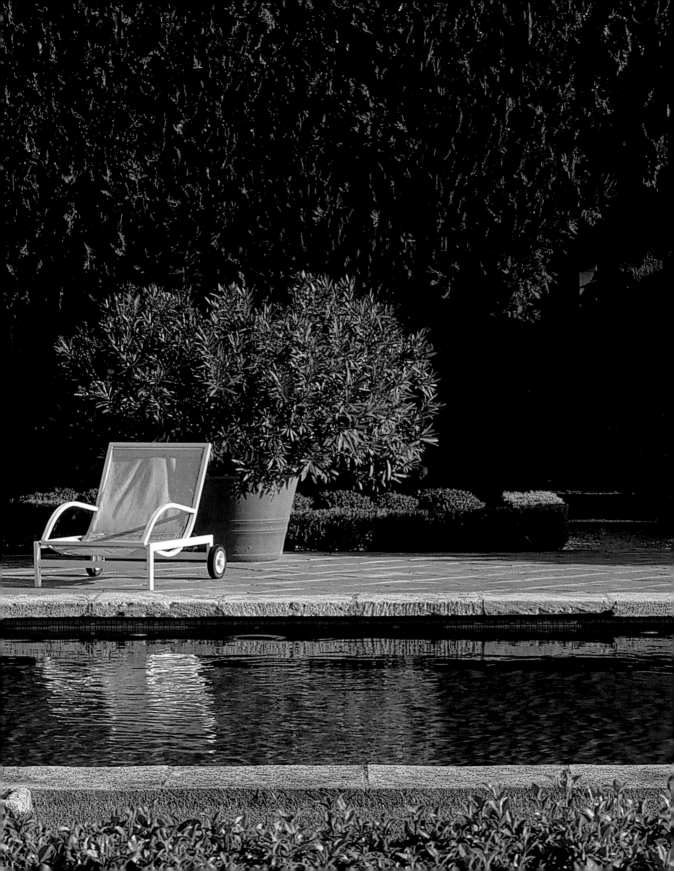

If there is any place where the brilliant, spectacular Mediterranean light becomes even more sublime and powerful, it is in the lands to the south, among which Cádiz, Spain, stands out. Drenched in this marvelous light are these two pools, slightly different in shape and size. The first, square and smaller, dates back to the 1960s, and was part of the original grouping before its renovation and expansion. Once the renovation work had begun, the owners wanted to add another pool for swimming. The new pool was built to resemble the older one. They employ the same construction techniques and materials, so they blend perfectly with each other. Both were designed with straight, severe lines. Three bands of different materials accentuate their shape. A band of terra-cotta separates the pool from the inviting carpet of grass that covers the garden. This is followed by a rougher surface of embossed marble (marble treated to keep it from being too smooth, polished, and slippery) and another band of terra-cotta. The interior is painted white to achieve that evocative blue color that invites the visitor to come in for a swim.

The new pool, intended mainly for swimming, has steps on each end. These consist of two unadorned, parallel stainless steel poles, crowned by round black pieces, supporting four stainless steel steps. These underwater stairs were inspired by traditional everyday stairs but boast a modern design.

The refined garden surrounding the pools, which rest at the foot of a typical Andalusian building, recalls the site's Mediterranean origins. The green hues and the subtle chromatic touches of the orange trees make it a special place in which to enjoy the sun, leisure time, and sports.

Cádiz, Spain

To Live in Paradise

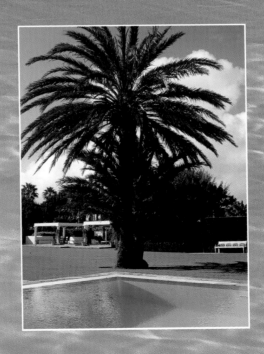

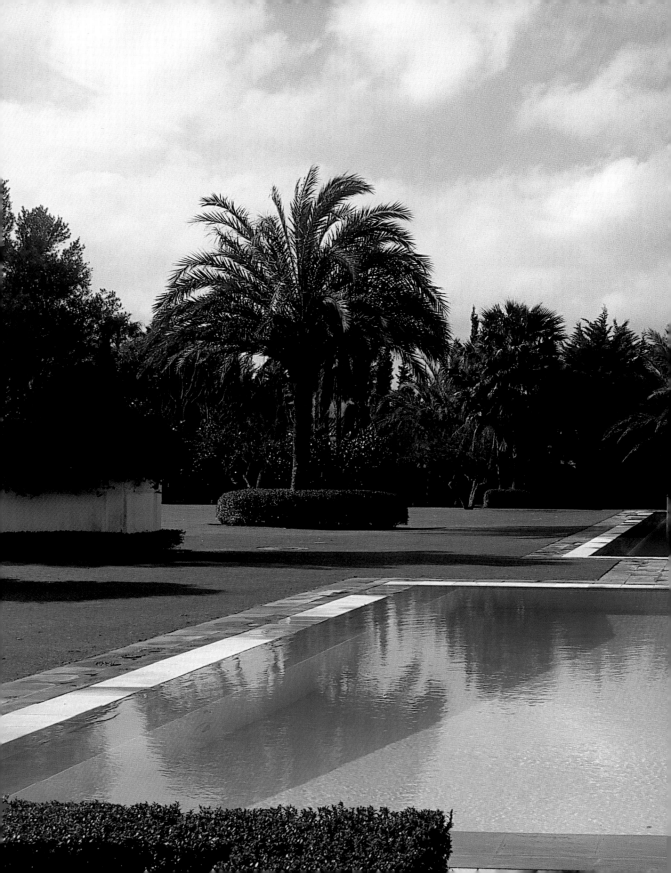

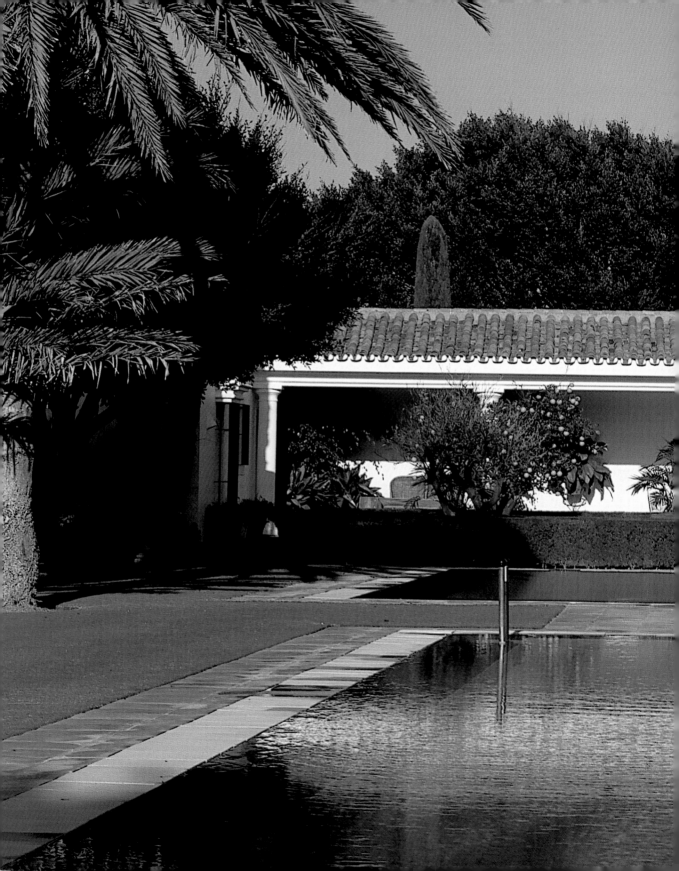

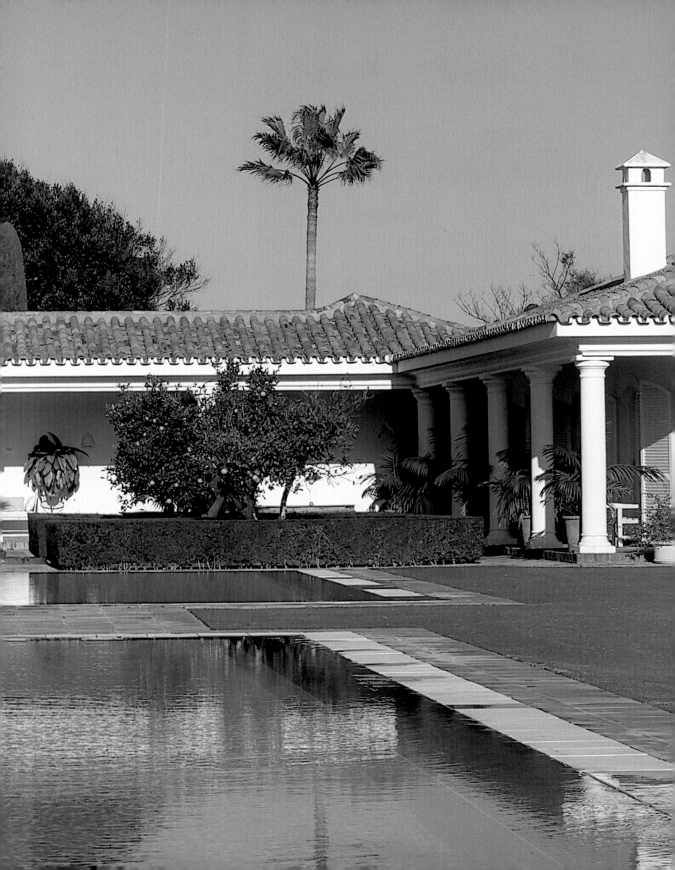

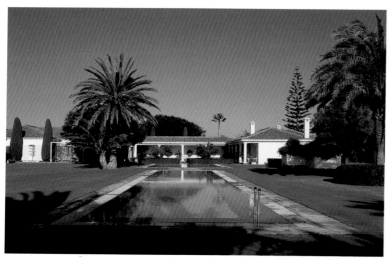

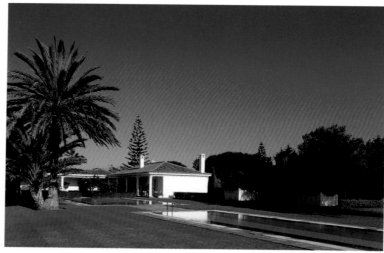

This traditional setting takes its inspiration from typical Andalusian structures. In this beautiful scene, light and water have become the center of attention.

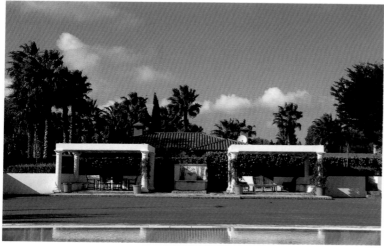

The pool closer to the house's semi-covered porches was inspired by traditional ponds whereas the second was designed for swimming. One of the few differences between them is the inclusion of access stairs in the rectangular swimming pool that subtly interrupt its contours.

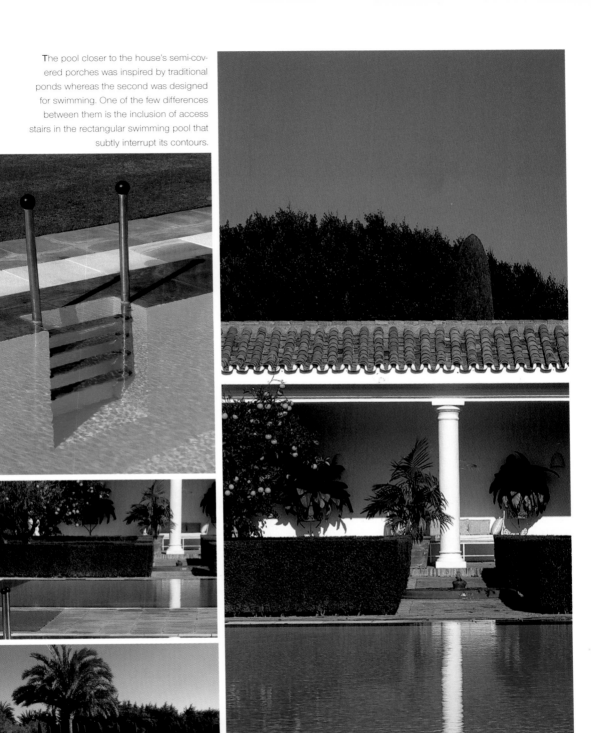

This splendid garden, which extends generously to the east and west of the property, was conceived as a succession of individual spaces, chromatically differentiated but united by an imaginary straight line. On one side, this line takes the form of a waterway, and on the other, it blends with the green hues of the grass that carpets the entrance to the rear gardens.

From the central point of the magnificent restored house, painted a vanilla color, extend four classical gardens. Two of them include conceptually different ponds: one for visual appreciation and the other for swimming. The studied landscaping invites reflection while it sparks the stroller's secret internal creativity with a rapid succession of different spaces, lovingly landscaped and united by organically vivid visual effects and perspectives.

The area opposite the porch, previously the site of a dismal metal sheep shed, now contains a serene pond which reflects the warm light of Provence and the shadow of plane trees. Massive solid rock spheres— symbols of perfection—align themselves with balanced precision on ancient bases in front of the pond.

Another highlight is the stylized Aeolian fountain, also in the form of a circle of vegetation, from which crystalline water flows as a soft breeze blows. Fish, ducks, and frogs inhabit this water area, and water lilies in velvet tones dot the surface. A water channel flows from the pond, and extends between a long line of olive and cypress trees, terminating some 262 feet later in a small pool shaped like a half moon, surrounded by iris and willows.

Saint-Rémy de Provence, France

Classical Spirit

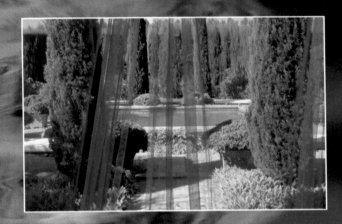

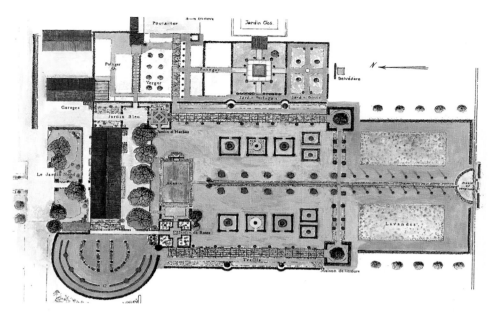

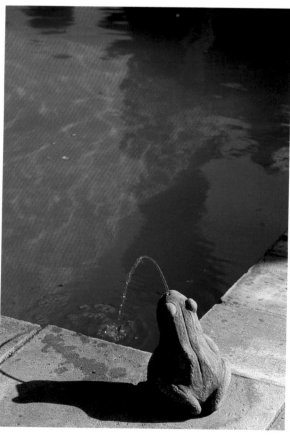

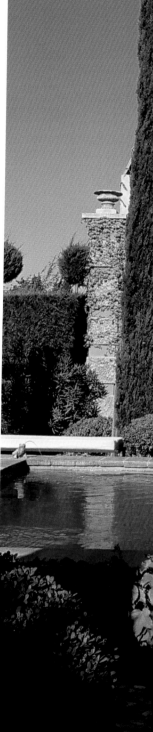

Nature plays a pervasive role in this classical composition. The carefully formulated landscaping has given way to vegetation that accents the stone structures scattered throughout the garden, creating a harmonious blend of natural and man-made elements.

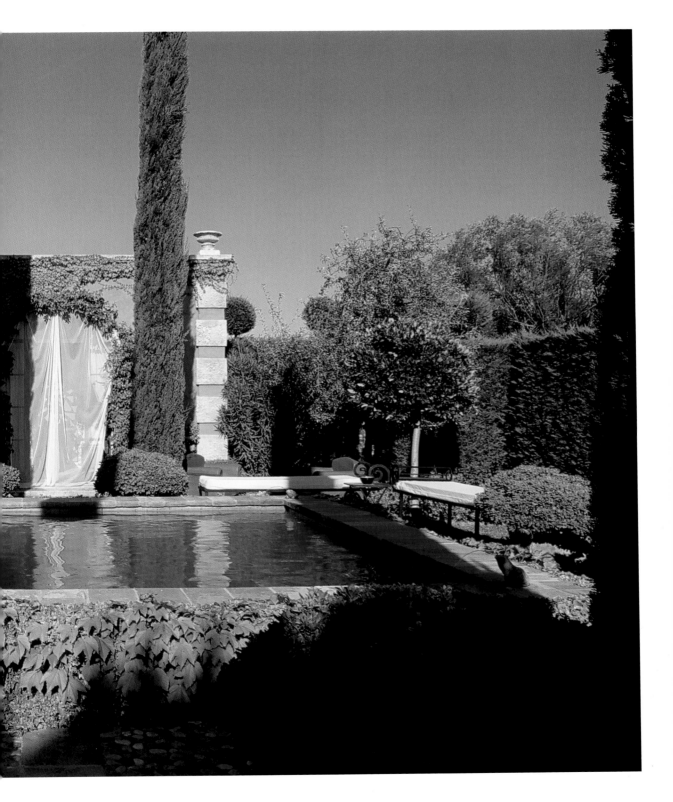

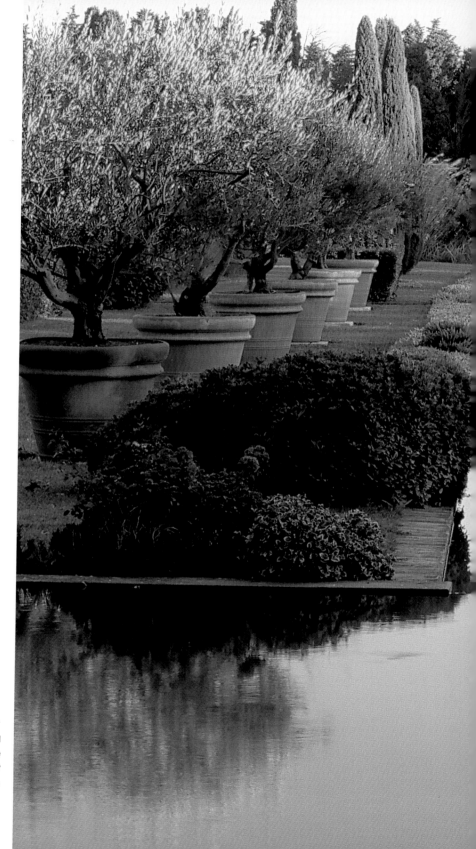

Although conceived as individual
elements in a sequence, the spaces are
united by a straight waterway edged by
a long line of olive and cypress trees.

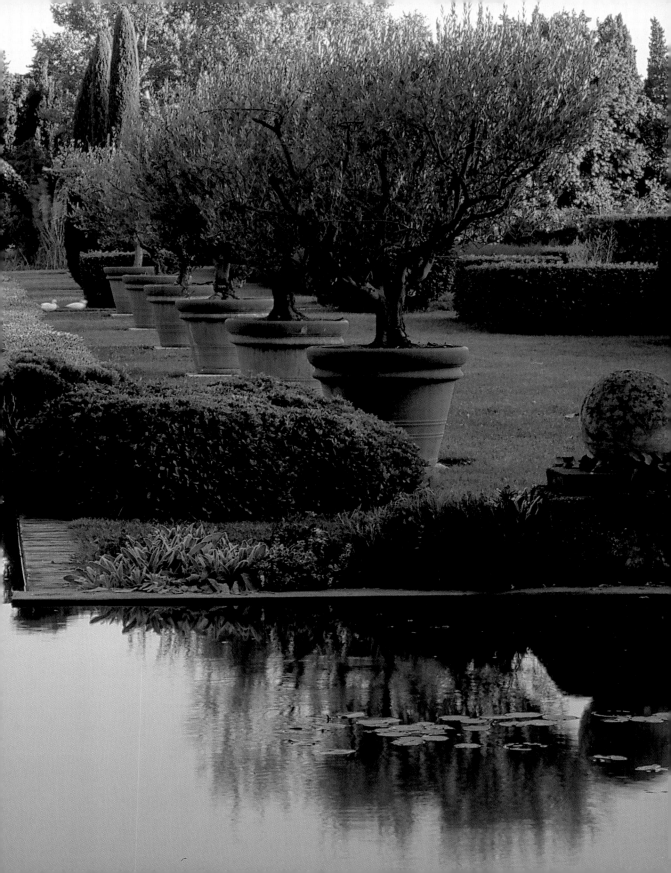

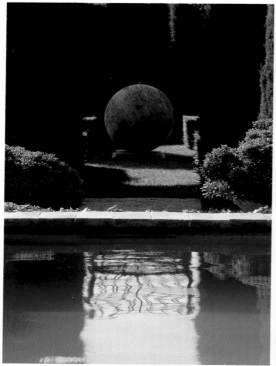

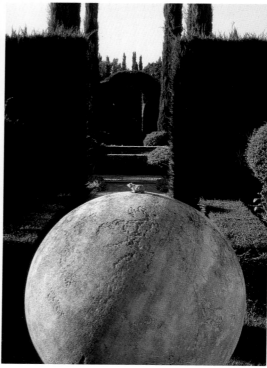

A series of massive stone orbs fixed on ancient bases harkens back to the classical notion that spheres represent perfection and completion.

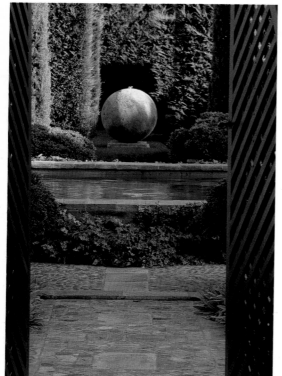

The high shrubbery and the gate enclosing the pool area give a feeling of seclusion. A maze of vegetation and waterways within the isolated garden area creates a sense of magic and mystery amidst an orderly landscape.

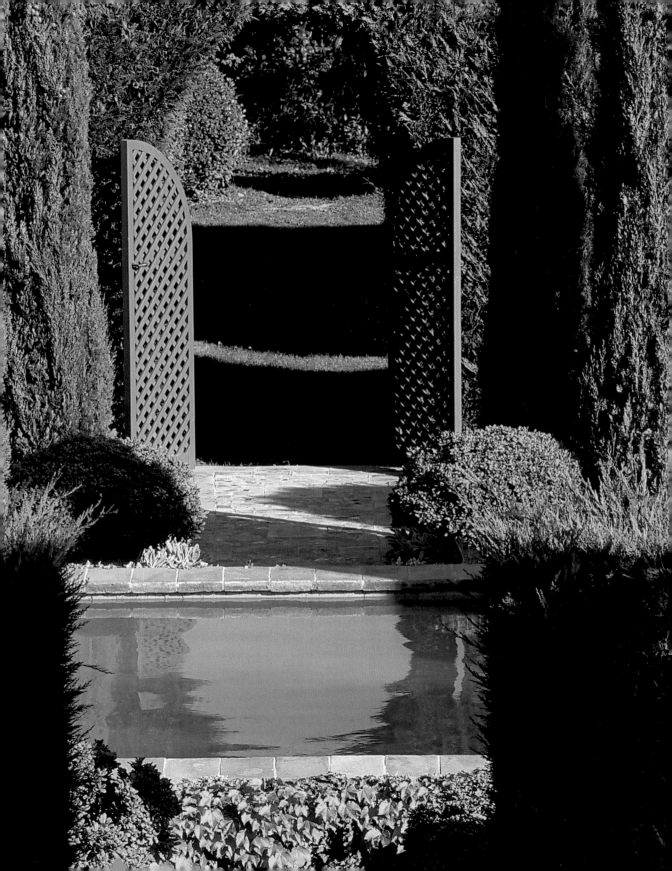

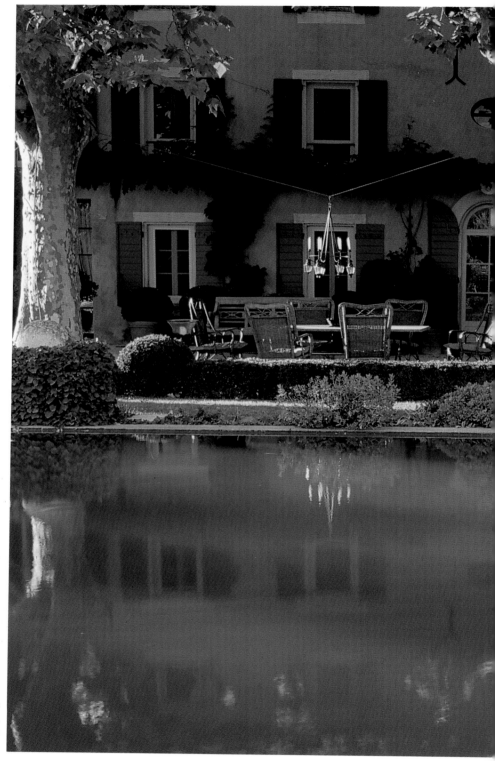

The silhouettes of the plane
trees, chosen to provide shade,
are reflected in the pond
opposite the porch.

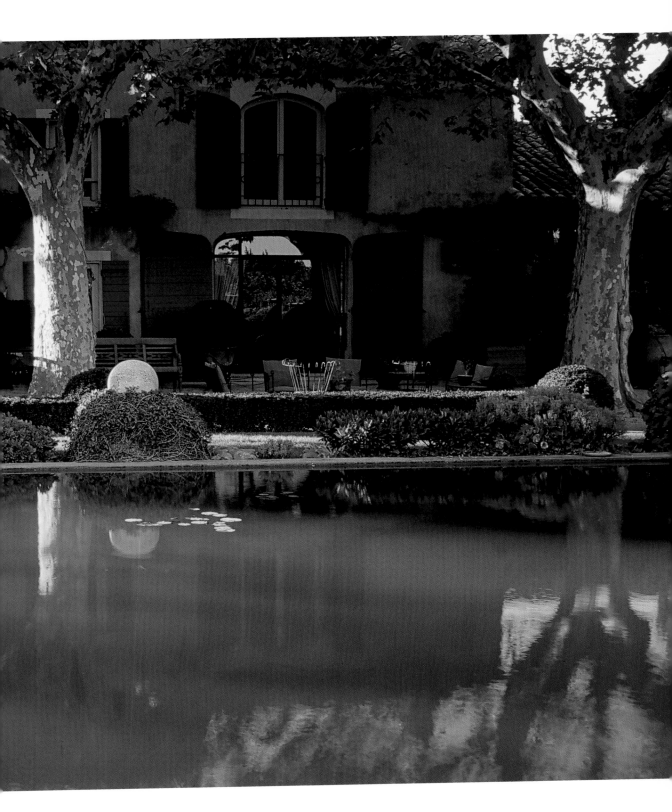

eeking out from a small, steep cove, the exceptional location of this pool captures all the beauty of the landscape, which seems to extend toward infinity. Its irregular, wedge-shaped perimeter, with soft, unusual curves, stops at the edge of the cliff, and accommodates three different levels. At the sharpest bend, a first step facilitates entry into the pool. A second skirts the side and forms a kind of underwater bench for relaxing, and the deepest part is at yet a third level.

A single material was used inside the pool and the area surrounding it: lime cement, with a typically Mediterranean texture and tonality. Also typically Mediterranean are the pines, which provide the only note of color in this universe of dazzling luminosity.

The design of this pool, built without ornamental trim but with rounded edges, is more about aesthetics and leisure than swimming. Admiring the scenery is paramount, albeit comfortably settled in the water.

This beautiful and powerful landscape is in constant motion, subject to the will of the light. The pool becomes a serene vantage point from which to contemplate at any time of day the play and subtle changes of light— by any standard, a privilege.

Ibiza, Spain

Vantage
Point

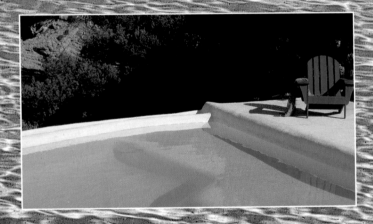

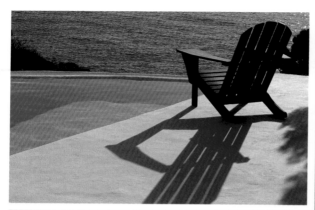

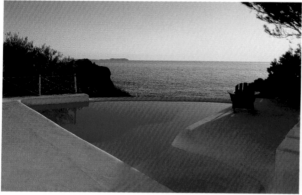

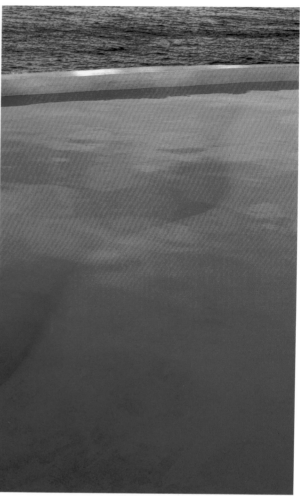

The immensity of the sea and the infinity of the horizon can be enjoyed from any of the pool's three levels. The pool's exceptional location makes it possible to enjoy the sunset from a unique vantage point.

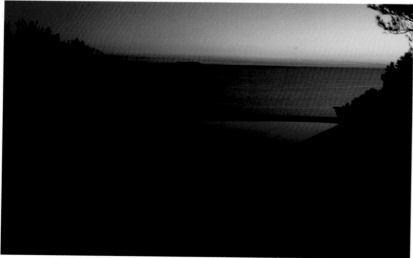

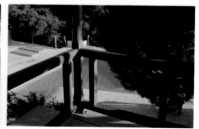

The pines provide a note of color in this composition dominated by white and blue.

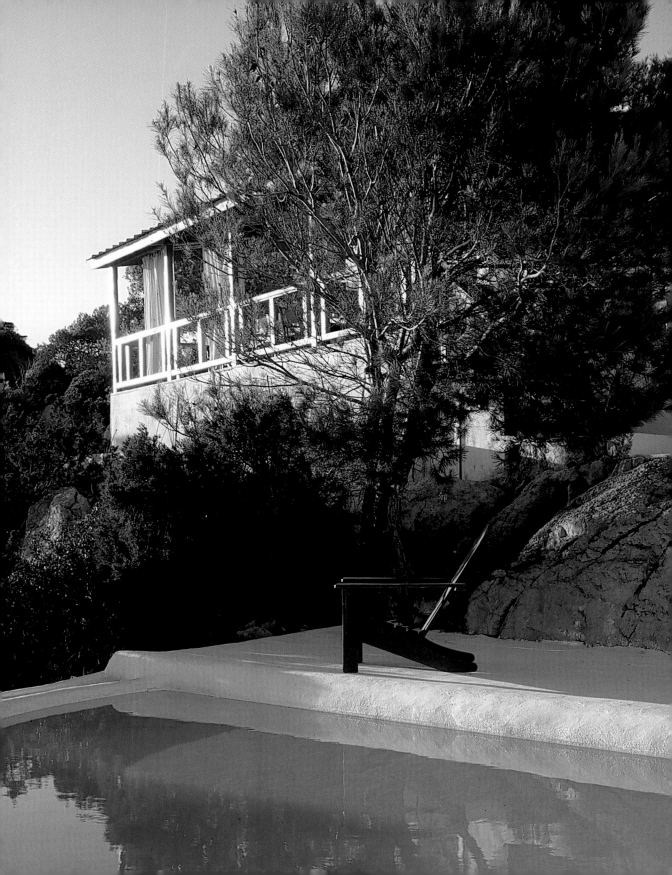

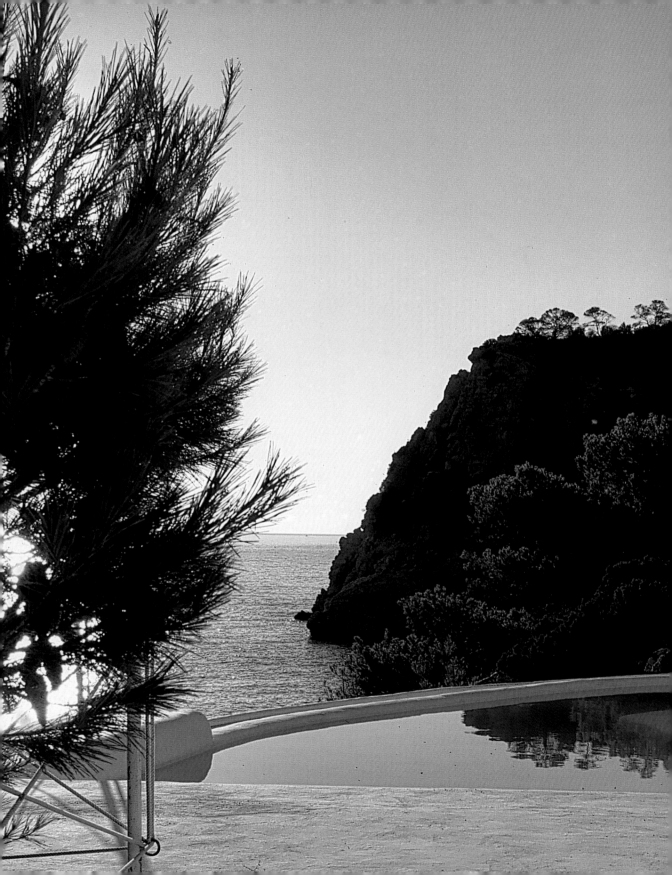

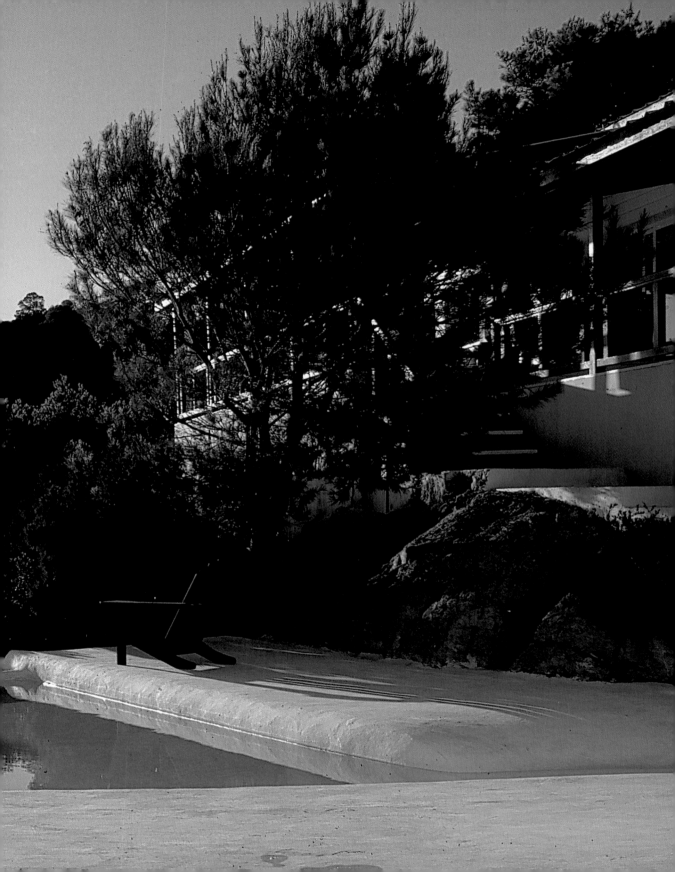

The passage of years has left its patina on this complex landscape composition, to which the pool is a worthy addition. The presence of many ponds, parterres, and beautifully paved paths that leisurely lead to different areas of the garden, makes the pool a secondary but perfectly integrated element in this kaleidoscope of plant life.

Surrounding the pool area are several pavilions, whitewashed and coated with a layer of lime mortar. These small structures provide the only note of color in a composition featuring earth tones and an extensive fan of greens. Amid the columns, custom-made benches provide a place to chat in the shade. The inside of the pool, also whitewashed, enhances the continuity of the materials and the colors of the setting.

The surrounding area features a low garden that includes papyrus, which grows in the ponds, and cyca, a very slow-growing Japanese plant species. The plants are combined with various trees, including ancient olives, which symbolically preside over the entrance to the pool area. In this composition, the vegetation has been sculpted, molded, and dominated by the hand of man, transformed according to his concept of beauty.

Located on an upper level, separated from the garden by a dividing wall, is an orchard of fruit trees surrounded by grass. The distribution of the different garden areas, the constant presence of water, and the serene meandering paths, were inspired by cloister orchards and gardens.

Ibiza, Spain

The Patina
of Time

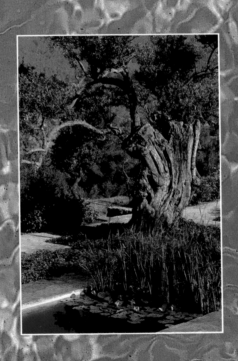

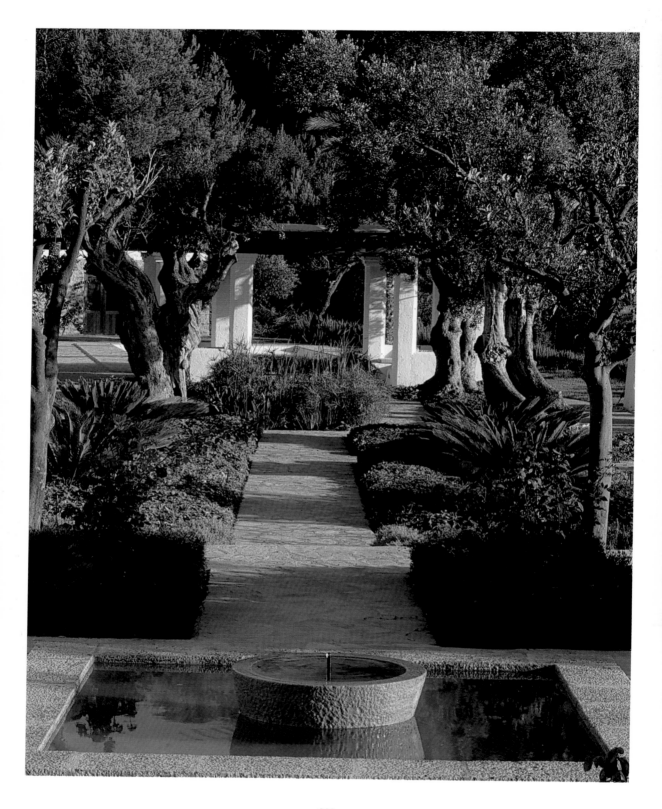

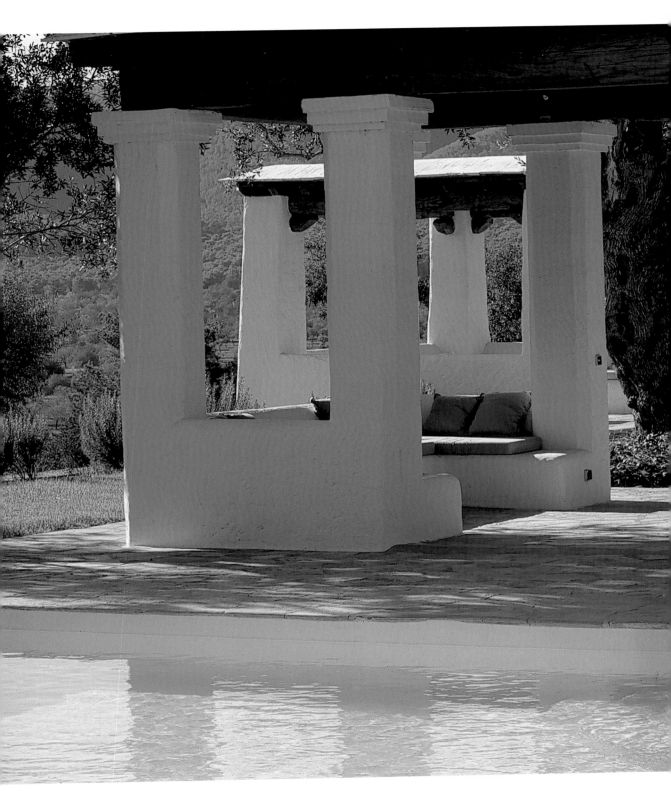

Above the pool, set apart by a low dividing wall, is a row of vines leading to an
orchard of fruit trees. At the back, a restored stone hut coated with a layer of
lime mortar houses the garden tools.

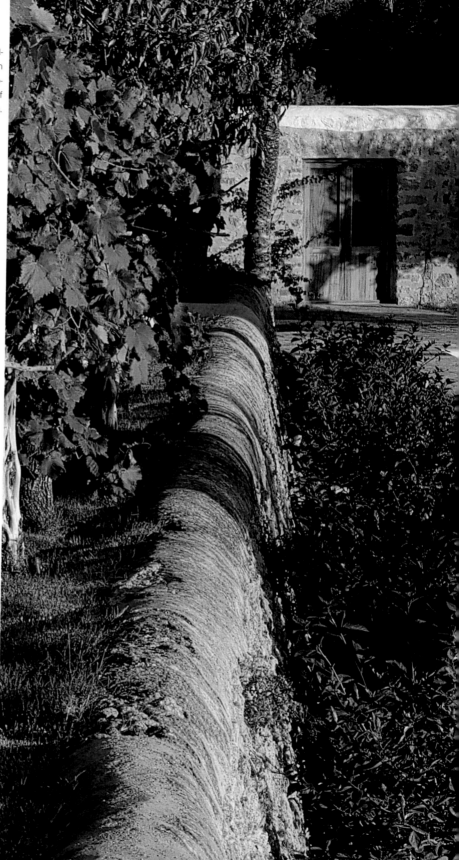

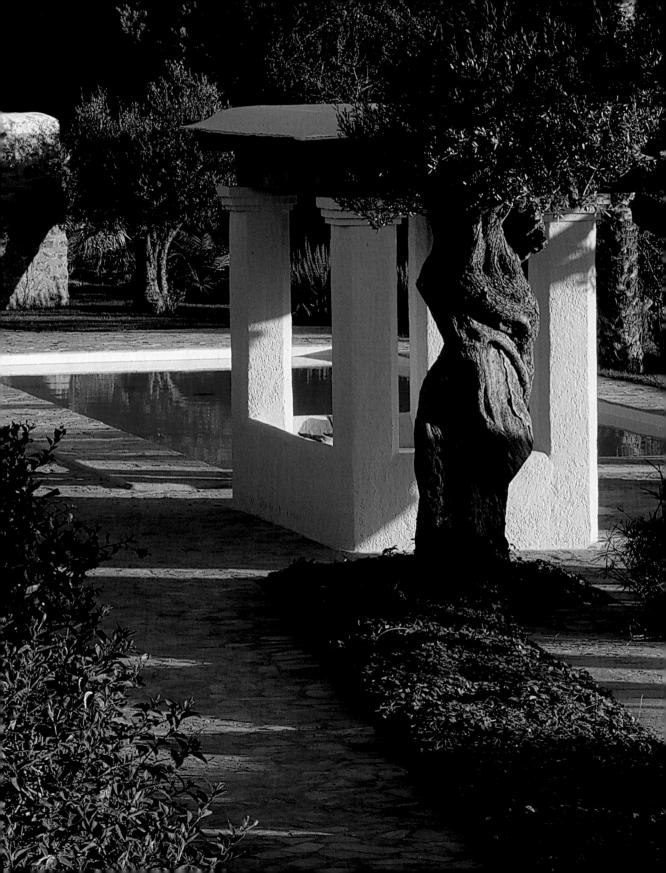

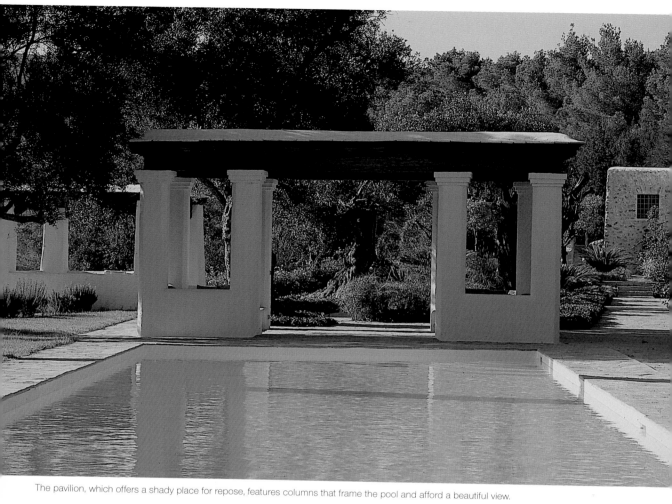

The pavilion, which offers a shady place for repose, features columns that frame the pool and afford a beautiful view.

A cloister's orchards and gardens inspired the constant presence of water and the serene appearance of the paths.

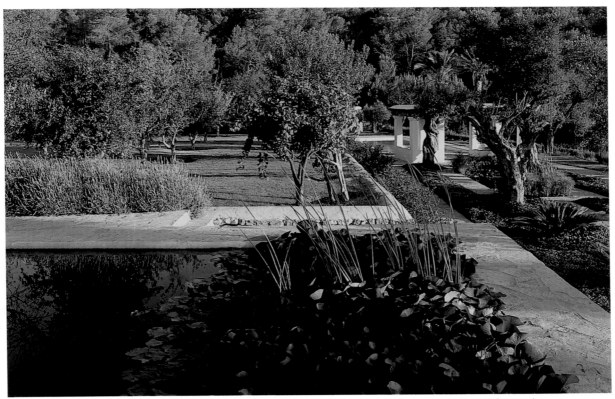

Two plant species are prominent in this garden setting: papyrus, which grows in the ponds, and cyca, a very slow-growing species.

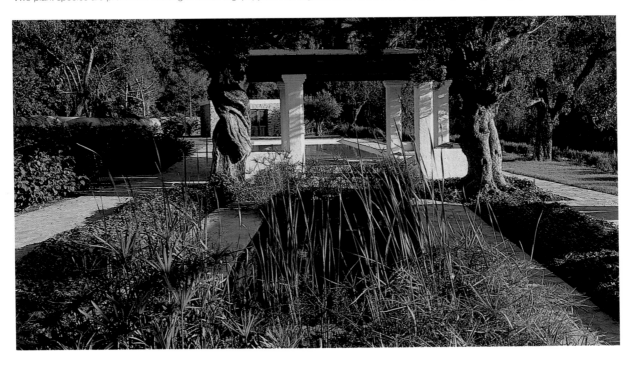

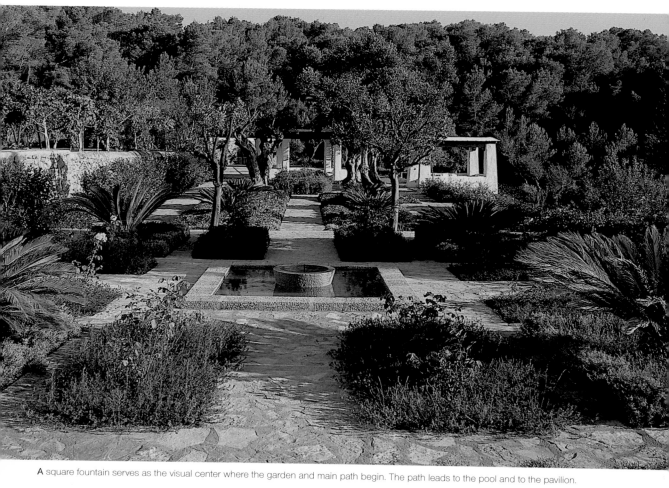

A square fountain serves as the visual center where the garden and main path begin. The path leads to the pool and to the pavilion.

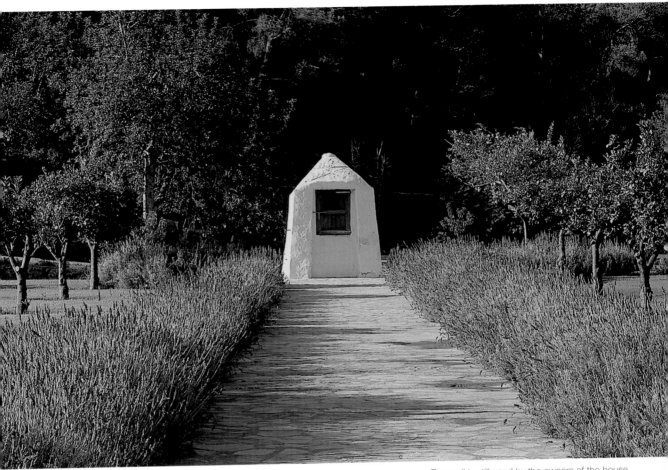

The well is still used by the owners of the house.

M elting into the immense horizon on this island is not just a privilege but a singular tribute to its natural beauty. Through the use of carefully placed gradients, a linear geometry that creates spectacular perspectives, and a palette based on just one color, blue, a magnificent composition has been achieved that extends visually to the depths of the sea and sky.

One of the keys to the grouping is the exterior profile of the swimming pool, which seems to be on a level with the sea. To enhance this effect, the interior of the pool has been coated white, increasing the contrast of tones while creating a white geometric border, like a visual interlude between the intense blue of the sea and the crystalline hues of the pool water.

The simple lines of the two porches, combined with unusual materials such as cement—which crowns the pool and covers its entire perimeter— and iron—which acts as the principal support of the exterior structure—are the key elements to the pool's integration with the surroundings. The use of these two construction materials makes it possible to play with new textures and add character to the grouping while they concede the starring role to the majesty of the landscape.

The decoration has followed the same principle: intelligent design and innovative materials for outdoor furniture with a distinctive style.

Ibiza, Spain

The Magic of a Setting

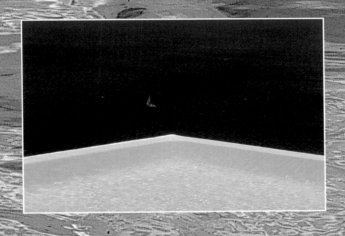

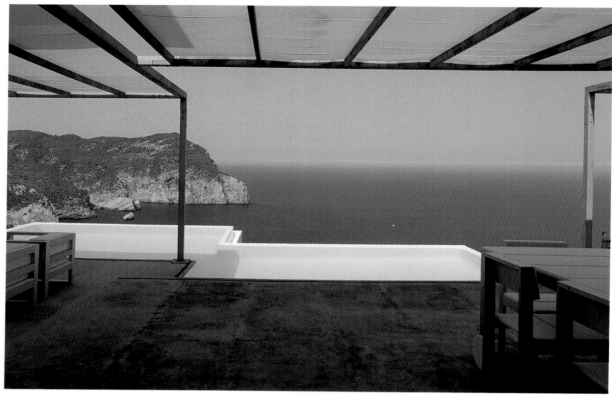

The pool features two levels of water in the shape of a *Z*, whose exterior perimeter stretches out spectacularly over the bay.
Seen from the porch due to a subtle gradient, the turquoise water seems to blend with the immensity of the Mediterranean Sea.

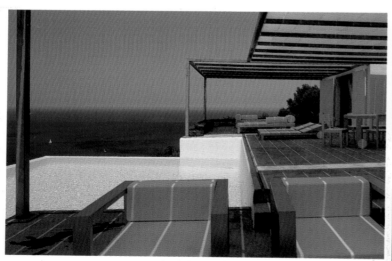

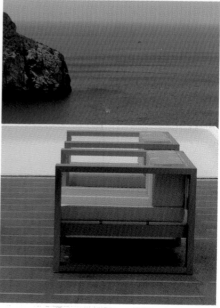

Innovative materials and furnishings with
a contemporary style were chosen for
the exterior decoration.

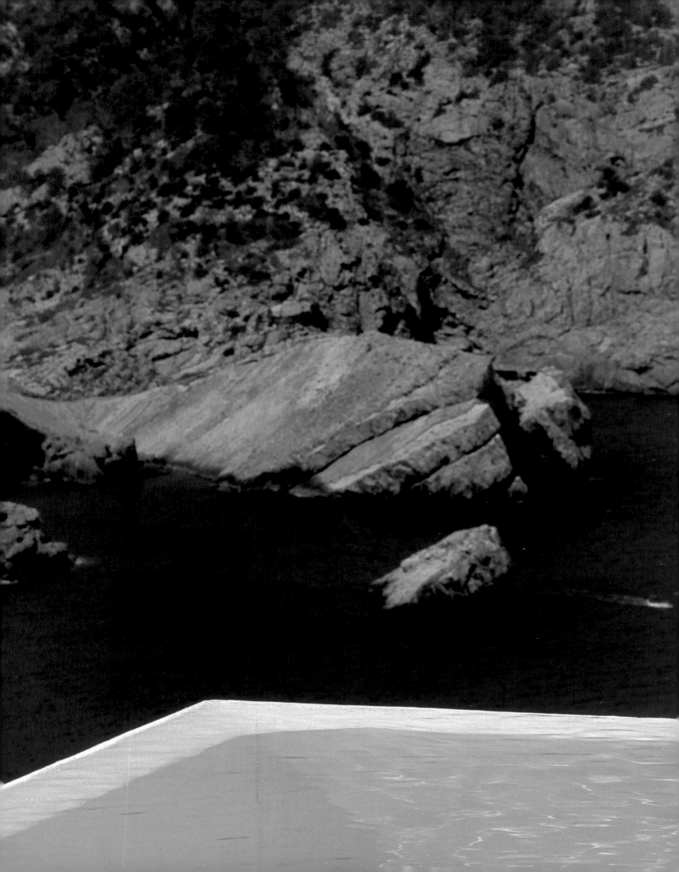

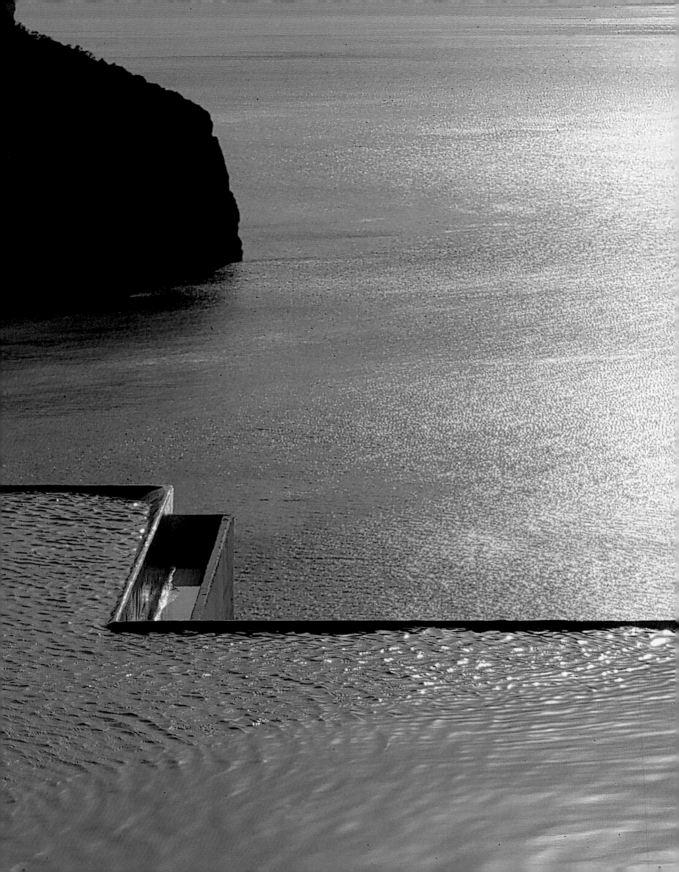

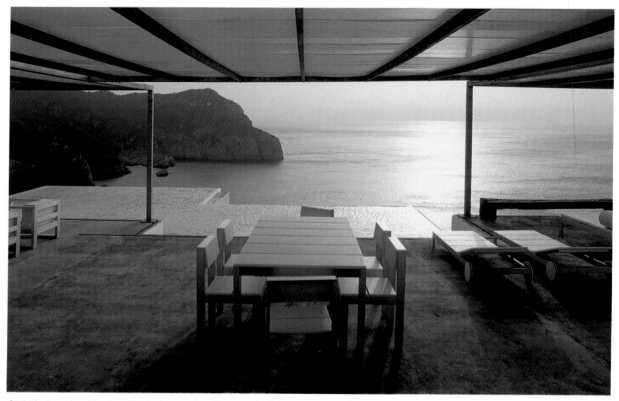

At dusk, the colors blend and the textures soften. The grouping takes on an aura of serenity in perfect harmony with the setting but always conceding the feature role to the beauty of the landscape.

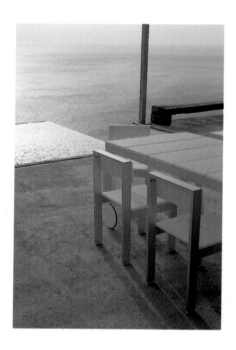

Changing with the light, the color of the pool water seems to merge with the sea. The different textures of the water, in constant motion, create moments of incredible beauty, as if it were a spectacular kaleidoscope.

One color, white jade, and one material, a clay-like quarry stone, are the two key elements that serve as a thread between the main building and the pool to produce a homogeneous architectural volume. Starting from one of the side walls that shelter the house's winter porch, the pool becomes the logical extension of the house.

To accentuate the integration of both spaces, the pool was structured on two levels that merge into one: the level that starts at the winter porch, where three large windows shaped like sliding doors open up, and another that starts at the summer porch, where the stairs to the pool are located. Thus, the water does not just surround the interior and exterior recreation areas, but is also a calm, restrained, modern element with a highly refined style.

The ubiquitous white stone surrounds the property like a protective cloak, embellishing the house and adding an element of surprise with its unique clay-like texture and smooth luminosity, which highlight the linearity of the grouping and add a certain formal dynamism. In keeping with this approach, the summer porch was paved with the same material, uniting the pool with this exterior area. A thin netting, manipulated by a sophisticated mechanism, serves as a minimalist canopy in an area intended basically for sunbathing during the day and as a summer porch at night.

As for the garden, its elegant sward of grass brings out the luminosity of the stone. At the main entrance to the house, a pine tree more than fifty years old welcomes visitors and is the only vertical element in a garden that prefers to spotlight the architectural work.

Miami, Florida, USA

Minimalist Character

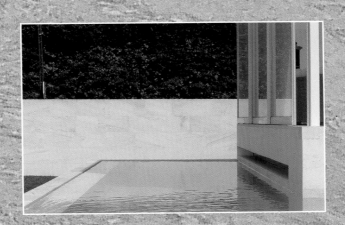

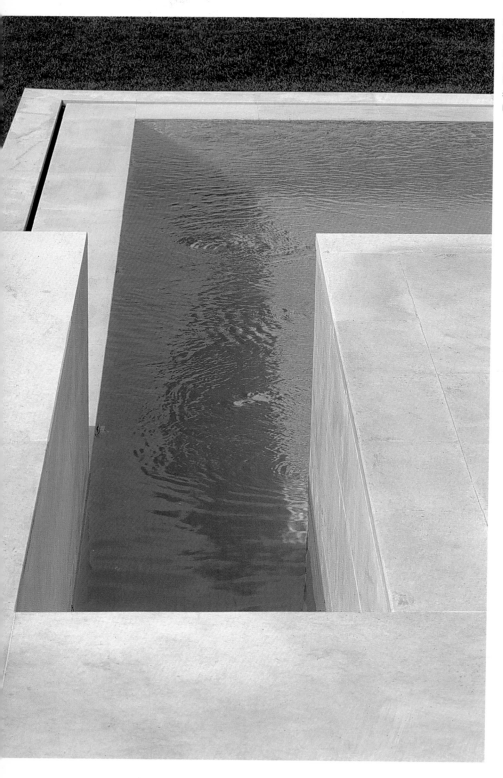

Opposite the luminous summer porch is the entrance to the pool, a narrow stairway between two wide, low walls that function as a solid banister. The pool was built of the same clay-like material as the house.

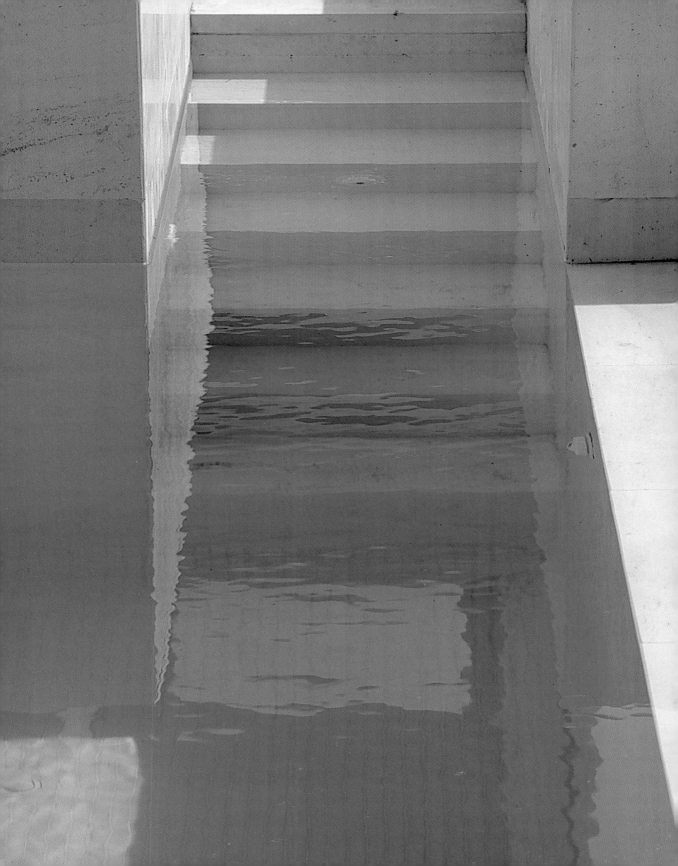

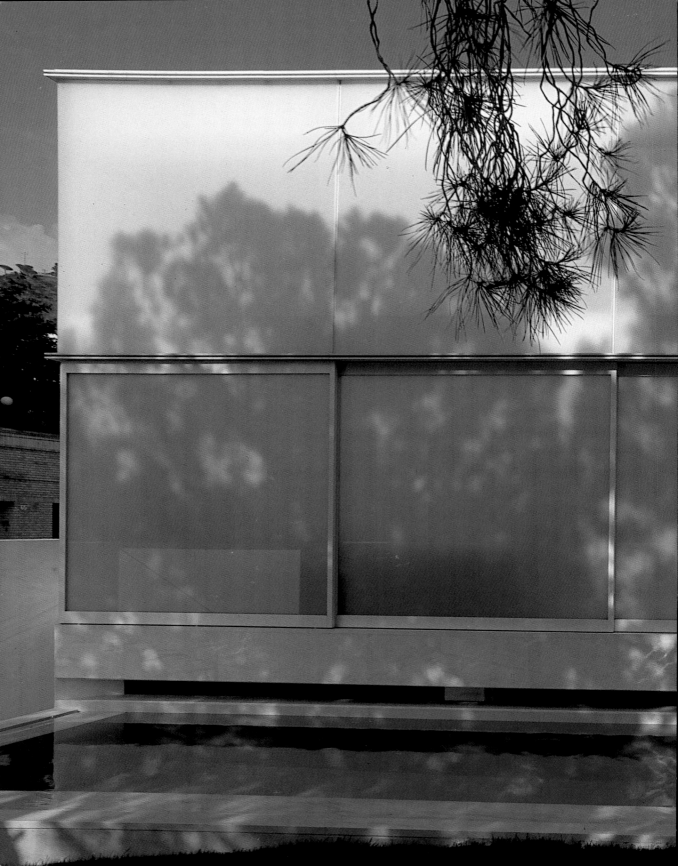

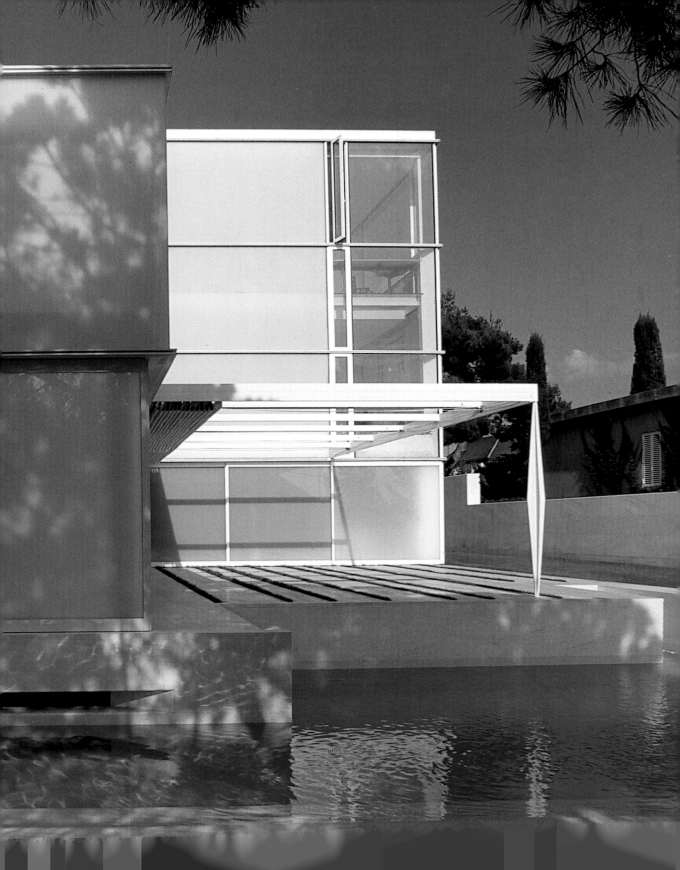

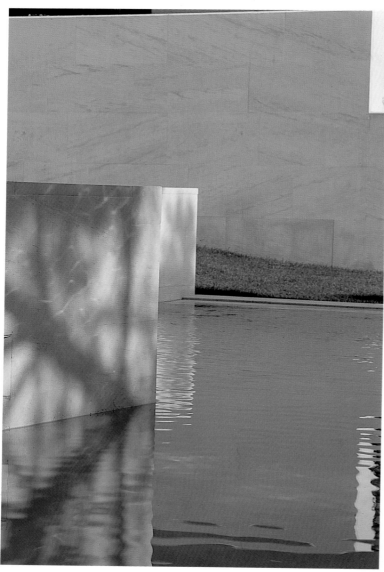

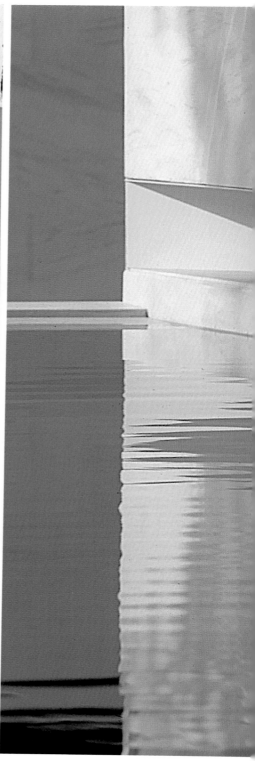

The horizontal opening provides light to the underground garage. At the back, the water glides over the low wall in a flat cascade.

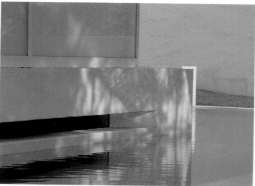

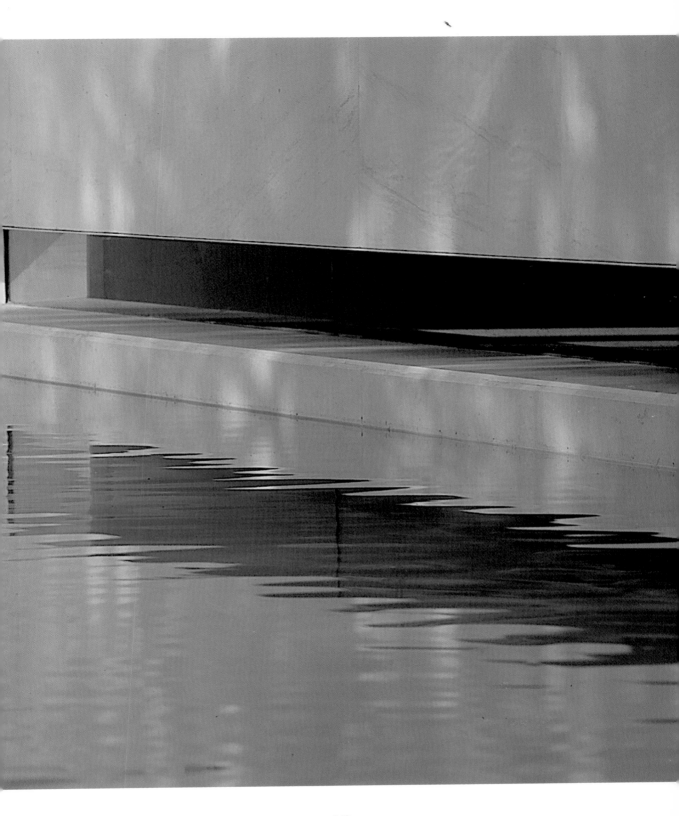

This rectangular pool sits between two long, dry stone dividing walls and is surrounded by a soft tapestry of grass. The principal goal of the design was to overcome the problems presented by the site, a narrow band surrounded by walls of varying heights. Therefore, its excessive linearity had to be compensated for, and smaller areas had to be created on the two shorter sides, where the presence of small and medium-high walls physically and visually cut any expansion.

To break the rigidity of the straight lines and to add volume, the principal wall was used as support for dense vegetation that could spread out like a natural cascade. This greenery, comprised mainly of a spectacular bougainvillea and various common plant species, softens the harshness of the dry stone and isolates the area, ensuring a peaceful, intimate setting.

A limestone rim puts the finishing touch on this sheet of calm water and houses the ingenious channels that return water to the pool to prevent the grass from flooding.

An informal porch was created in front of a rear wall. A unique ochre canopy makes this spot a pleasant niche, perfectly integrated into the grouping. At the opposite end, three steps break up the dividing wall while joining the two side walls. This solution, based on one material, stone, made it possible to construct a formally balanced area for sunbathing. Several stylized chaise lounges of tropical wood complete the setting and add a note of color.

Santorini, Greece

Rural
Symmetry

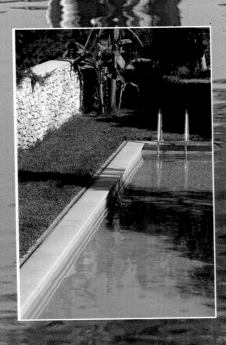

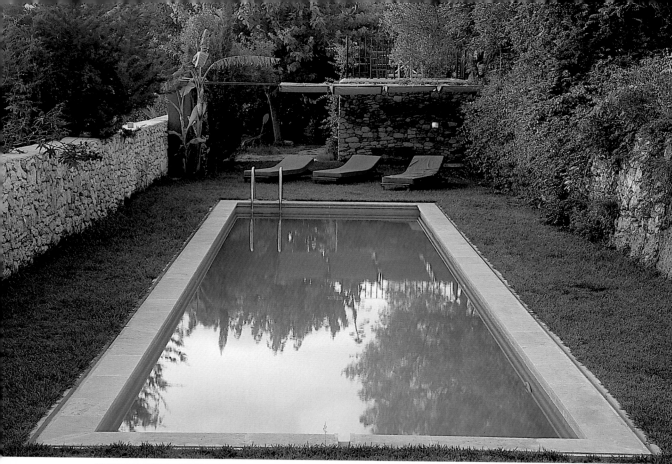

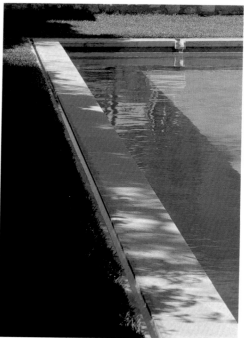

The ochre canopy offers a segue from the open space to the niche containing the pool. This pleasant corner, which serves as an informal porch, is covered with the same soft grass that covers the entire area.

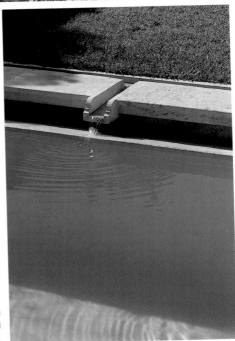

The pool is located on a narrow strip surrounded by dividing walls of varying heights. The dense vegetation that spreads out over the dry stone like a natural cascade adds volume and breaks up the excessive formal linearity.

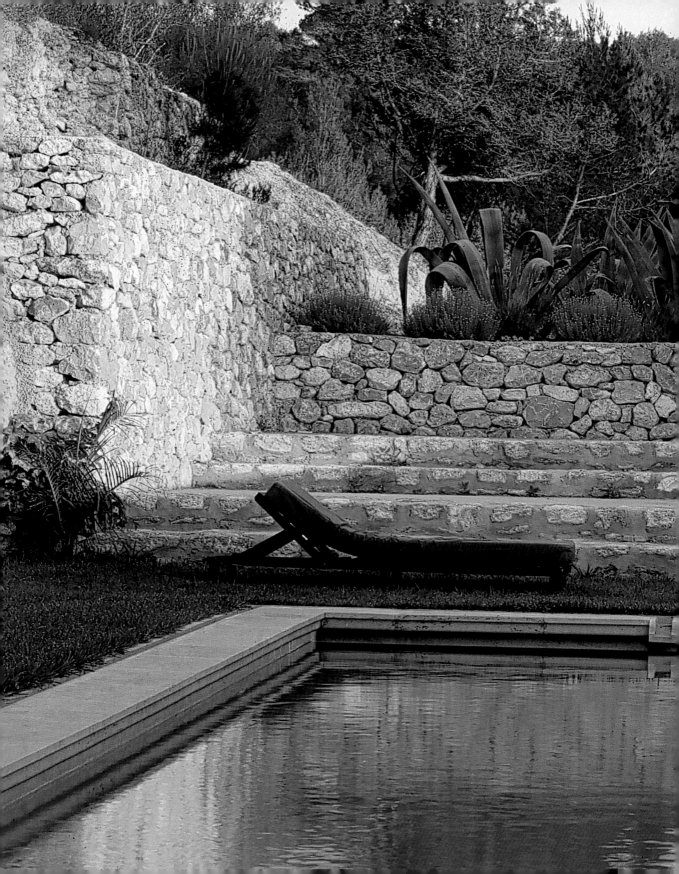

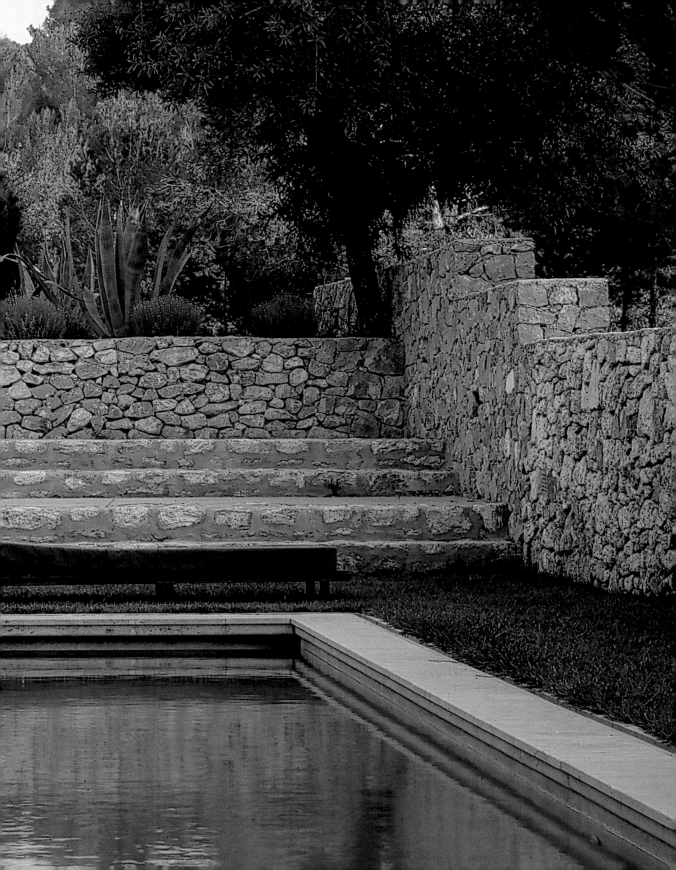

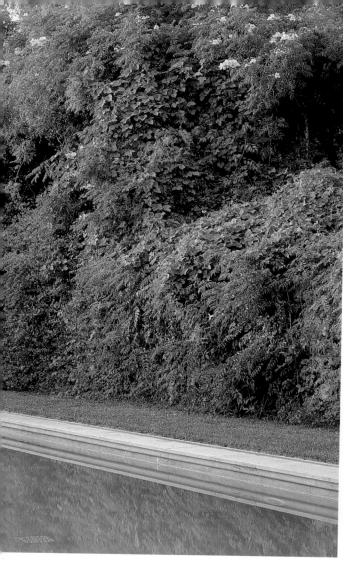

Dense vegetation diminishes the harshness and linearity of the multi-level stone wall. The pool area is enclosed in a veritable jungle of greenery, giving a sense of warm intimacy.

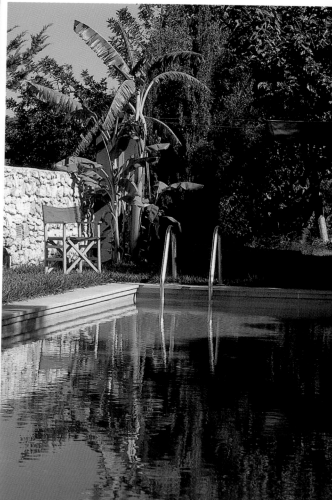

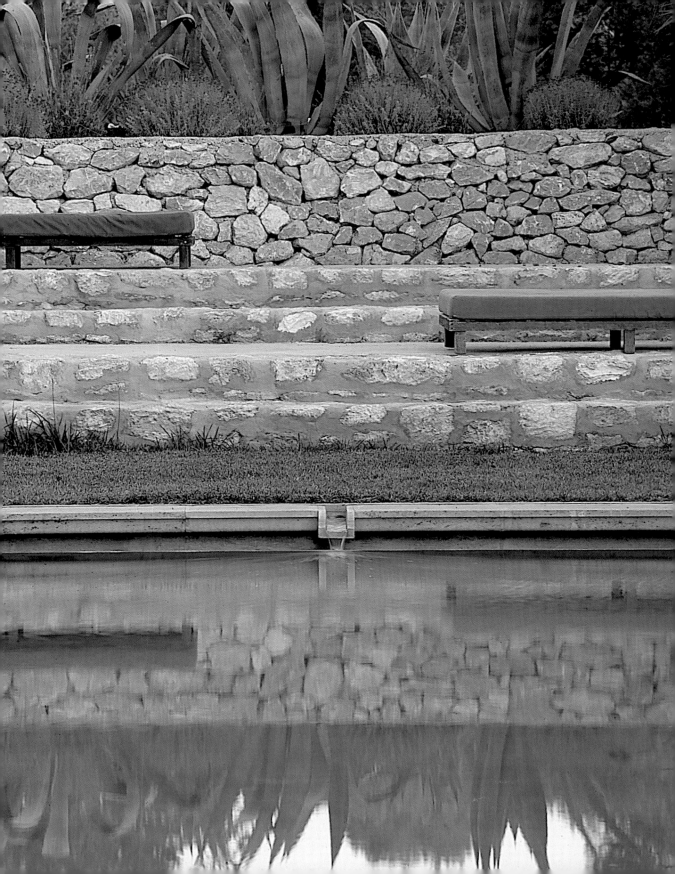

The pool rests peacefully in this orderly garden, its balanced volume contrasting with the carefully laid out setting. This L-shaped pool melts seamlessly into the whole. Its white, geometric outline breaks the soft grass around it and makes it seem to expand beyond the continuous, fluid space.

At the smallest, narrowest part, a stone wall with a spout provides a constant flow of water, encouraging circulation with the peaceful murmur of a fountain. This utilitarian sculpture is the center of attention. It visually isolates a section of the pool while providing an original solution to the problem of formally balancing the long structure. Visually enhancing the studied landscaping, it also softens the grouping's linearity.

The green shades of the surrounding plant life and the white finish of the pool's edge provide visual order in the natural setting, closing the composition and affording protection from curious eyes. As a result, the space is open but intimate and inviting.

The pool and garden are naturally integrated in a single plane. The shapes lend themselves to a restrained, peaceful setting in which the elements interrelate smoothly and continuously.

Girona, Spain

Carpet of Water

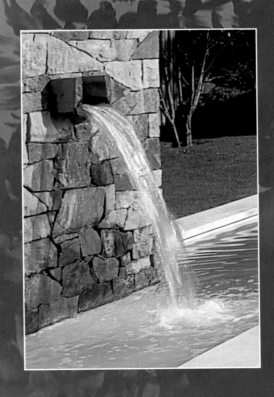

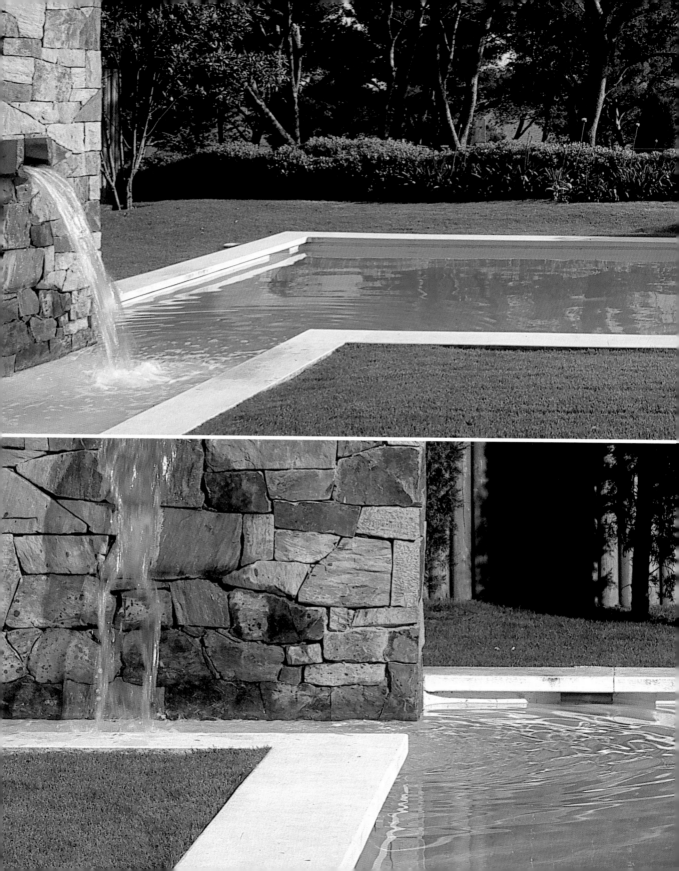

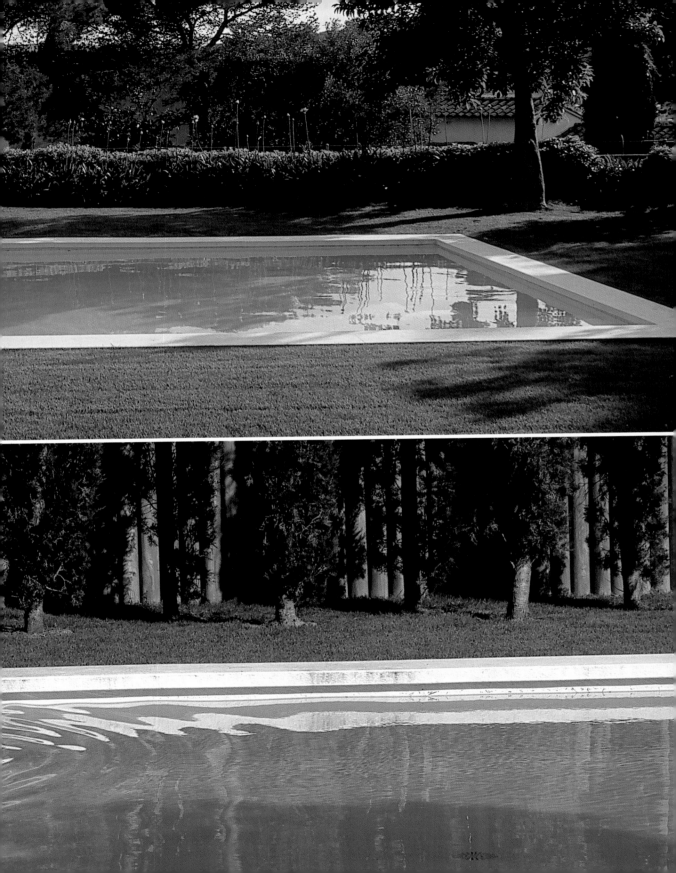

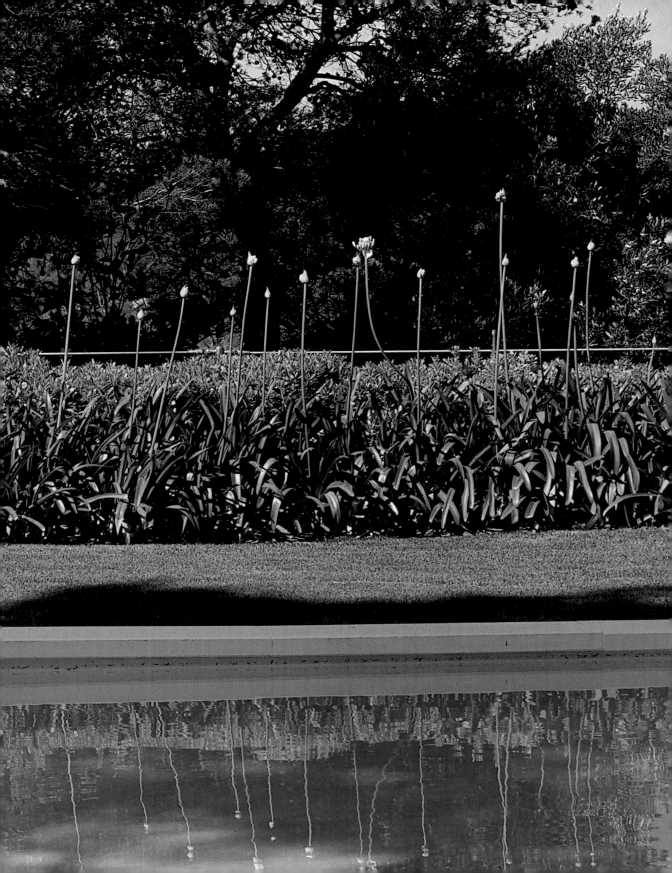

Like a teardrop from the sky, this pool, with its evocative, recognizable shape, surrounded by rectangular sandstone tiles, inspires awe in all who see it. This is a community pool serving a group of attached houses in Barcelona. It occupies a small, irregular space between the rear of the houses and the dense garden. The pool and the landscaped area are separated by a low wall of wooden slats sitting atop a stone base which continues beyond the wall to reach the stairs leading to the pool. Topping it all off is a manicured hedge, part of the garden itself.

Severe in its details, the pool is minimalist in every sense of the word. That austerity of form and material becomes its best quality, since a variety of resources and materials are glaring in their absence.

The interior of this pool, noteworthy for its simple, clean lines, is entirely covered with navy blue mosaic tiles. The harshness of the dark, intense blue is softened by the light color of the paving surrounding the pool, which is carried over into the lower part of the house's walls. That strong dark/light contrast is even more striking against the green background of the cypresses and other vegetation in the garden.

The four steps leading into the water, submerged and completely hidden, were placed in the narrowest, most rectilinear part of the pool. They invite the visitor to enter silently and double as an improvised bench when the pool is not too crowded.

The intense colors, the simple steps that beckon the visitor to slip into the water, and the unique enclosure become the dominant features of this relaxing space.

Barcelona, Spain

Dressed in
Blue

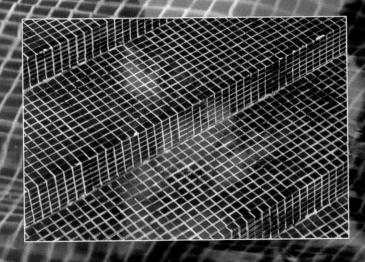

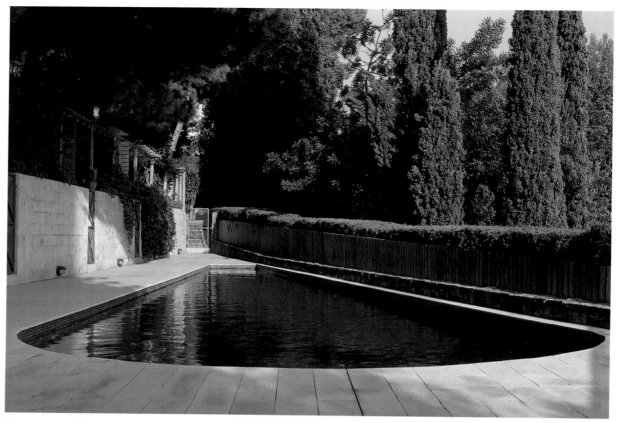

The pool, proportioned, restrained, and striking, is evocatively shaped, having been adapted to the special features of the available space.

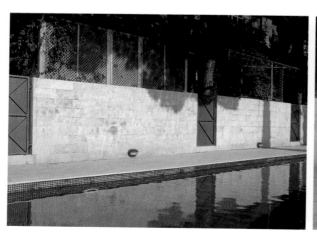

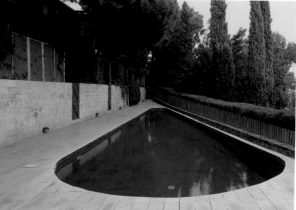

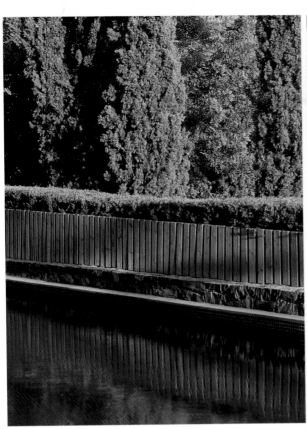
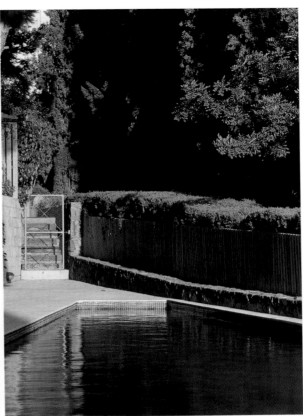
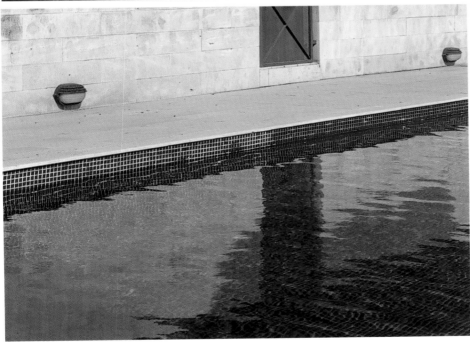

This ancient reservoir, restored and converted into a swimming pool perfectly integrated with the original structure of the house, is sheltered by a 200-year-old wall. The pool's charm comes from the bewitching turquoise color of its water and the luminosity of an antique ochre wall that functions as the project's starting point.

To blend the pool's profile into the setting, the designer chose a sandstone trim whose sand color complements the rest of the materials. At one end, a small retaining wall, also covered with stones, becomes an informal diving board or sunbathing area. Behind it, lush vegetation flourishes, hiding a stone guest house from view.

The ends of the pool are characterized by very diverse landscaping: at one end, the color and splendor of freely growing vegetation; at the other, the precision and simplicity of a monastic cloister. The worlds with two landscape treatments are joined by a path with rounded edges, which runs rectilinear and parallel to the pool, sharply interrupting the green grass of a small orchard of fruit trees.

At the end of the path, a few steps down, a fountain offers strollers the coolness and musicality of its crystalline waters. The details were created to delight and soothe the senses through the power of nature's beauty and simplicity.

Tuscany, Italy

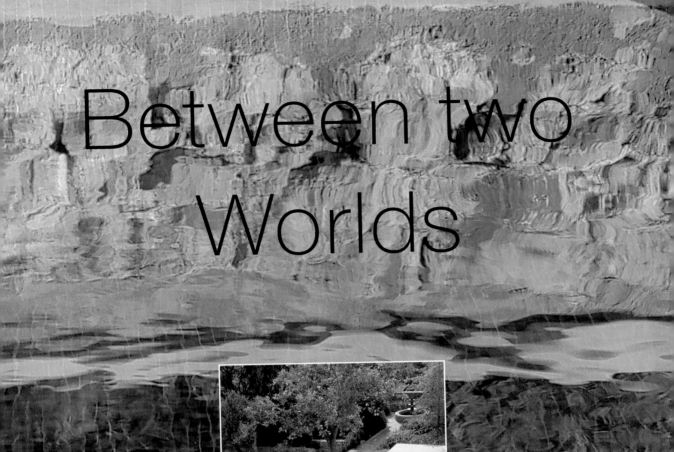

Between two Worlds

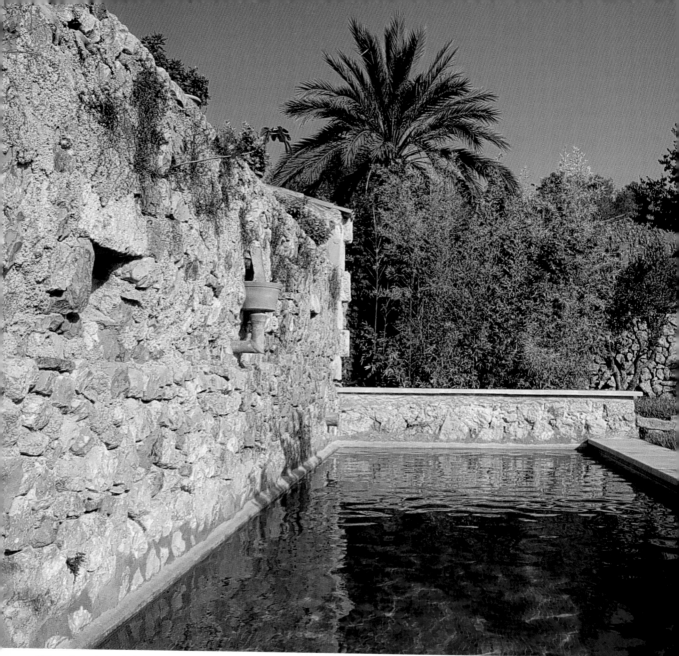

This rectangular pool trimmed with
sand-colored stone is protected by a
200-year-old wall. At one end, a low
retaining wall serves as a diving board.

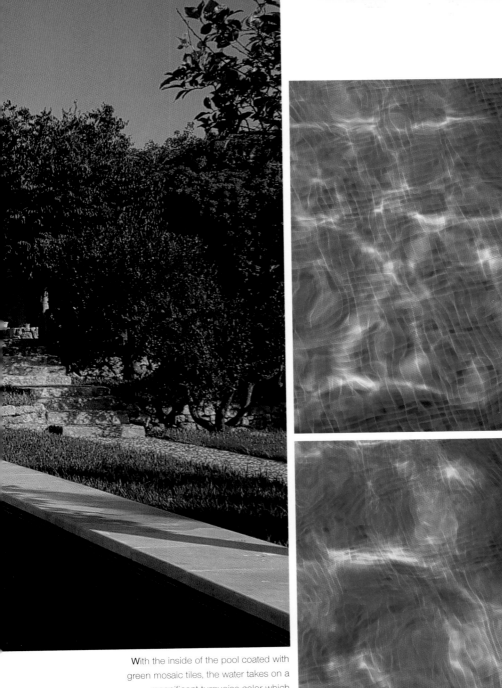

With the inside of the pool coated with green mosaic tiles, the water takes on a magnificent turquoise color which highlights the luminous ochre color of the ancient wall that shelters it.

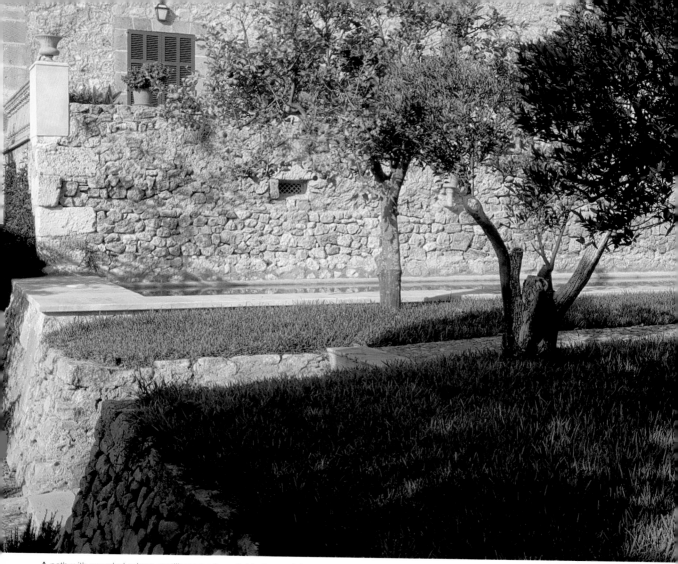

A path with rounded edges, rectilinear and parallel to the pool, interrupts the green grass of a small orchard of fruit trees.

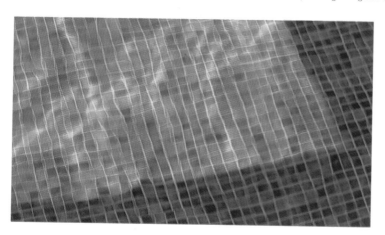

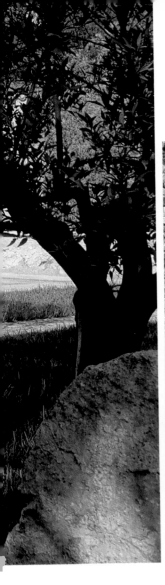
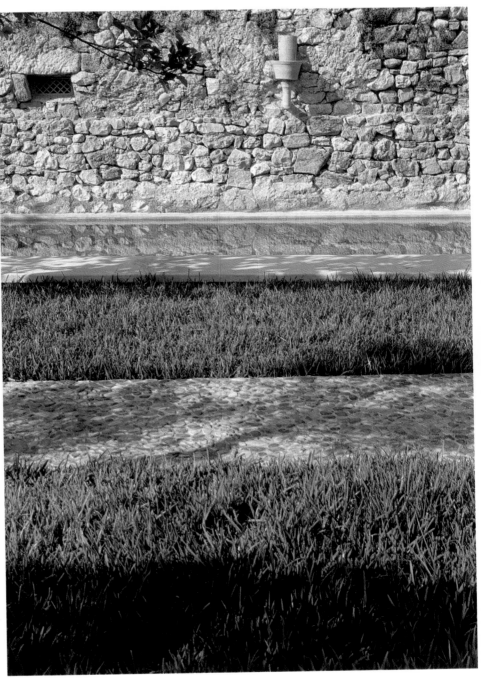

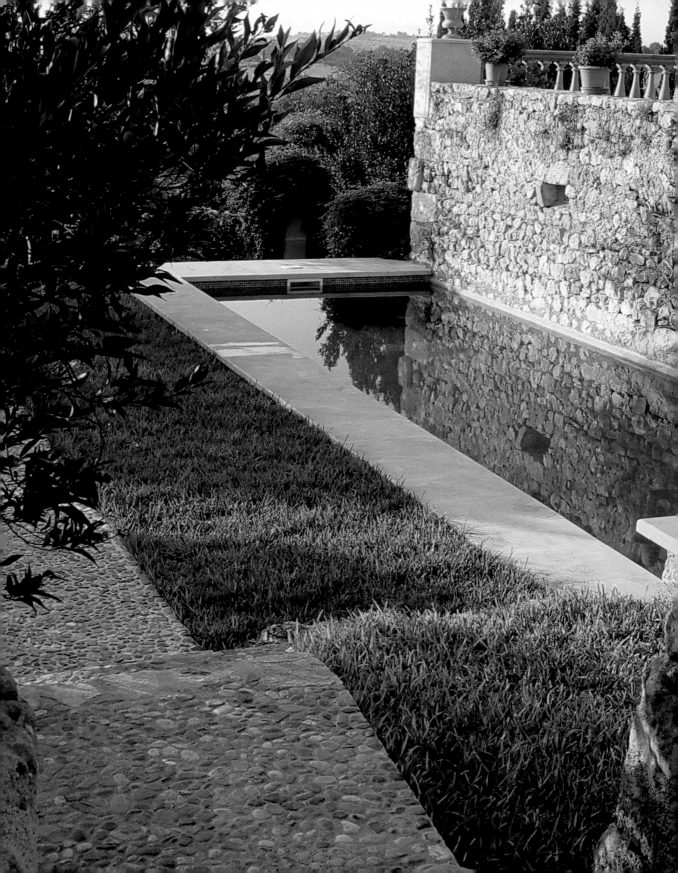

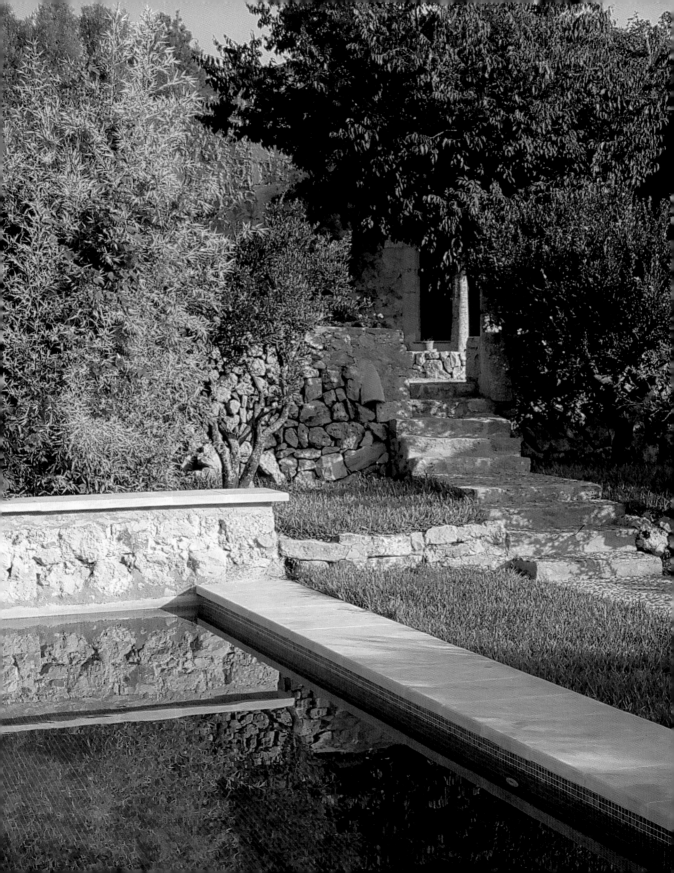

This long, narrow urban pool is surrounded by the striking geometric forms of a cube-shaped building, a long wall of gray concrete, and a thick, green rectangle of grass. The straight lines of the other structures and the austerity and paucity of the materials used accent the pool's linearity and rectangular shape.

Slate covers the entire outside perimeter as well as the sides and bottom of the pool. Access to the water is facilitated by submerged steps that stretch across the entire narrow end. The dark gray of the slate is in stark contrast to the white of the house's facade and the iron slats, also white, that camouflage the doors leading to the pool from the ground floor of the house.

Minimalist lines, restrained and simple, create a balanced, modern composition that makes the best use of the opportunities the land offers and the restrictions it imposes.

The result is an intimate niche, private, quiet, and up-to-date, protected from curious eyes, in which to savor the fresh air and restful setting.

Barcelona, Spain

Urban
Essence

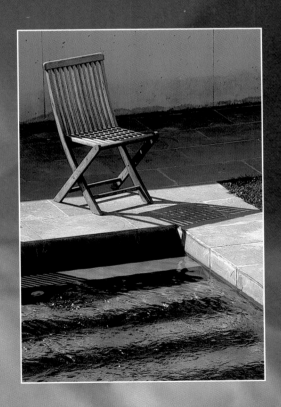

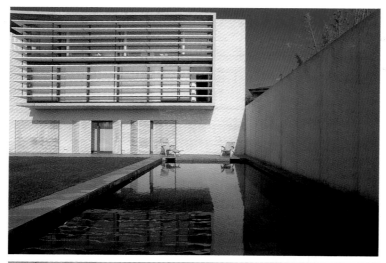

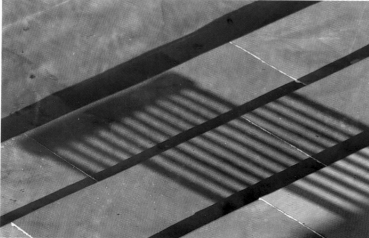

The lines and shape of the building emphasize the pool's straight edges. This urban design, composed entirely of straight lines and right angles, has minimalist features ideal style for a metropolitan setting.

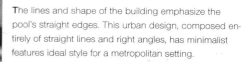

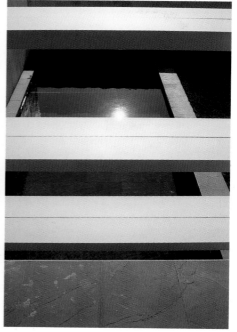

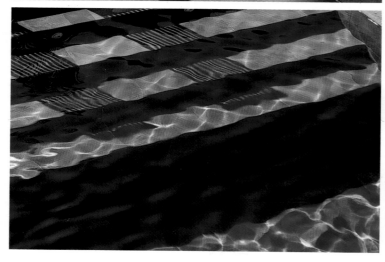

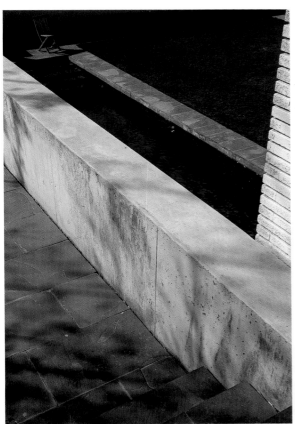

The evocative color of the water, which reflects everything around it, is the result of the use of rectangular sheets of slate. The pool and the grass resemble two nearly identical compositions separated by the subtle walkway, also slate. They complement each other and form part of a cosmopolitan urban landscape.

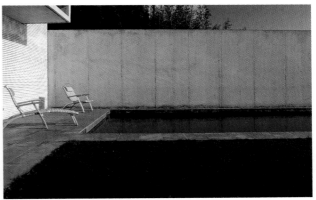

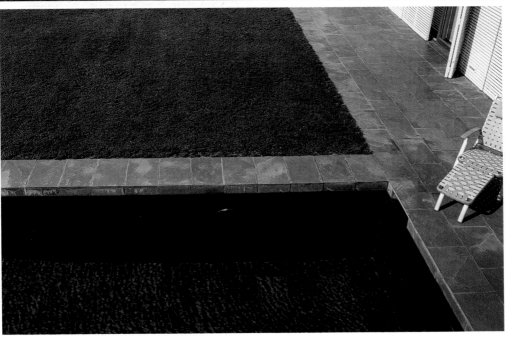

Refined and almost monastic, this swimming pool recaptures the identity of the Roman *thermae*, the ancient public baths known for their importance as social centers. But here the aesthetic of Roman civilization has been replaced by an austere, restrained style that comes to life only with the caress of sunlight.

Built as an independent structure attached to the main dwelling, the pool is sheltered from the wind by three high, intensely white walls. The palm and pine trees surrounding the house peek over the walls. The pool's rectangular shape occupies almost the entire space, leaving just a narrow strip that functions as both ornamental trim and walkway.

The continuity of the white color enhances the formal balance of the composition. The chromatic contrast is accentuated through the use of the color indigo, which the clients requested to coat the pool's interior. Throughout the day, the play of light and shadow imparts volume and geometry to the grouping. At nightfall, the heat accumulated during the daylight hours keeps the water warm.

In addition to providing physical pleasure, this unique pool is also an intimate, private space, ideal for meditation.

Ibiza, Spain

Private
Space

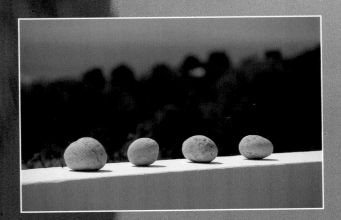

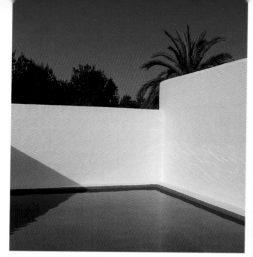

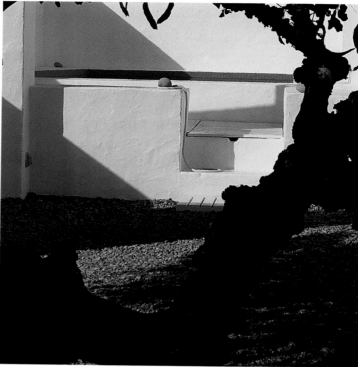

Beyond the twisted trunk of an old carob tree, the different levels of the pool are visible. The key to its formal balance lies in the restrained style and two-color chromaticism.

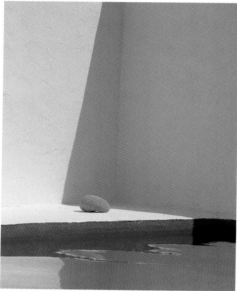

The pool's linearity offers bright, colorful geometric perspectives, such as the one that can be enjoyed from the entrance. A narrow strip of blue color frames the water, giving it visual depth. Access is by two built-in steps. Levels and gradients are balanced by the continuity of the white color.

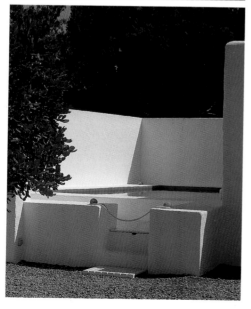

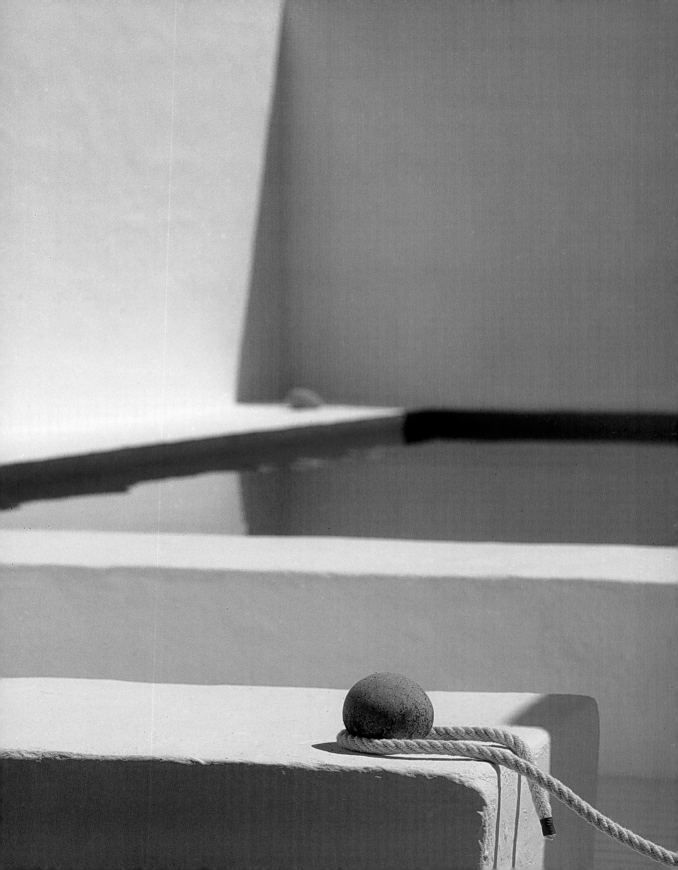

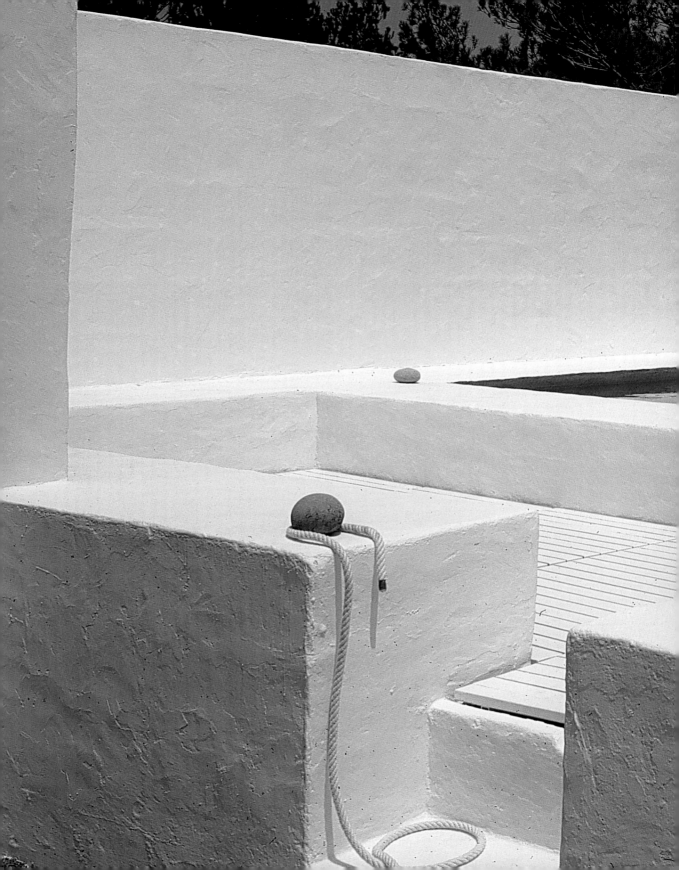

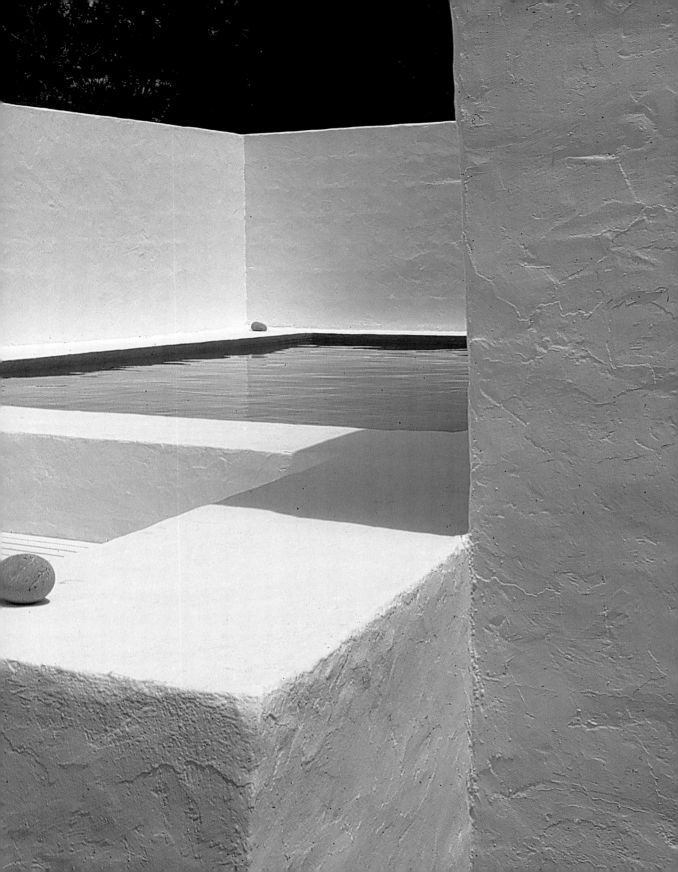

This refreshing urban pool, near downtown Barcelona, invites the visitor to test the waters and forget the suffocating heat, enjoy the autumn breeze, recall the good weather during the coldest months of the year, and long for summer as soon as the first rays of spring sun arrive. Restrained, contemporary, and austere décor defines these exteriors. The long, narrow pool is ensconced in a corner of the understated garden.

It belongs to a house built between party walls, and abuts one of them. On the lower part of this wall, running its entire length, is a large, rectangular white unit that functions as a plant container. This closes off a part of the pool and features a rectangular spout that supplies it with water. Its severe rectangular shape is softened by the springy carpet of grass around it and the deck of tropical wood that comes to the water's edge.

The same tropical wooden deck completely surrounds the pool, which is coated with mosaic tiles in different shades of green. This touch gives the water a charming color that pays homage to the plant life all around it. Facing each other on the shorter ends are stainless steel steps, so simple as to be practically invisible. In the middle of the end bounded by a brick wall is a diving board, also of tropical wood, resting on four stainless steel legs. Lounge chairs and benches with sleek lines and white cushions complete the grouping. Across from the diving board are the shower—a striking structure with white walls—and a large sculpture. The overall effect is that of a pool protected from indiscreet glances, and a tranquil niche removed from the hustle and bustle of the city.

Barcelona, Spain

An Urban Oasis

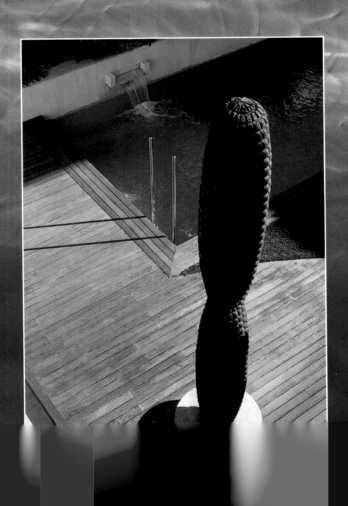

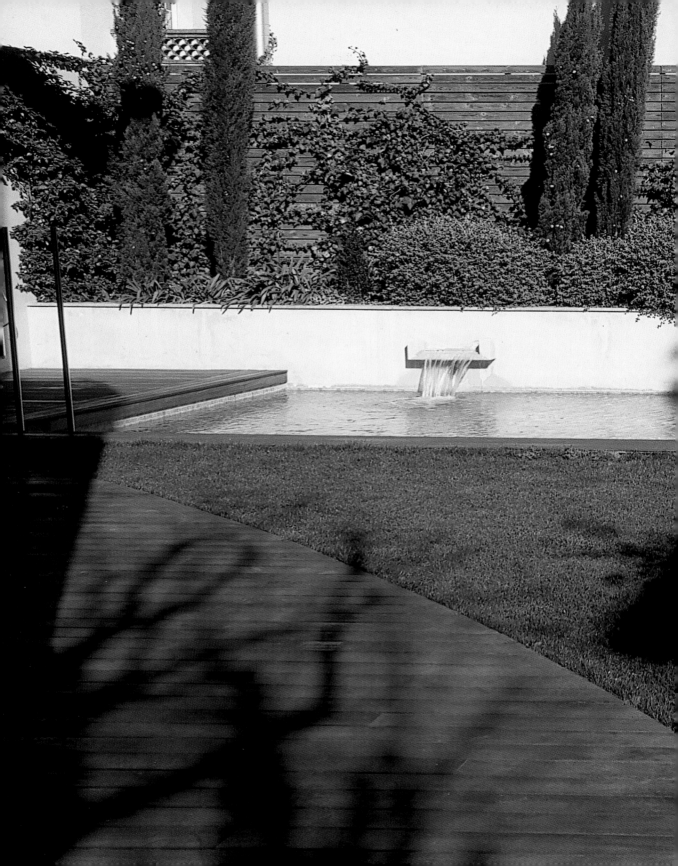

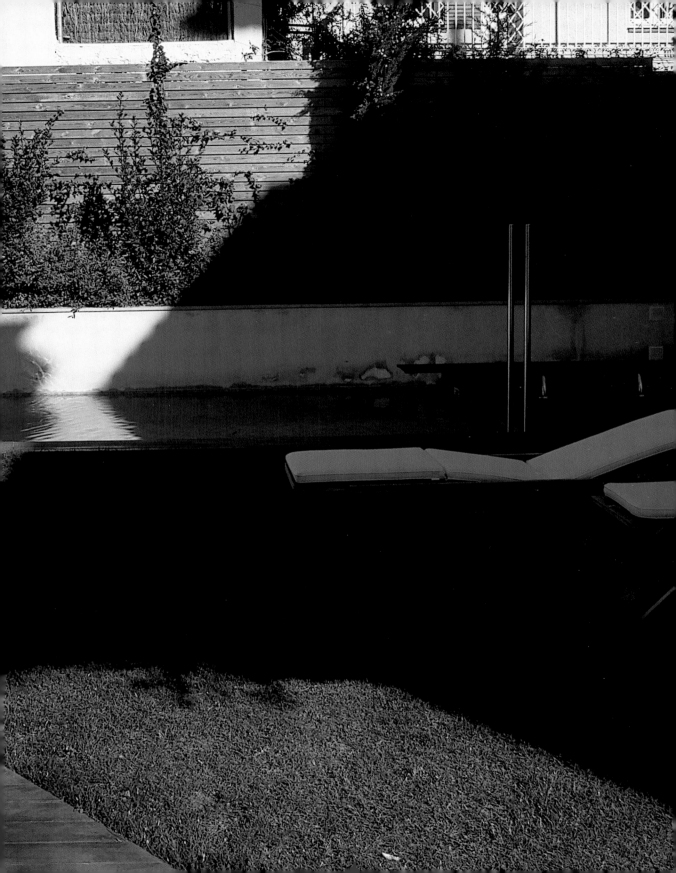

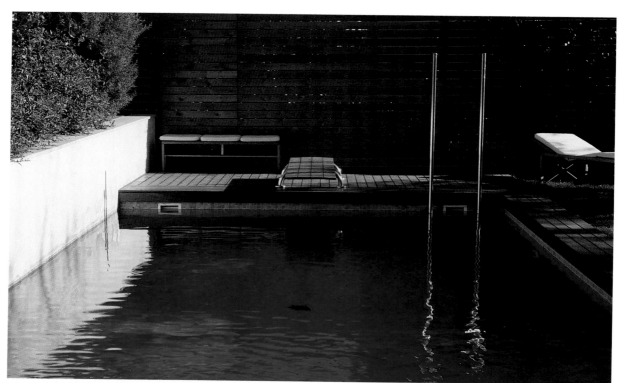

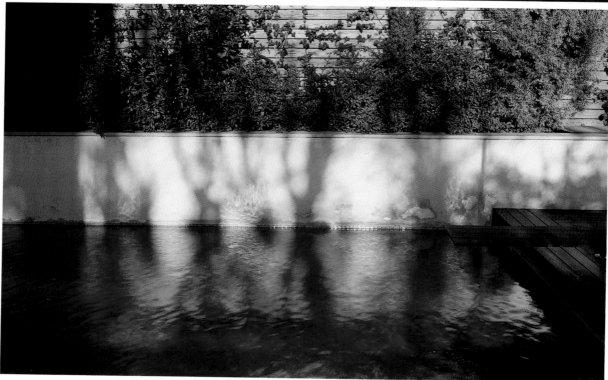

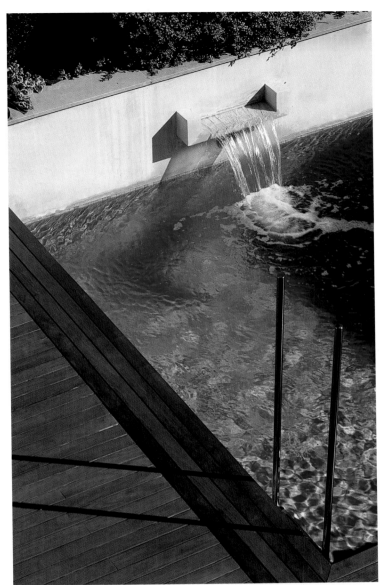

Protected by one of the party walls between which the house was built, this rectangular pool is surrounded by a deck of tropical wood and a long masonry plant container. The wood is visually dynamic, integrates the entire area on a single plane, adds a touch of warmth, and unifies the materials and textures.

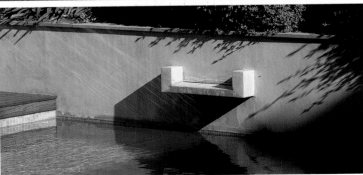

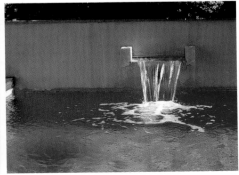

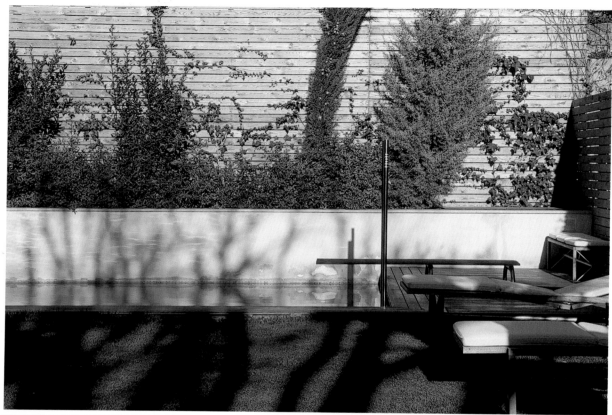

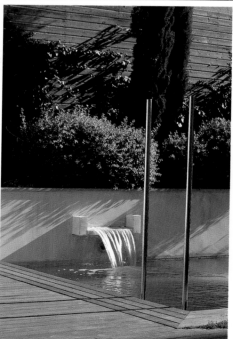

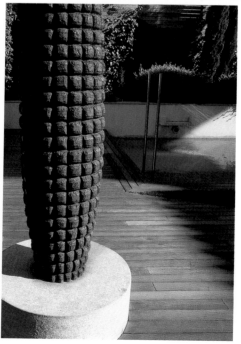

The peaceful ambience offers a retreat from the nonstop movement of city life.

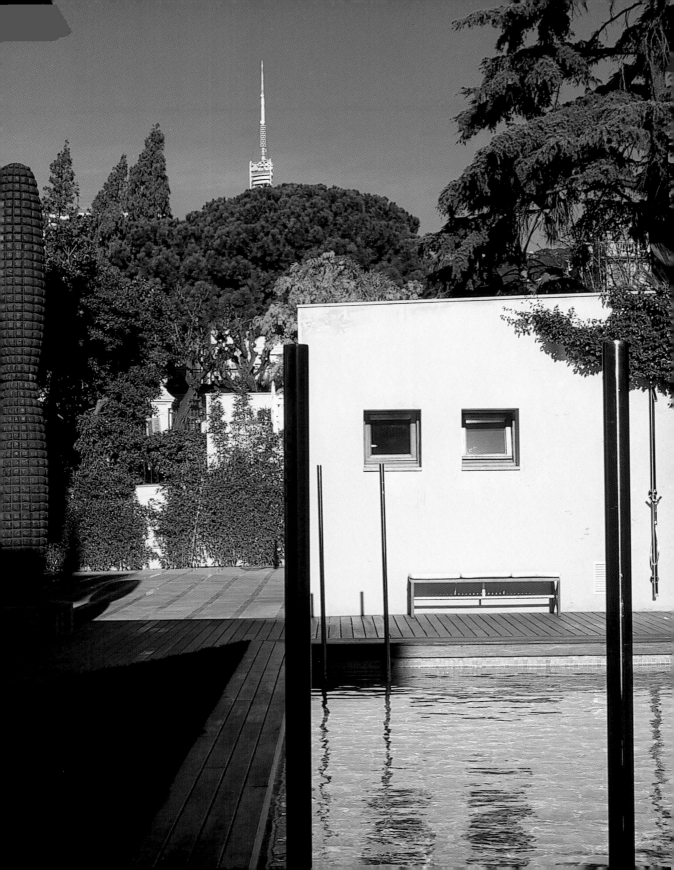

At the height of the Moorish splendor of Cordoba, Spain—during the tenth and eleventh centuries—there were more than three hundred bathhouses. Over time, the Christian kingdoms returned to power, and bathhouses disappeared or fell into disuse.

Just yards from Cordoba's mosque, these new Moorish baths resemble those of antiquity. They were built to restore one of the most widely practiced Muslim customs.

The *hamam* (an Arabic word meaning "bath") was a public building intended as a meeting place for people from all social strata. Nowadays, these baths are bringing back an entire era in order to recover a tradition, becoming a place of rest, a place to refresh body and mind, and a place to meet for all those who seek pleasure and health in the water.

The Medina Califal Moorish baths recreate all the splendor of an era while adapting to modern needs. As a result, it is a place where the visitor can travel back to the past and soak up the magnificence of a time that can never be repeated. These are the largest public baths in Europe, with approximately 11,000 square feet of floor space, half of which is devoted to thermal pools.

In keeping with tradition, the baths are divided into spaces that serve as courtyard and dressing room as well as cold, warm, and hot rooms, inspired by the Roman baths. Great attention was paid to the details, so the architectural solutions and decorative touches echo the geometry of the mosaics, the carving of the arches, the plinths, latticework, capitals, materials, and even the constant, hypnotic murmur of the flowing water, the most typical aromas of the era, and the essence of Moorish culture.

Córdoba, Spain

Memories of the Past

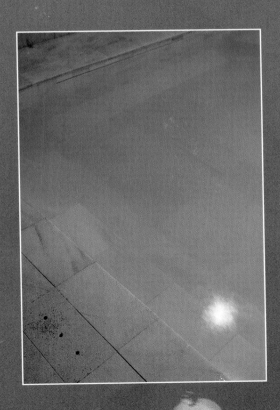

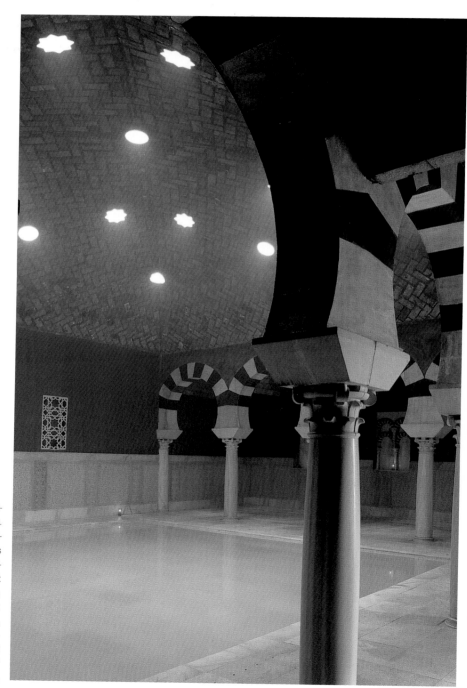

Light and water are essential considerations in Moorish architecture. Light, which is filtered through openings in the vaulted ceilings, molds the space and makes the walls vibrant screens on which plays of light and shadow are projected. Water, the omnipresent, undisputed star, symbolizes life itself. These baths, true to Moorish culture and construction methods, employ marble and stucco to reflect all the splendor of the civilization they honor.

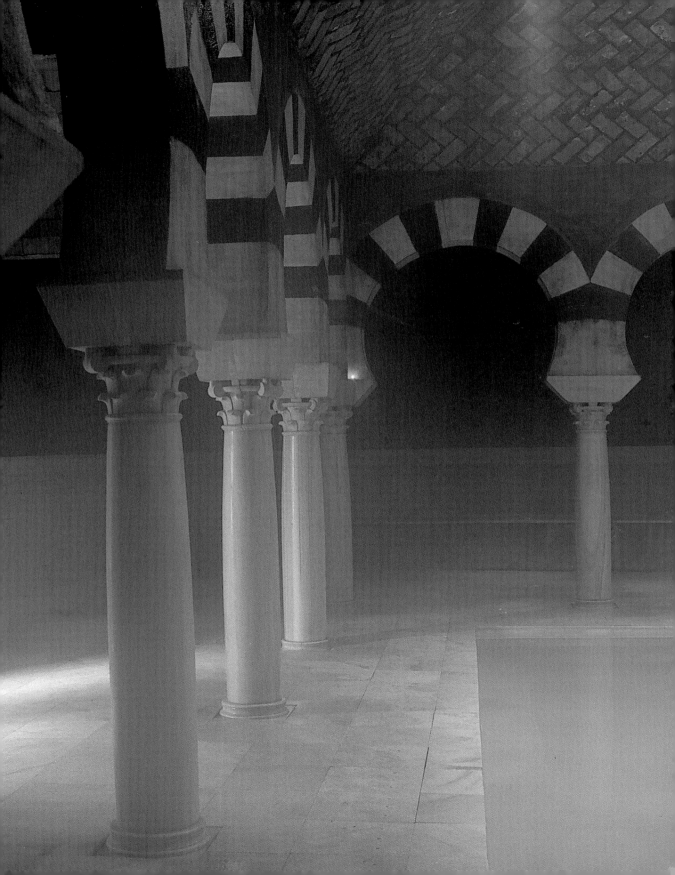

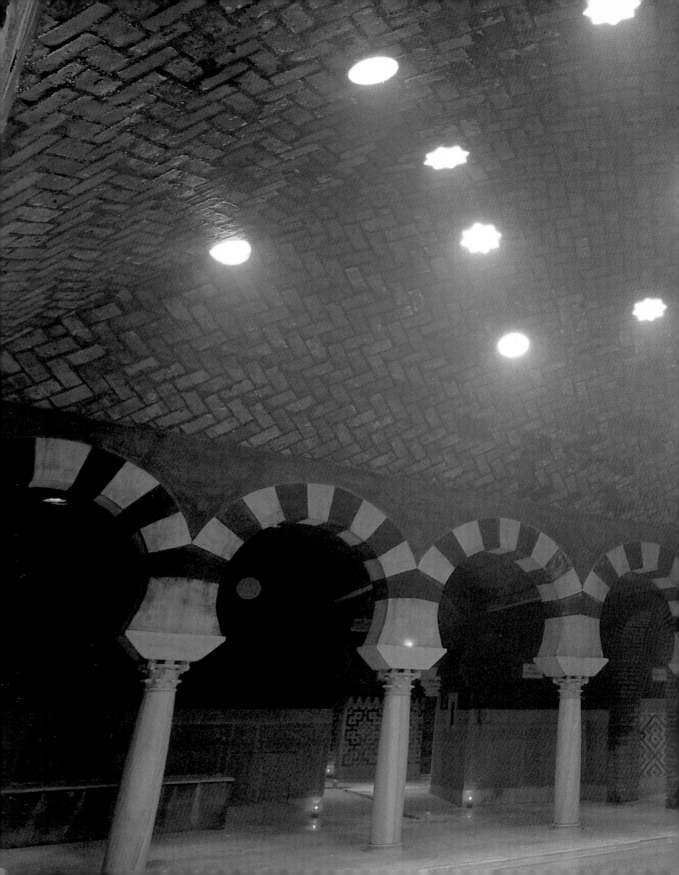

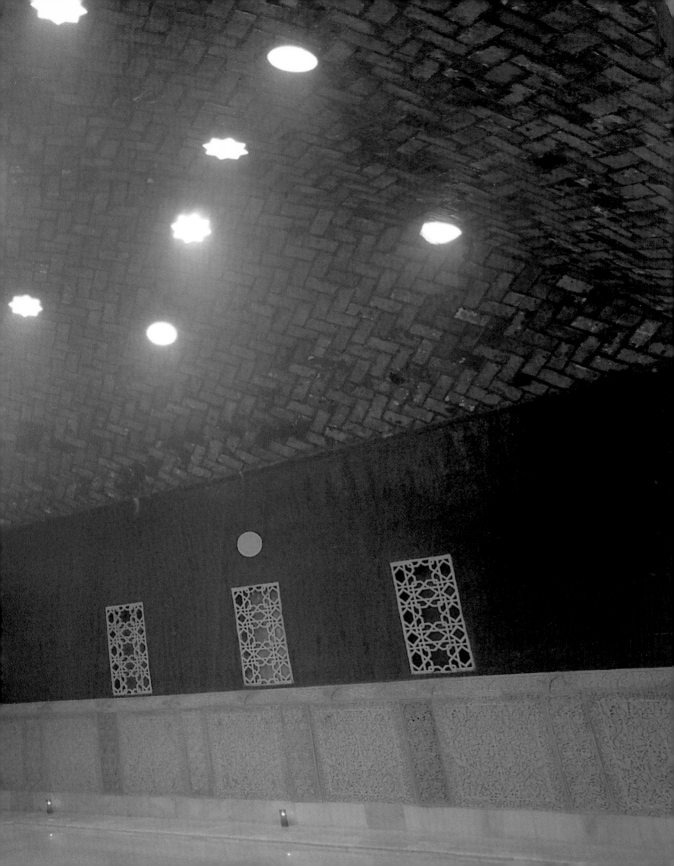

Despite its apparent symmetry, this project on the island of Mallorca is in keeping with the tradition of oriental architecture, based on discontinuity, broken lines, and the lack of a single focal point.

Flanked by majestic palm trees is a swimming pool whose edges are elegantly submerged in the water. To the right and on the same level as the still surface of the water, a small square building with a vaulted roof, fronted by a refined, rectilinear porch, rises up like a burst of color. It is an amazing *hamam*, whose interior, in the shape of an octagonal star, follows the guidelines of Arabic symbolic geometry. Two colors, purplish blue and soft ochre, dominate the room and filter the exterior luminosity, inviting one to remain under its protection.

Opposite, a second structure demands attention: erected with strong posts, a large *jaima*, or traditional Berber tent, stands in the purest Arab style. Also situated on the same level as the water, the tent's imposing presence is accompanied by a new element, the sound of the wind whipping the fabric.

Exotic shapes and uncommon textures are combined in this project, where space and rhythm acquire a multiple dimension based on the most subtle emotions and senses.

Mallorca, Spain

Nomadic
Sensations

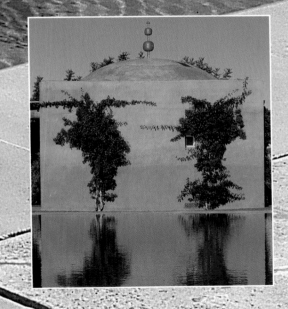

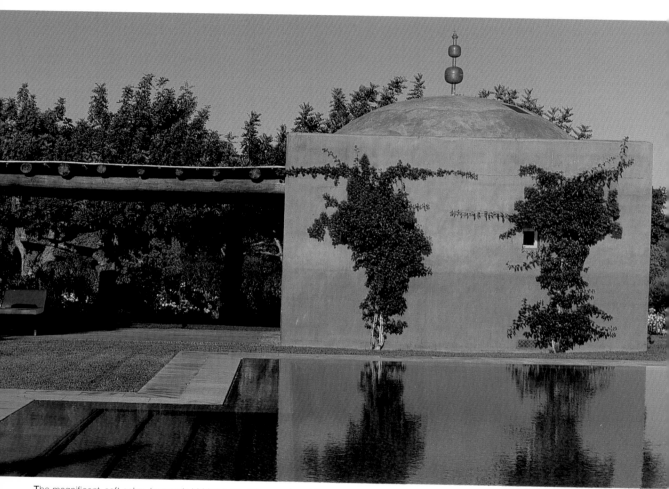

The magnificent, soft ochre *hamam* is hidden behind the porch and façade.

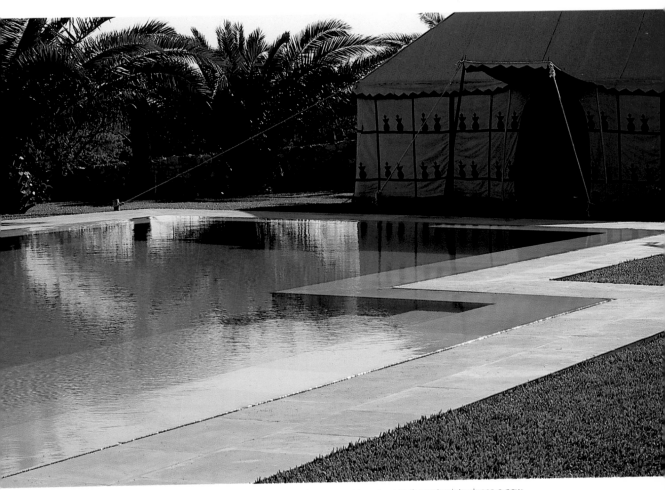

The presence of a *jaima* with harmonic proportions, fixed with solid posts reaching down to the water, introduces a new element: the sound of the wind hitting the fabric.

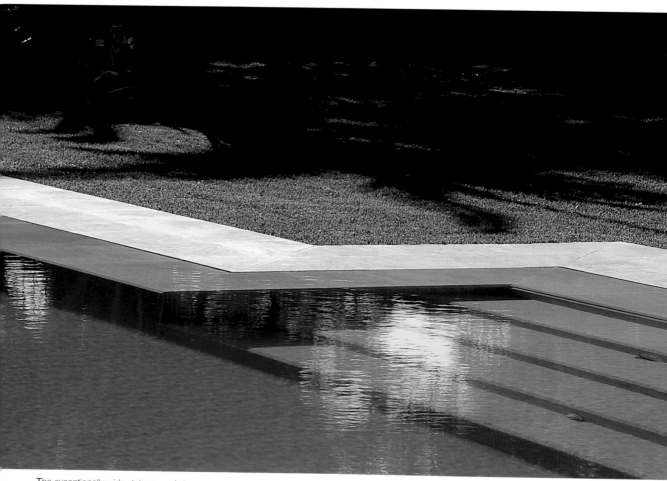

The exceptionally wide stairway and steps, in combination with the slightly sloped, submerged edge, provide a touch of restrained elegance. The color of the outer perimeter was selected to blend with the ochre tones of the *hamam*'s walls.

Despite its square exterior shape, the interior of this amazing *hamam* follows the guidelines of Arab symbolic geometry and is shaped like an octagonal star. Water as a source of life and wealth is the great central character of this oriental-style project.

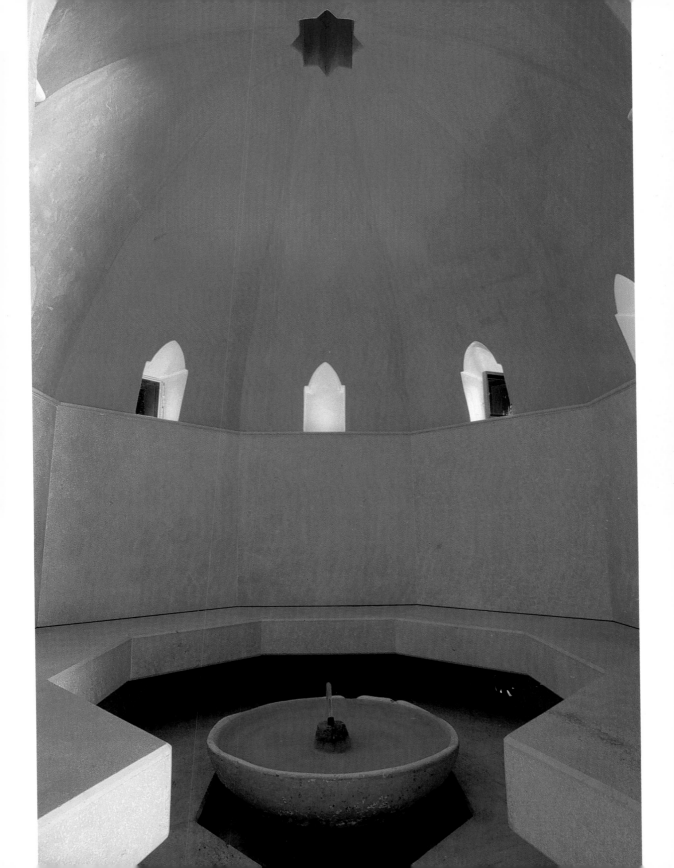

Hidden amid the thousand-year-old stones of a nineteenth-century building in Marrakech, this small pool pays homage to water as the source of life. The building that houses it is an old *ryad*, a grouping surrounding a central courtyard, typical of the region. The pool was added during a renovation that was faithful to the house's original plan and features. Partly covered, it resembles a traditional *hamam*. Its irregular but geometric lines are practically hidden. A small rectangular area, reminiscent of typical Moorish pools, is uncovered. The entire perimeter (inside and bottom) is gray cement, which has the effect of darkening the water.

In one of the interior niches, a little above water level, a lounging area includes a mat with a backrest and head support. In the middle of the interior section, a small animal-shaped faucet ensures that the water—in true ritual fashion—flows constantly. Its soft sound can make it easy to forget everything else.

As in the other rooms, the light creates images of powerful beauty, playing with the decorative colors and the various niches in the walls, which keep part of the pool half hidden. The double play of light—natural from the outside, and artificial from within—produces a strong calming effect.

This space combines vestiges of the Moorish past with more western, modern forms. Both styles merge seamlessly, as if they had always existed side-by-side. All the ornamental elements, subtly combining eastern and western styles, come from a local antiques dealer.

Marrakech, Morocco

Peaceful
Pool

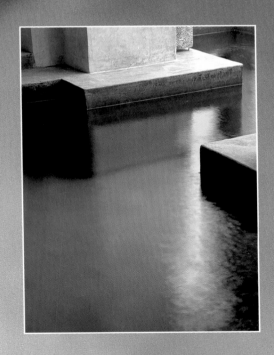

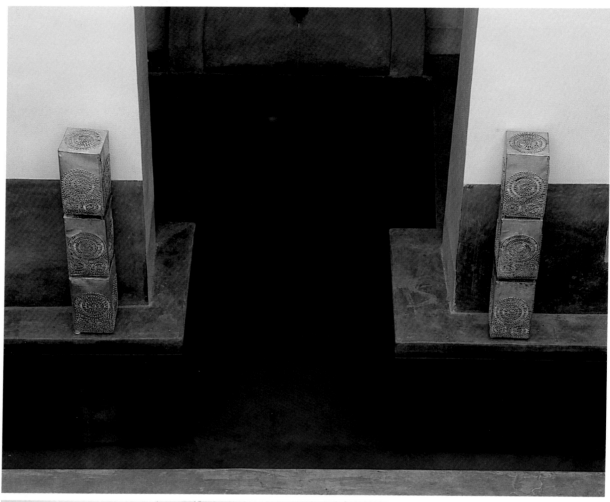

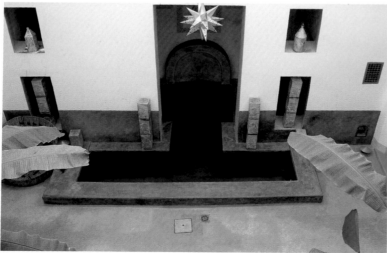

This project achieves the perfect fusion of the original, restored structure and the new pool. The pool, dark against the white walls that partially conceal it, is integrated without visually changing the composition.

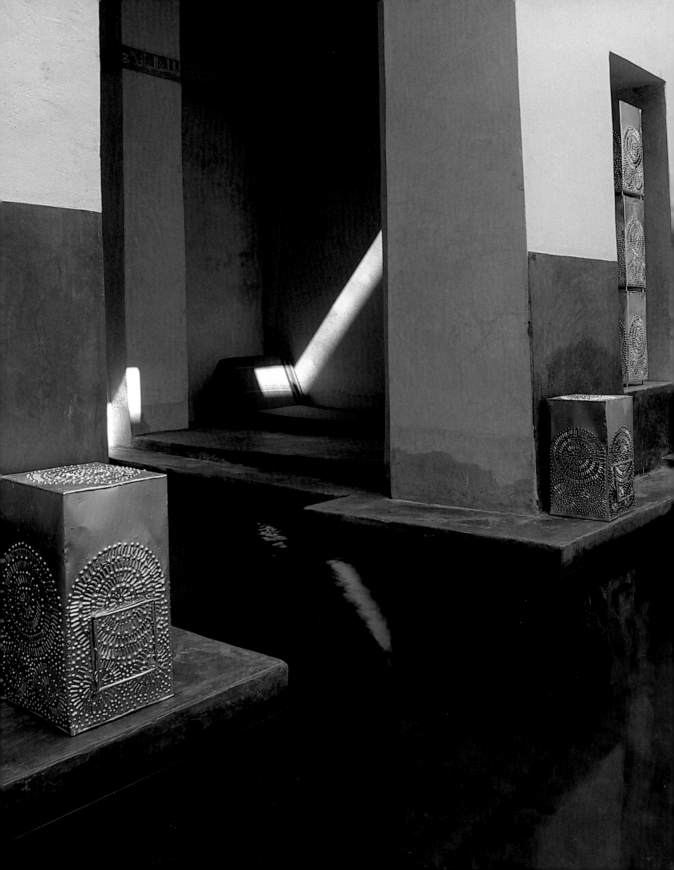

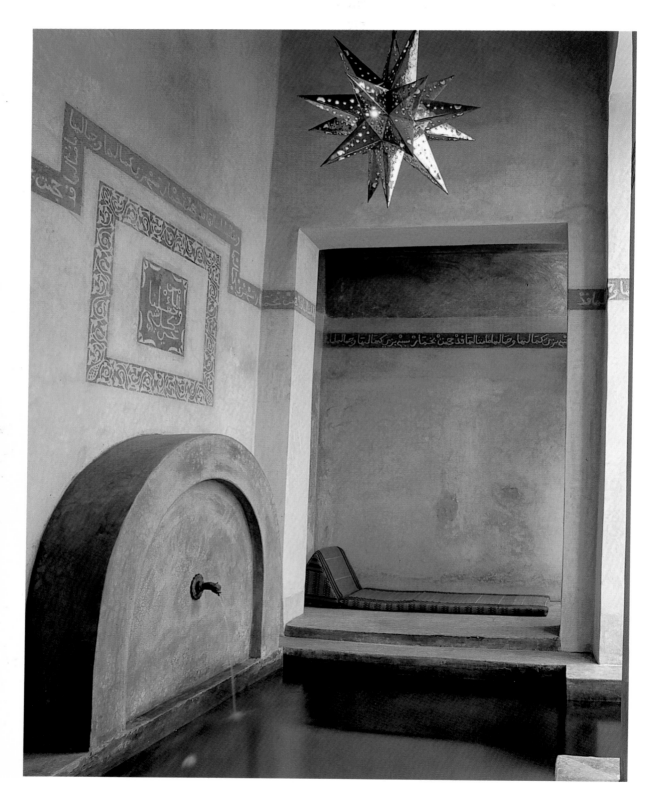

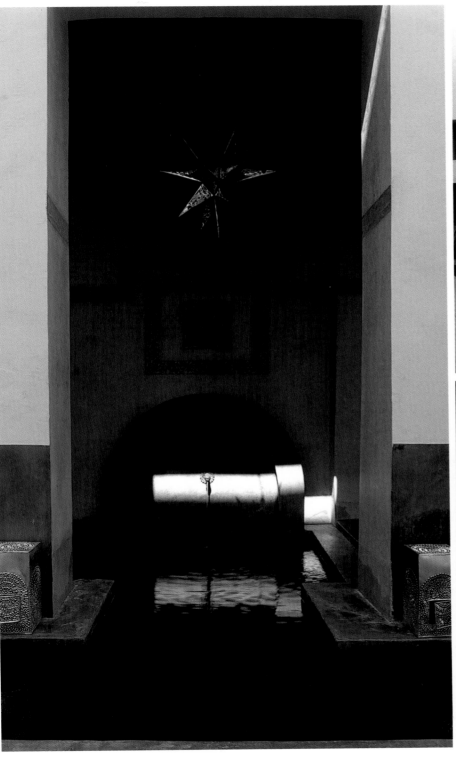
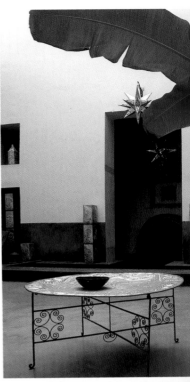
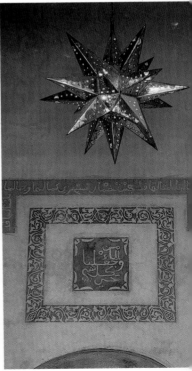

Drawing inspiration from Moorish-Andalusian architecture and staying as true as possible to the features of the original structure, this old Marrakech *ryad* was restored. The pool and garden—both perfectly integrated with the whole—are new.

Situated in an interior courtyard, the pool is a clear example of how mosaics are used in Morocco, even today. The complex is a fluid succession of spaces in which the green hues of the pool water break the continuity of the flooring while maintaining a visual connection.

The water rests placidly in this pool, surrounded by a rectangle of ceramic tiles. This restrained, elegantly colored geometrical border graces the upper edge and contrasts with the mosaics that cover the inside. The pool is crowned by a circular marble fountain, filled with multi-colored roses in a square recess. Water springs eternally from this fountain and flows through a small channel into the pool.

The pool is flanked by plants, emphasizing the long narrow lines that divide the ceramic floor. These neatly arrayed green plants provide a distinct contrast to the white of the walls and arches that surround the grouping, the solid old wood of the restored doors, and the lively colors of the flowers and oranges.

Marrakech, Morocco

Soft Murmur
of Water

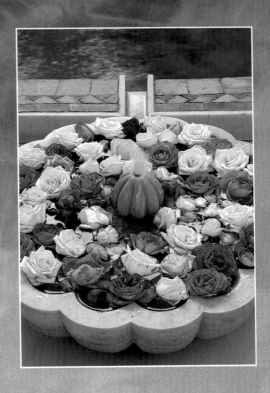

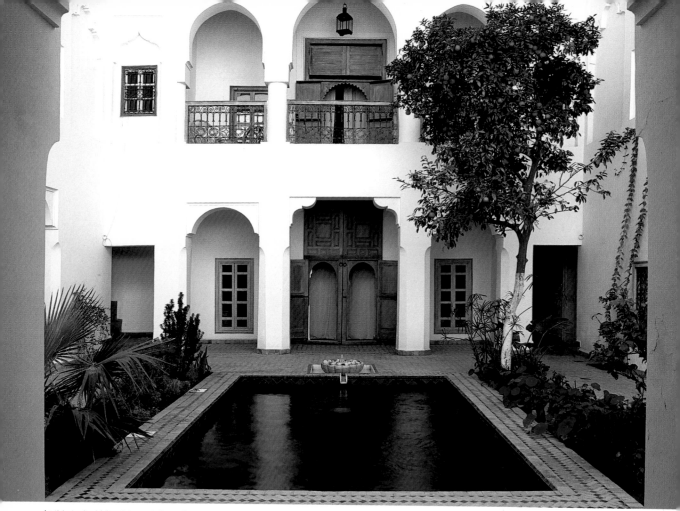

In this typical Moorish pool, the reflection in the water recalls the image of the Alhambra, considered by many Muslims to be the lost paradise.

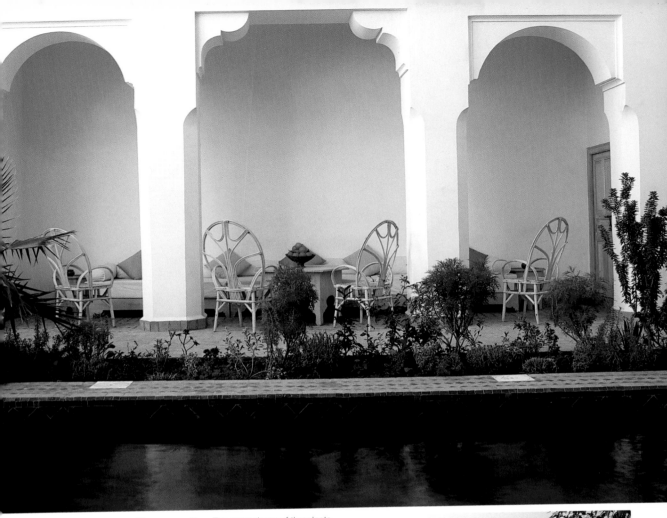

etation is an important element of the composition. The green hues of the plants complement the interior of the pool and contrast with the white walls and warm-colored flowers and fruits.

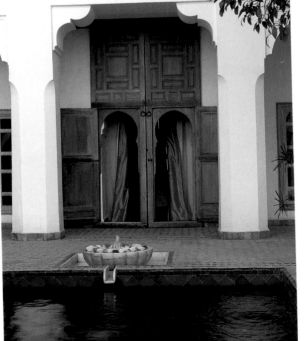

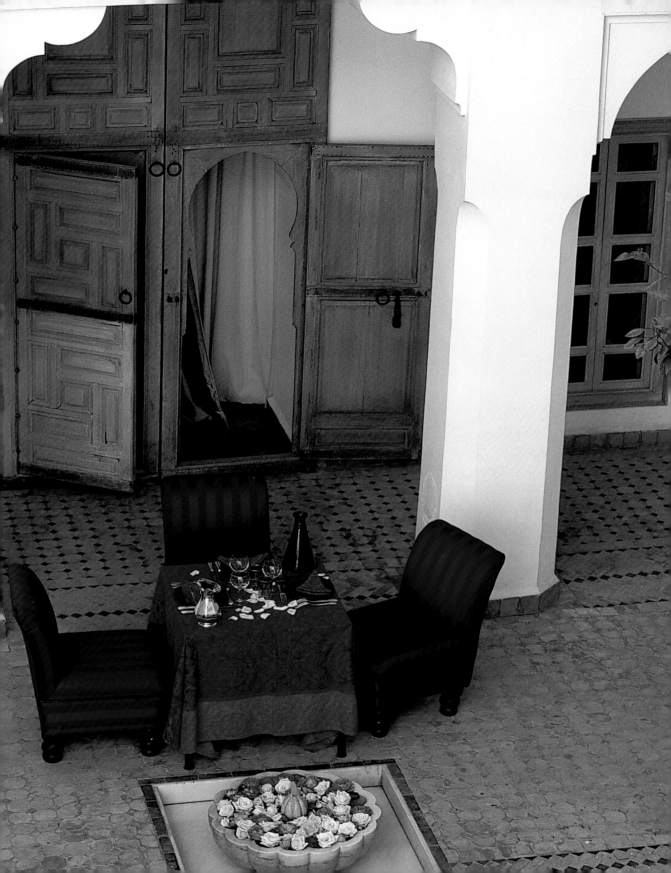

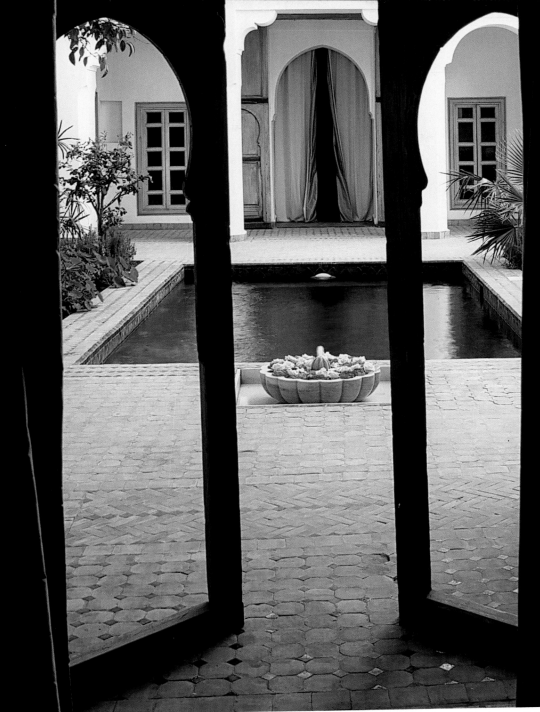

A geometric structure of ceramic tiles marks off the low marble fountain at the end, which continuously feeds the pool.

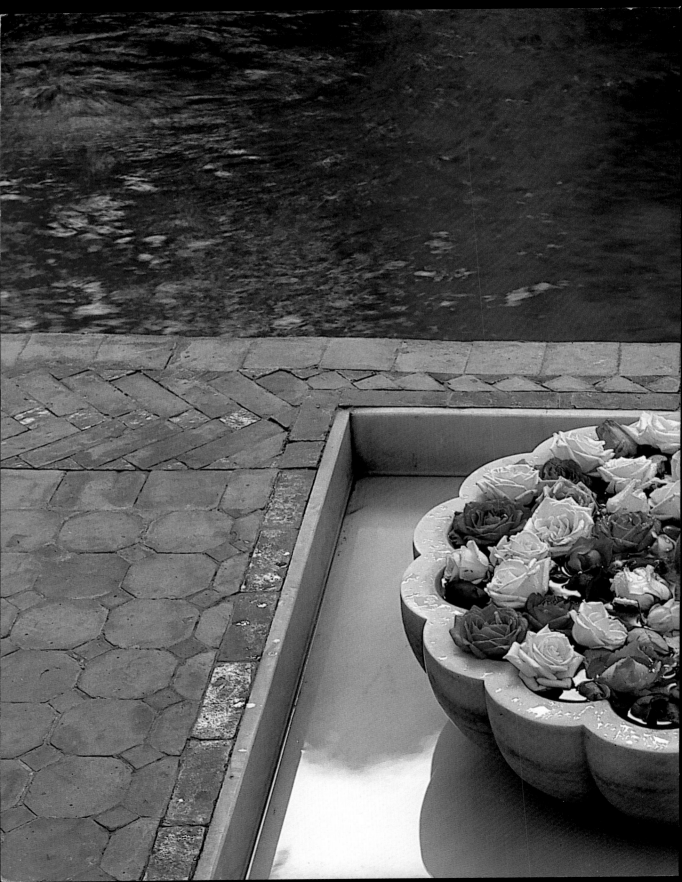

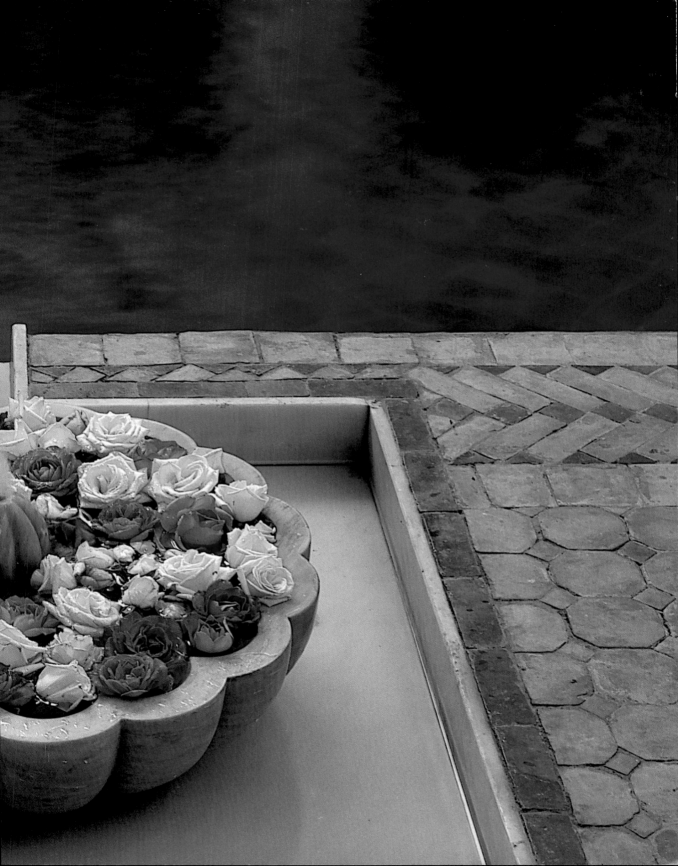

In Marrakech, in the interior courtyard of an old, renovated *ryad*, this semi-covered pool makes simplicity and tradition its best allies. It was conceived as a small pool hidden behind the solid walls of the building that protects it from the wind and unwanted glances. With exquisitely pure lines, the pool follows the tradition of Moorish structures. The color palette was chosen specifically to unify the space. A single material, tinted with a Moroccan technique known as *tadlack*—which creates an effect similar to colored cement—was used for the interior of the pool and the surface that surrounds it.

The light, neutral colors give the water its crystalline, transparent hue, and a typical Moroccan lamp hung from the center of the ceiling illuminates the space when the sun deserts it.

A discreet round pump ensures continuous circulation of the water, which creates natural background music that can be heard all over the courtyard. The visible areas and the outside are finished with small ceramic pieces, while the covered part has rounded edges but no finished border. The surrounding courtyard is every bit as austere as the pool itself.

Space, light, and color combine to create a simple, restrained spot, rich in nuance. The result is a restful niche where the water is the star, and a person can relax, gazing at the charming, subtle changes created by the play of light.

Marrakech, Morocco

Renewed
Tradition

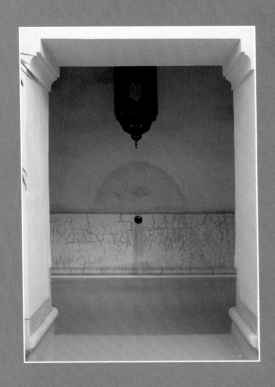

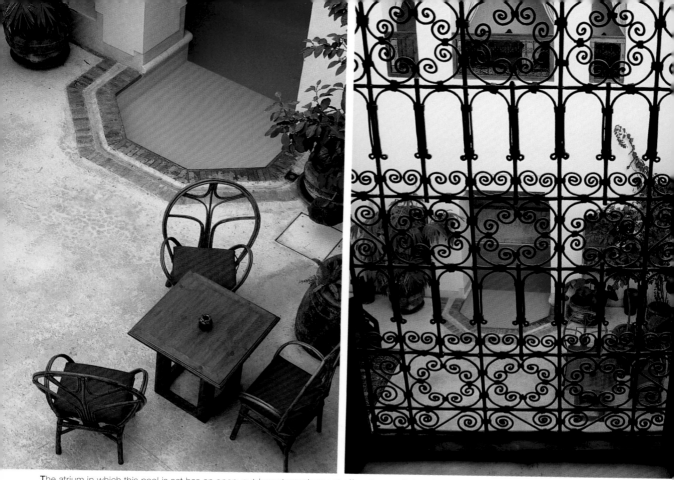

The atrium in which this pool is set has an open, outdoor atmosphere yet offers the comfort and protection of the indoors.

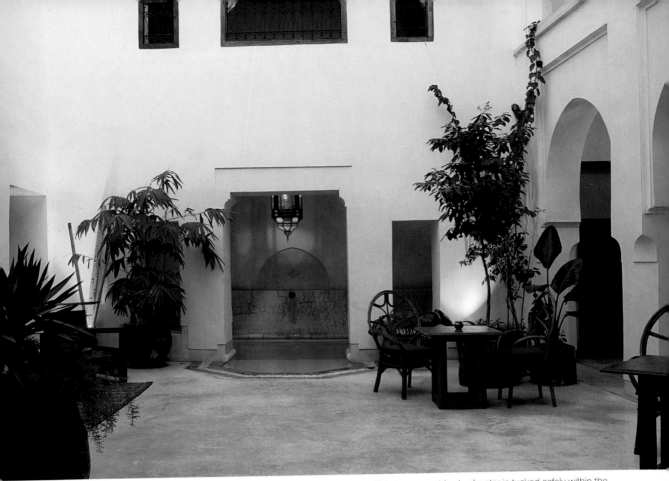

The minimal decor of the courtyard corresponds to the minimalist nature of the pool. This transparent body of water is tucked safely within the protective walls of the *ryad*, whose sharp lines and severe white color highlight the pool's simple shape and turquoise color

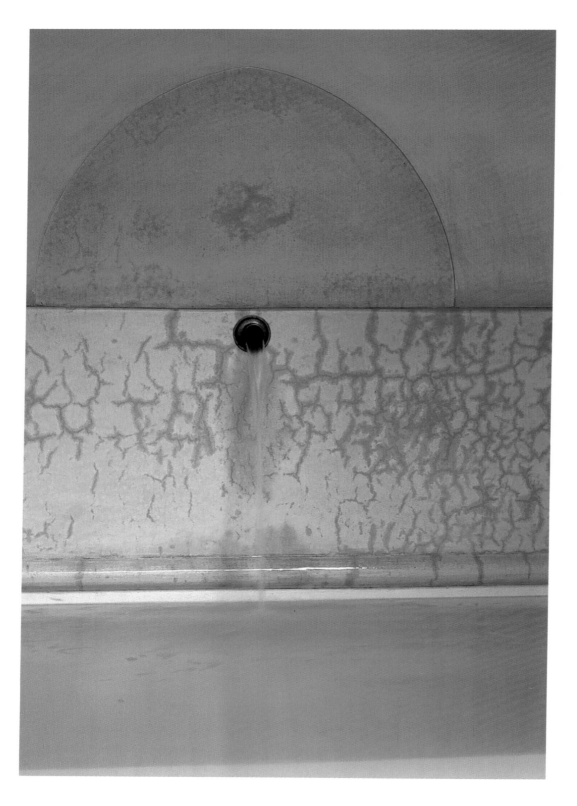

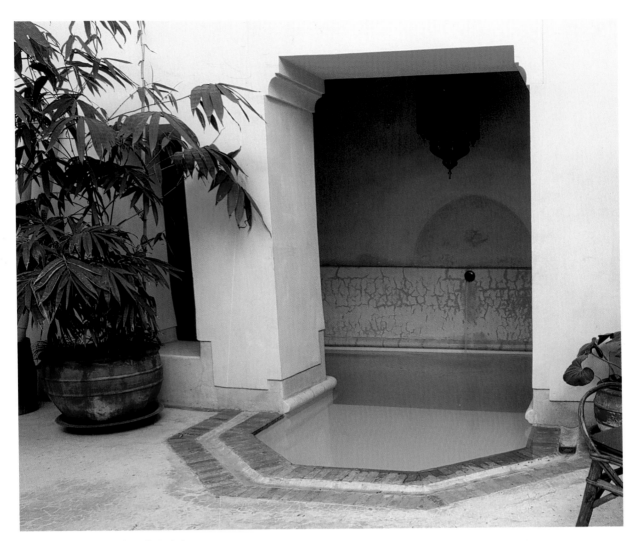

The renovation of this old *ryad* (a typical
Moroccan structure built around a central courtyard) was true to the original
design. The pool, while not a part of the
original structure, was built in the same
style and is integrated harmoniously into
the complex.

A few miles from Marrakech, in the enchanting town of Ouled Ben Rahmoune, this hotel offers the guest a special way of getting to know the area's traditional lifestyle complete with Western luxuries and all the comforts of a hotel. The grouping highlights the elegance and simplicity of a severe rural style with open courtyards, colorful gardens, terraces, and small arches reaching skyward.

The name of the hotel—Caravanserai—derives from two Persian words: *Karawan* (caravan) and *sarai* (inn). When the camel caravans on the silk or gold route were nearby, they always spent a few days at a *caravanserai* where they could bathe, change clothes, and prepare to do business. It was a place to rest and recover one's strength. In exactly that same spirit, and in keeping with the culture, refinement, and sensuality of Morocco, this hotel complex, inspired by traditional Moroccan architecture and using local construction techniques and materials, was designed.

Protected by the surrounding structure, this magnificent, simple pool is in perfect harmony with its setting. Made with the same materials, colors, and techniques used for the building, the pool sometimes seems to blend right in with the walls. Only the discreet blue or green—depending on the time of day and the lighting—reveals it for what it really is.

Like a carpet of water, the pool lies within the surrounding structure, placid and discreet to the visitor's eyes. Its straight lines harmonize with the grouping. To avoid breaking that spatial continuity, the stairs, located in each of the four corners, are submerged in the water. The spectacular stepped entrance beckons to the visitor, while the submerged masonry bench provides a place to rest. The entire edge and interior of the pool were constructed using a Moroccan technique known as *tadlack* (for an effect similar to colored cement). Inside, strategically distributed points of light illuminate the water at night, creating charming images.

The result is an inviting, magical space, which tempts the visitor to abandon himself to peace and quiet, relaxation, and reflection.

Ouled Ben Rahmoune, Morocco.

Captivating
Calm

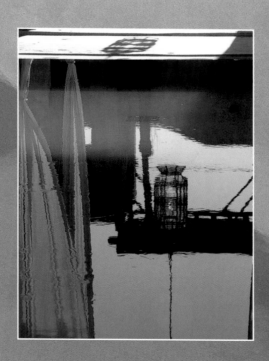

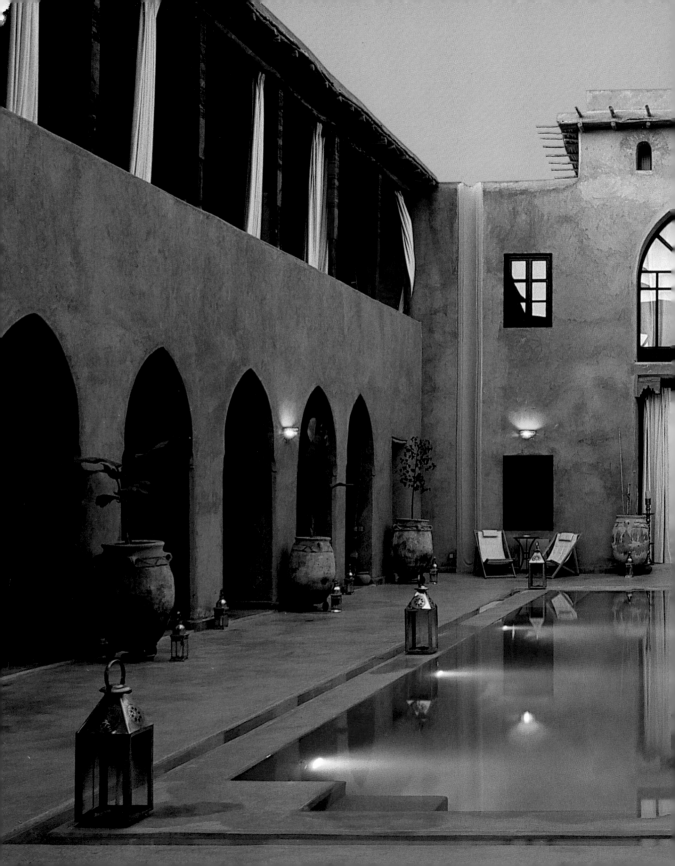

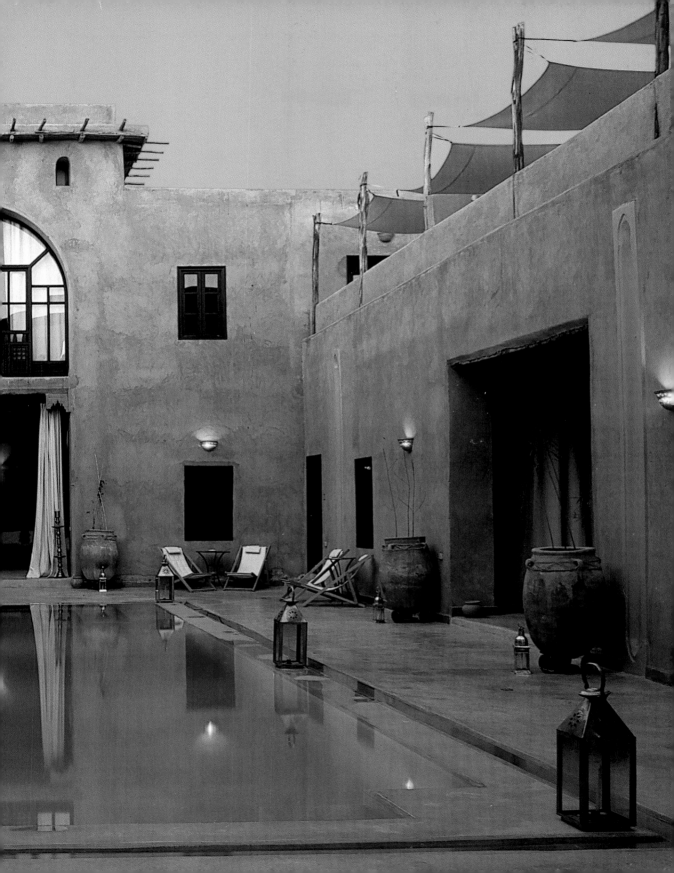

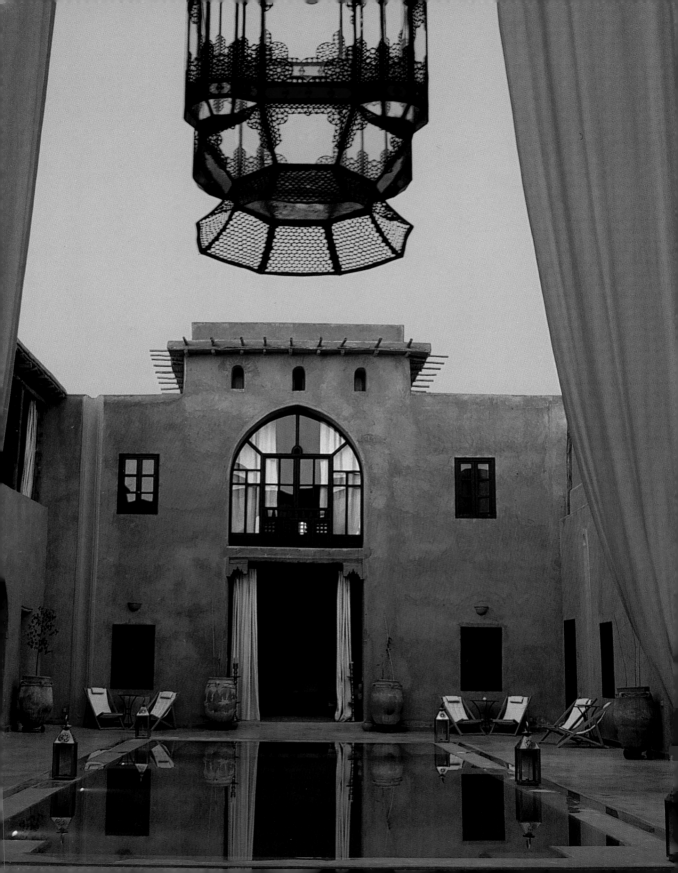

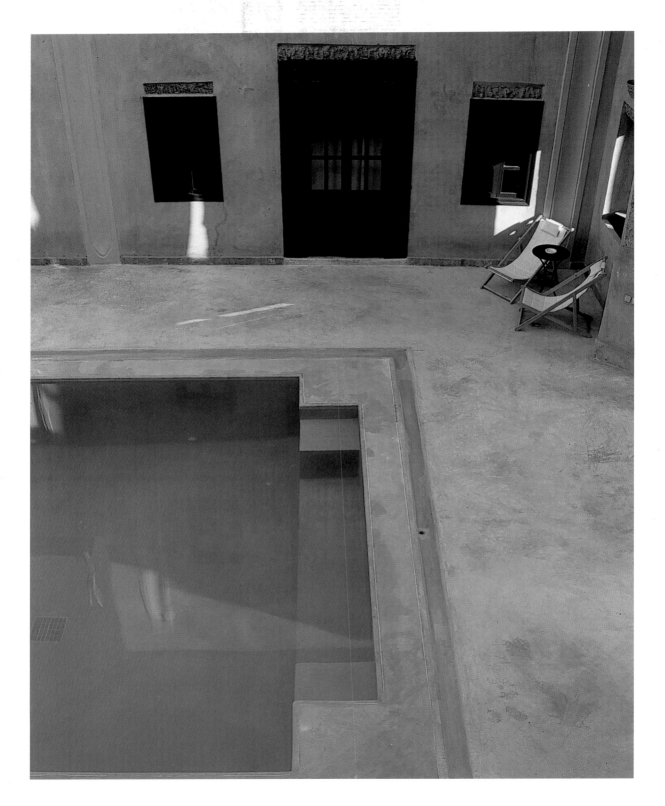

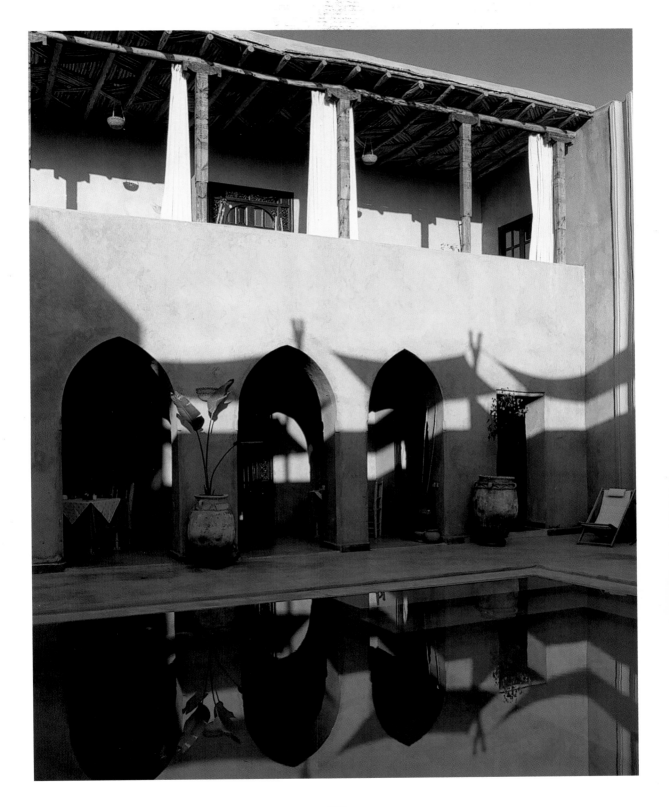

Pool designers:

Sophisticated Geometry **Design: Valentin de Madariaga & Ernesto Merello, Architect, Carmen Brujó, Decoration**
The Value of the Past **Design: Charles Boccara, Architect**
Water in Continuous Motion **Design: ADA Maurice Sauvinel & Ronald le Bévillon**
In the Heart of a Quarry **Design: Guillermo Maluenda, Architect, Josep Armenter, Coordination**
Play of Shapes **Design: Boyer-Gibaud, Percheron, Architect**
Chromatic Personality **Design: Angels G.Giró & Luis Vidal**
Perfect Blend **Design: Victor Esposito**
Inspired by the Past **Design: Thomas Wegner**
Bordering on the Theatrical **Desing: Rudy Ricciotti, Architect**
A Small Oasis **Design: Antonio Obrador, Estudio Denario Arquitectura**
Passion for the Traditional **Design: Duque de Segorbe**
The Eternal Cycle of Water **Design: B.B.& W. Estudio de arquitectura. Sergi Bastidas, Wolf Siegfried Wagner**
The Reinterpretation of Water **Design: Charles Boccara, Architect**
In the Garden of the Imaginary **Design: A.D.A. Maurice Savinel & Roland le Bévillon**
A Stream Amid the Rocks
Color Contrasts **Design: B.B.& W Estudio de arquitectura. Sergi Bastidas, Wolf Siegfried Wagner**
Hidden in a Garden **Design: Ely Mouyal, Architect**
A Mirror between the Earth and Sky **Design: Wolf Siegfried Wagner**
Hymn to Sensuality **Design: Valentin de Madariaga & Ernesto Merello, Architect**
Traditional Inspiration **Design: Charles Boccara, Architect**
Exercise in Contrasts **Design: Patrick Genard, Architect**
Zen Symmetry **Design: Lluís Alonso & Sergi Balaguer, Architect**
Classical Personality **Design: Bruno, Alexandre & Dominique Lafourcade**
To Live in Paradise **Design: Valentin de Madariaga & Ernesto Merello, Architect**
Classical Spirit **Design: Bruno, Alexandre & Dominique Lafourcade**
Vantage Point **Design: Françoise Pialoux**
The Patina of Time **Design: Rolf Blackstad, Architect**
The Magic of a Setting **Design: Ramon Esteve, Architect**
Minimalist Character **Design: Aranda, Pigem, Vilalta Architect**
Rural Symmetry **Design: Christopher Travena**
Carpet of Water **Design: Javier Barba, Architect, Anna Esteve, Landscaping**
Dressed in Blue **Design: Carlos Ferrater, Architect**
Between two Worlds **Design: Guillem Mas. Engineer**
Urban Essence **Design: Carlos Ferrater, Architect**
Private Space **Design: Erwin Bechtold**
An Urban Oasis **Design: Patrick Genard, Architect**
Memories of the Past **Design: Juan Jose Bormujo, Architect**
Nomadic Sensations **Design: B.B.& W. Estudio de arquitectura. Sergi Bastidas, Wolf Stegfried Wagner**
Peaceful Pool **Design: Chez Amídou. Decoration**
Soft Murmur of Water **Design: La cour del Mirtes, Jérôme Vermelin & Michel Durand-Meyrier**
Renewed Tradition **Design: Christophe Simeón, Architect, Catherine Neri, Decoration**
Captivating Calm **Design: Charles Boccara, Architect, Max Lawrence, Mathieu Boccara, Coordination and Decoration**

The authors would like to extend special thanks to the homeowners for opening their doors, to the architects for their creativity, and to the following people and groups for their help and collaboration during the development of this book.

Baños Arabes "Medina Califal", Gabriel Vicens & Mamen Zotes, Hoteles les Terrasses (Ibiza, Spain), Hotel Lindos Huéspedes (Pals, Spain), Hotel Les DeuxTours (Marrakech, Morocco), Hotel Caravanserai (Marrakech, Morocco), Hotel Casas de la Juderia (Seville,Spain), José Gandia (Gandia Blasco S.A) Valencia, Jean Paul Lance & Jalal Alwidadi, Jordi Millet, Laure Jacobiak, Mercedes Echevarria, Nona Von Haeften, Olivia Vidal, Philippe Gillot, Pan con Tomate (Ibiza, Spain), Unicorn and Coconut Company (Mallorca, Spain), Rafael Calparsoro, Riad Mabrouka, Riad El Mezouar, Victoria Martos, Xavier Farré, XYZ Piscinas.

And:
Aïcha, Alexandra, Antonia & Tomeu, Antonio, Antonio Jr., Bern, Bernadette, Carlos, Carmen & Manolo, Cecilia, Christian, Chris, Clay & Annie, Mimia, Danielle & Susan, Erwin & Cristina, Familia Pialoux, Isabel, Judith, Maria, Mari Carmen, Manolo, Mercedes, Mohamed, Mustapha, Nasima, Nora, Nuria, Olivier, Rachid, Said, Sarah, Stanislas.

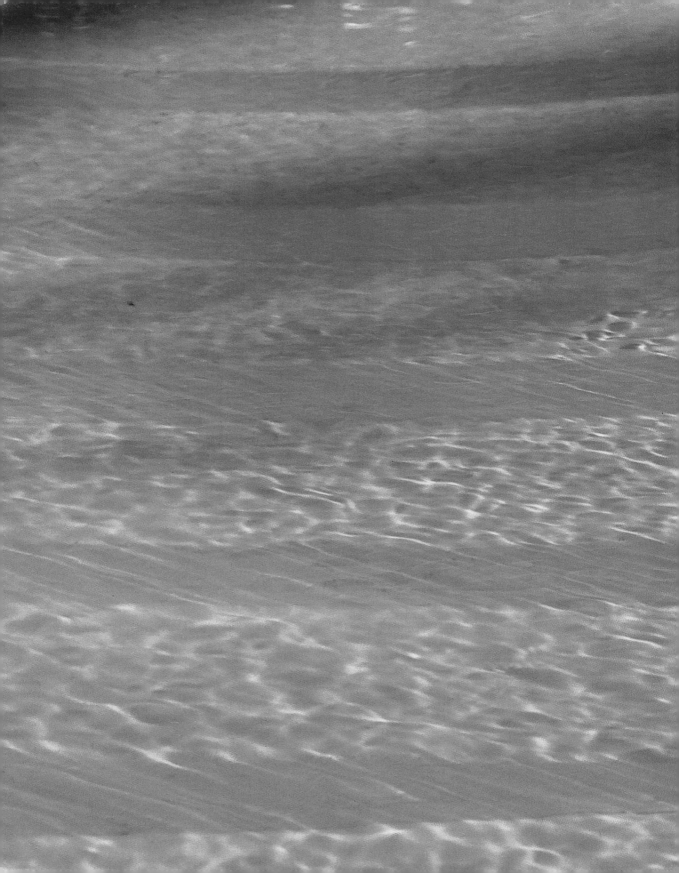

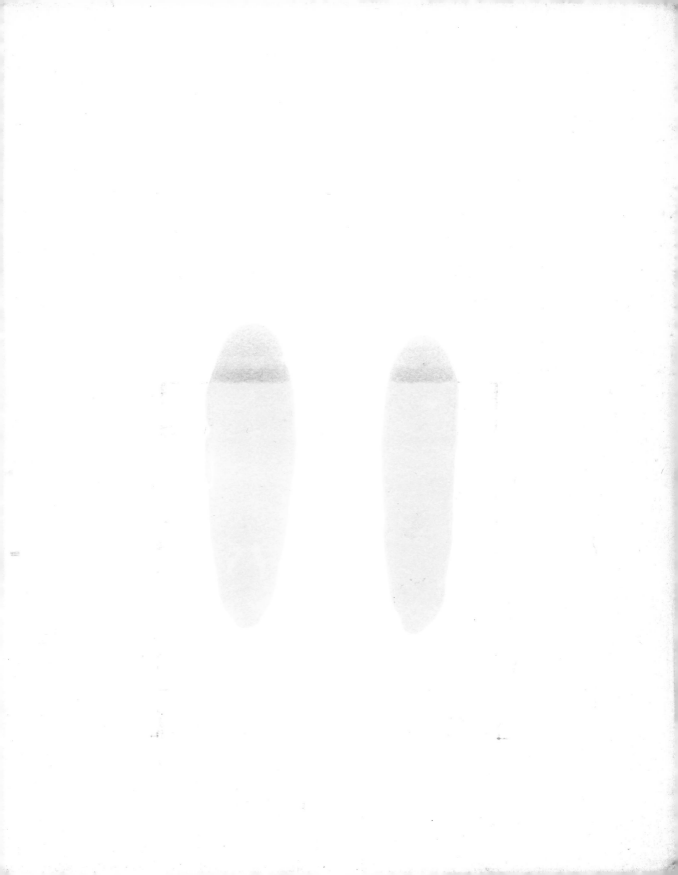